An Introduction to the Scots Law
of
SUCCESSION

An Introduction to the Scots Law of SUCCESSION

D. R. Macdonald, B.A., LL.B.,

Solicitor, Lecturer in Law
University of Dundee

EDINBURGH
W. GREEN & SONS LTD.
Law Publishers
St. Giles Street
1990

First published in 1990

ISBN 0 414 00916 9

Printed in Great Britain by
the Alden Press Ltd., Oxford

PREFACE

The law of succession, by its nature, has immense importance in any country. It impinges on everyone, without exception, at some point. Patterns of inheritance reflect the attitudes of society towards property ownership, the family, and the distribution of wealth between rich and poor. Yet no modern work provides a broad overview of the law of succession in Scotland. Some aspects of the law have been well served—Professor Meston's classic study of *The Succession (Scotland) Act 1964* is an instance—but others remain relatively untouched. In a modest way this book attempts tentatively to fill that gap.

This book is an introduction to the subject for students and others who come to it afresh. It tries to set out the principles, explain them and put them in their context, and where appropriate to offer comment on them. However, I have also attempted to include sufficient detail for it to be of value to students taking the Diploma in Legal Practice and to legal practitioners. In particular, emphasis is given to executry procedures, while reference is made to the effect of different types of clauses commonly found in wills. Finally, taxation cannot be ignored, and apart from an inevitably brief introduction to the subject, its implications are highlighted where appropriate at various points in the rest of the text. While a work of this nature perforce cannot examine many topics in depth, I have tried to warn of the pitfalls which may occur in practice.

The use of "he" or "she" in the text to describe someone usually has no legal significance. There are a few rare exceptions; I hope I have made them clear in their context.

I owe a debt to Professor Meston of Aberdeen University, who initially stimulated my interest in this area of law. My thanks go to those colleagues with whom I have discussed aspects of the subject, and in particular to Dr R. D. Leslie of Edinburgh University for his comments. I must also warmly thank Dr James Furnell for reading and commenting on the proofs, and Peter Nicholson of Messrs W. Green & Son Ltd. for his assistance and encouragement while the book has been in preparation. I am, of course, responsible for any defects which remain.

I have tried to state the law as at 1 September 1989, but have referred where appropriate to the Scottish Law Commission's proposals for reform in Consultative Memoranda 69, 70 and 71. The Commission's final Report was issued early in 1990, and it has proved possible to add a survey of its contents in Chapter 15.

Department of Law,   D.R.M.
University of Dundee.
March 1990.

CONTENTS

TABLE OF CASES

ALPHABETICAL TABLE OF STATUTES

ABBREVIATIONS AND AUTHORITIES

Anton	A. E. Anton, *Private International Law*, 1967.
Bankton, *Inst.*	Andrew McDouall, Lord Bankton, *Institute of the Laws of Scotland in Civil Rights*, 1751–53.
CGTA	Capital Gains Tax Act 1979 (c. 14).
CTO	Capital Taxes Office.
Clive	E. M. Clive, *The Law of Husband and Wife in Scotland* (2nd. ed., 1982).
Currie	J. G. Currie, *The Confirmation of Executors in Scotland* (7th. ed., by A. E. McRae, 1973).
Elder	A. H. Elder, *Forms of Wills*, 1947.
Encyclopaedia	"Wills and Succession" in *The Laws of Scotland: Stair Memorial Encyclopaedia*, Vol. 25, by M. C. Meston and others, 1989.
Ersk., *Inst.*	John Erskine of Carnock, *An Institute of the Law of Scotland* (8th ed., 1871).
Ersk., *Prin.*	John Erskine of Carnock, *Principles of the Law of Scotland* (21st ed., 1911).
Gloag & Henderson	W. M. Gloag and R. Candlish Henderson, *Introduction to the Law of Scotland* (9th ed., by A. B. Wilkinson and W. A. Wilson, 1987).
Goudy	H. Goudy, *Law of Bankruptcy in Scotland* (4th ed., 1914).
Halliday	J. M. Halliday, *Conveyancing Law and Practice in Scotland*, Vol. I (1985) and Vol. IV (1990).
Henderson	R. Candlish Henderson, *The Principles of Vesting in the Law of Succession* (2nd. ed., 1938).
IHTA	Inheritance Tax Act 1984 (c. 51).
J.L.S.	Journal of the Law Society of Scotland.
L.Q.R.	Law Quarterly Review.
McBryde	W. W. McBryde, *The Law of Contract in Scotland*, 1987.
McDonald	A. J. McDonald, *Conveyancing Manual* (4th ed., 1989).
McLaren	John, Lord McLaren, *Law of Wills and Succession* (3rd. ed., 1894); supplement by D. O. Dykes, 1934.
McMillan	A. R. G. McMillan, *The Law of Bona Vacantia in Scotland*, 1936.
Macphail	I. D. Macphail, *Evidence*, 1987.
Meston	M. C. Meston, *The Succession (Scotland) Act 1964* (3rd ed., 1982).
Miller	J. Gareth Miller, *The Machinery of Succession*, 1977.
Morley	M. F. Morley, *Accounting for Scottish Executries and Trusts*, 1984.
Morris	J. H. C. Morris, *The Conflict of Laws* (3rd. ed., 1984).
Murray	C. de B. Murray, *The Law of Wills in Scotland*, 1945.

Parry & Clark	J. B. Clark, *The Law of Succession* (9th. ed., 1988).
S.L.C.	Scottish Law Commission consultative memoranda: No. 69, *Intestate Succession and Legal Rights*; No. 70, *The Making and Revocation of Wills*; No. 71, *Some Miscellaneous Topics in the Law of Succession*; all 1986.
S.L.T.	Scots Law Times.
Stair, *Inst.*	Sir James Dalrymple, Viscount Stair, *Institutions of the Law of Scotland* (Tercentenary ed., 1981).
Walker	N. M. L. Walker, *Judicial Factors*, 1974.
Walker, *Prin.*	D. M. Walker, *Principles of Scottish Private Law* (4th. ed., 1988).
Walkers	A. G. Walker and N. M. L. Walker, *The Law of Evidence in Scotland*, 1964.
Wilson	W. A. Wilson, *The Law of Scotland Relating to Debt*, 1982.
Wilson & Duncan	W. A. Wilson and A. G. M. Duncan, *Trusts, Trustees and Executors*, 1975.

Further reading on specific topics is listed at the end of each chapter.

CHAPTER 1

PROOF OF DEATH AND OF SURVIVORSHIP

INTRODUCTION

1.1 The law of succession governs how a person's property passes on his death. Succession to property depends on proof or legal presumption that the person whose estate is to be distributed has died, and that the potential beneficiary has survived him. If an interest in property passes before death it is not a right of succession; it may instead involve a trust in favour of the beneficiary or an outright transfer by gift.

While death and survivorship are essential to give the beneficiary a vested—indefeasible—right, they are not always sufficient: vesting may be postponed till some later event such as the beneficiary's reaching a certain age. Conversely, if the beneficiary predeceases, his offspring may step into his shoes and take his interest in his stead: this can result from the rules of representation (in intestacy) and (in testate succession) the *conditio si institutus sine liberis decesserit*.[1]

PROOF OF DEATH

1. General requirements

1.2 Death itself is an imprecise concept; questions of brain death as opposed to physical death may arise in modern medicine. Issues of medical ethics aside, the position is ordinarily straightforward. Death must be proved in order to permit inheritance; the executor must aver precisely the date and place of death to obtain confirmation, and must prove this if challenged.[1a] Under the Registration of Births, Deaths and Marriages (Scotland) Act 1965[2] an extract from the Register of Deaths is "sufficient evidence of the death," but is not conclusive proof.

2. Disappearance: the legal background[3]

1.3 Difficulties arise where a person has disappeared and is not heard of again. Scots common law had no rule presuming him to have

---

[1] Discussed at paras. 4.15, 4.25, and 10.21. For vesting see chap. 11.
[1a] Currie, pp. 124–125.
[2] s. 41(3).
[3] See generally Scot. Law Com. Report No. 34 (1974).

died after a period of seven years. There was a strong presumption that life continued to the extreme limits of human age: 80 or 100 years according to Stair.[4] To rebut it required proof "beyond reasonable doubt"[5] or "positive proof,"[6] a higher standard than the ordinary standard in civil cases of proof on the balance of probabilities. Rebuttal depended on the special circumstances of each case: lapse of time was only one factor, insufficient by itself, coupled with other evidence such as a dissipated or dangerous lifestyle. So death was held proved in *Greig* v. *Merchant Company of Edinburgh*[7] where a wife wished to claim a widow's pension: the husband had been absent for 10 years; on medical evidence his alcoholism would have killed him within that time. But in *Secretary of State for Scotland* v. *Sutherland*,[8] where a husband had left his wife and not been heard of for 42 years, he was presumed still alive (though aged 72) on the grounds that this merely proved how successful he had been in avoiding his wife.

Difficulty of proof aside, the common law was felt defective. Its justification went once rapid modern communications made it unlikely for someone to disappear completely for years yet still be alive. It effectively quarantined the person's property for a generation. An action to declare death was probably only effective against the parties to the action. If death could not be proved, the only remedy was to appoint a factor *loco absentis* to administer the missing person's estate.[9]

Legislation remedied some but not all of these defects. The main problem was fragmentation of the legal rules, so that a person might be treated as alive for some purposes and dead for others. The Presumption of Life Limitation (Scotland) Act 1891[10] allowed death to be declared after seven years' disappearance: but it affected only succession to property, and permitted restitution to the disappeared person if he reappeared in the following 13 years. The Divorce (Scotland) Act 1938[11] allowed dissolution of a marriage, but had no effect on property rights. Neither Act gave a right to pension or life assurance benefits.

3. The Presumption of Death (Scotland) Act 1977

1.4 The Act answers most criticisms of the previous law; common law actions are still competent but will be rare. By its main provisions:

---

[4] *Inst.*, IV. xlv. 17 (19thly).
[5] *Bruce* v. *Smith* (1871) 10 M. 130, at p.133.
[6] *Fife* v. *Fife* (1855) 17 D. 951, at p. 954. See also *Tait* v. *Sleigh*, 1969 S.L.T. 227.
[7] 1921 S.C. 76; and see *X* v. *S.S.C. Society*, 1937 S.L.T. 87.
[8] 1944 S.C. 79.
[9] Still useful where the 1977 Act does not apply.
[10] Which replaced a more limited Act of 1881.
[11] s. 5.

(1) If someone is thought to have died, or has not been known to be alive for a period of at least seven years, anyone having an interest may raise an action to have him declared dead. So the pursuer might be a spouse, or a potential beneficiary, or the Lord Advocate for the public interest. Both the Court of Session and the sheriff court may have jurisdiction on grounds of the domicile or habitual residence of the missing person or his spouse (if that is the pursuer). The sheriff may—and must if the Court of Session so directs on application by a party to the action—remit the case to the Court of Session if the issues are important or complex (section 1).

(2) Proof is on the balance of probabilities. If death is proved, the decree states its date and time; if it is uncertain when within a period of time the person died, the end of the period is chosen. In the case of seven or more years' disappearance, death will be held to occur at the end of the day seven years after he was last known to be alive (section 2).

The decree may also determine domicile at death and *any* question relating to *any* interest in property resulting from the death—*e.g.* where A's right to B's estate depends on the missing person C's death.

The court may appoint a judicial factor to manage the deceased's property, whatever its value. Thus, unlike ordinary appointments of judicial factors, there is no financial limit on the sheriff court's power. Note that if no decree is possible within the seven year period, because there is no proof of death, the main remedy is to have a factor *loco absentis* appointed over the property until the period is up.[12]

(3) The decree is effective and conclusive against *any* person and for *all* purposes, including the acquisition of rights to any person's property. It thus applies to insurance and social security benefits. It dissolves the missing person's marriage, even if the spouse did not bring the action (section 3).[13]

(4) Suppose in fact the missing person did not die, or died at a different date from that stated: (a) despite the decree the person remains liable for any crimes he has committed (section 3(4)); (b) the marriage remains dissolved by the decree and is not revived by its subsequent recall or by the person's reappearance (section 3(3), 4(5)); (c) supposing the spouse remarried *without* a decree dissolving the first marriage, it is a defence to a bigamy charge that for the seven years preceding the remarriage he had no reason to believe the missing person to be alive (section 13); (d) anyone having an interest may apply to have the decree varied or recalled (section 4(1)).

(5) The policy of the Act is to protect rights acquired under a decree—especially by a spouse—and to limit the missing person's

---

[12] See N. M. L. Walker, *Judicial Factors*, pp. 28–29.
[13] For criticism of this rule, see 1977 S.L.T. (News) 217.

right to recover his property if he reappears. So variation or recall will not automatically affect property rights acquired under the decree, *but*:

(a) If application for variation is made less than five years after the decree, the court *may* make "such . . . order . . . as it considers fair and reasonable in all the circumstances" (section 5(3)). Thus it may order restitution in kind or in cash. The order does not affect income accruing between the decree and its variation, nor the rights of third parties who acquired property for value.

(b) Special rules govern trusts and insurers. When making payments after a decree of death, insurers may (and trustees normally must) obtain insurance against its possible variation (section 6). If the court varies the decree, so far as practicable it will only order restitution of trust property still in the trustees' hands or, if previously distributed, its value when distributed. Insurers may recover capital sums—not annuities or periodical payments—if "the facts . . . justify," *e.g.* the sums were paid in error. (Note that insurance policies need not permit payment on a decree of death; they may require proof of *accidental* death.)

(c) The court may, on application by a trustee or a person entitled to aliment from the missing person, declare property not to be recoverable under a variation order (section 7).

(d) The court may order that inheritance tax be repaid to anyone entitled to a repayment (section 8).

(6) To obtain confirmation an executor formerly required to aver a precise date of death. The Act makes this unnecessary. If the person disappeared in Scotland, the decree is automatically effective for confirmation. An analogous foreign decree is sufficient (though not conclusive) evidence of death (section 10); the executor may use it in his averment (section 11). Similar rules apply to death in or loss from a ship, aircraft, hovercraft, or offshore installation (section 11).

(7) To ensure due publicity, (a) anyone possessing relevant information must disclose it if he knows that an action for decree or variation has been raised, unless rules of privilege, confidentiality or public interest apply; this duty applies explicitly to the D.H.S.S. (section 9); (b) decrees and variation orders are entered by the Registrar General in the Register of Deaths (section 12).

Proof of Survivorship

1. General

1.5 For a beneficiary to inherit from the deceased, it must be proved on the balance of probabilities that he survived him. "Survivance is in every case a matter of proof, and . . . when a claimant whose claim depends on proof of survivorship is unable to establish the fact of survivance, his claim necessarily fails."[14] Scots law requires no minimum period of survivance: a matter of seconds, if proved, is sufficient; once the beneficiary thus acquires a vested right of succession, on his own subsequent proven or presumed death that right passes to his own representatives.

The rule applies generally to testate and intestate succession. A special case is a survivorship destination, whereby property is owned in the names of "A and B and the survivor", the share of the first to die passing by accretion to the other on his death. Conversely a right of succession may depend on proof of another potential beneficiary predeceasing: this may occur in intestacy (the doctrine of representation), testacy (the *conditio si institutus sine liberis decesserit*), or under the express terms of a will (a legacy to X "if Y dies in my lifetime").

Failure to prove survivance may have drastic effects. A legacy will lapse, unless the *conditio* or the rules of accretion apply, and the sum will fall into residue or intestacy; failing intestate heirs the Crown will take as *ultimus haeres*.[15]

2. Common calamities

(a) Common law

1.6 Rigid insistence on this principle caused problems whenever it was uncertain in what order two or more people died: especially where they died in one "common calamity" such as a bomb blast. Evidence may be slight—disappearance in a shipwreck at an unknown moment within some period of time—and medical speculation necessary as to the precise time of death. At common law, in the absence of proof, there was no presumption as to who died first.

A trio of cases illustrates the effect of the rule. In *Drummond's Judicial Factor* v. *Lord Advocate*[16] a husband, wife, and children died in a bomb blast. The wife died intestate: her husband would inherit if he survived, but since there was no evidence of order of death and no other heir the Crown took as *ultimus haeres*. In *Mitchell's Executrix* v. *Gordon*[17] a husband, wife, and daughter died in an aeroplane crash; two children, and the daughter's son, survived them. Could the grandson claim his mother's share in the husband's intestacy (by

---

[14] *Drummond's J. F.* v. *Lord Adv.*, 1944 S.C. 298 *per* Lord Justice-Clerk Cooper at p. 302.
[15] See paras. 10.21 (the *conditio*), 10.17 (accretion), and 10.25 (residue).
[16] 1944 S.C. 298.
[17] 1953 S.C. 176.

representation) and under the wife's will (by the *conditio si institutus*)? His claims failed: both required proof of his mother's predeceasing the spouses (which was lacking); the share went to the surviving children. In *Ross's Judicial Factor* v. *Martin*[18] two sisters made separate but identical wills each leaving property to the other and to a charity if the other predeceased her. They died, the order uncertain, in a gas leak. The charity argued that the wills should be construed as one and the legacy implemented to give effect to the testators' intention: this failed because the words of the will were clear; the legacy failed and the intestate heirs inherited.

(b) Statute

1.7 It was generally felt that any presumption of survivance was better than none. English law now lays down two: the general rule is that where the order of death is uncertain the younger is taken to survive the older,[19] but where spouses die together and the older is intestate then neither is taken to survive the other.[20] *Hickman* v. *Peacey*[21] took "uncertain" to cover "virtually simultaneous": exact simultaneity is most unlikely.

1.8 In Scots law the Succession (Scotland) Act 1964 now lays down a general rule with two exceptions.

(1) Where two persons die in circumstances indicating that they died simultaneously or rendering it uncertain which, if either, survived the other, then the younger is presumed to survive the elder for all purposes of succession to property, legal and prior rights (section 31(1) (*b*)). However:

(2) Where the persons are husband and wife, it is presumed that neither survived the other (section 31(1) (*a*)). Note that this gives no answer where, as in *Ross's Judicial Factor*, "predecease" is required; survivorship destinations raise a similar point since they assume that one spouse survived the other.

(3) Where the elder left a legacy in favour of the younger or (if the younger fails to survive) to a third person, *and* the younger dies intestate, the elder is presumed *for the purposes of that legacy* to survive. For all other purposes the ordinary rule applies (section 31(2)). One is intestate if one leaves *any* part of one's estate undisposed of by will (section 36(1)).

The Act talks of "two persons." If a group is involved, it must be

---

[18] 1955 S.C. (H.L.) 56. *Wing* v. *Angrave* (1860) 8 H.L.C. 183 is an analogous English case.
[19] Law of Property Act 1925, s. 184.
[20] Administration of Estates Act 1925, s. 46(3). The aim is to stop a husband's estate going to his wife's relations.

analysed "in twos": each person's survivance of each other must be separately determined.

1.9 The Act only applies if proof of survivance is not possible. Proof is on the normal civil standard, balance of probabilities: *Lamb* v. *Lord Advocate*[22] rejected the idea, floated in *Hickman*, that a higher standard is ever required. Mere speculation not amounting to proof is insufficient.[23]

1.10 The Scottish Law Commission suggests two possible reforms:[24]

(1) A presumption of "predecease" rather than "survivorship." This would cover the point in (2); property held under a destination would pass in separate shares to each owner's heirs.

(2) A minimum period of survivance by the beneficiary. In practice many wills already include a "survivorship clause" to require 30 days' survivance, failing which a third person inherits. Otherwise the beneficiary inherits even if his death ensues minutes later: this has tax disadvantages and scarcely reflects the testator's true intentions.

3. Revenue law

1.11 If A is proved or presumed to survive B, inheritance tax (IHT) is in principle due on both A's and B's death. This would be unjust if they in fact die in one accident (albeit minutes apart), even though Quick Succession Relief[25] will apply to B's death. Two rules remedy this.

(1) If it cannot be known which, of two or more persons who died, survived the other(s), they are deemed to die at the same instant.[26] Now IHT is due on the estate immediately *before* death. So the effect is that property inherited by B from A suffers tax only on A's death, since it is not deemed part of B's estate for this purpose.

(2) Suppose under A's will property is held for B on condition he survives for a specified period less than six months, and it is transferred to him then (if he survives) or to an alternative beneficiary earlier (if he dies). Tax is due as if the transfer were made on A's death, *i.e.* once only and not also on B's death during the period.[27] This is why a will should include a "survivorship clause."

[21] [1945] A.C. 304.
[22] 1976 S.L.T. 151.
[23] *Re Beare* [1957] C.L.Y. 1361.
[24] Memorandum No. 71, paras. 3.2–3.8.
[25] Inheritance Tax Act 1984, hereafter "IHTA 1984", s. 141.
[26] IHTA 1984, s. 4(2).
[27] IHTA 1984, s. 92.

POSTHUMOUS CHILDREN[28]

1.12 Rights of succession are normally determined at the deceased's date of death. But where he leaves a child who is conceived but as yet unborn, it may be treated as actually born to allow it to inherit. "A child in the mother's womb is esteemed as already born, in all things that concern its own interest;"[29] *qui in utero est, pro jam nato habetur.*[30] The principle is not confined to succession: the child may have a remedy in delict for antenatal injury, either to itself directly or by the loss of a relative.[31]

The rule derives from Roman law and has rarely been disputed. It applies to wills, to entitlement to legal rights,[32] and to intestacy; the 1964 Act made no apparent changes. So, in *Cox's Trustees* v. *Cox*[33] where property was divided among "the descendants alive at the time of my death," that class included posthumous descendants unless expressly or impliedly excluded by the terms of the will.

The rule has two limits. First, the child must ultimately be born alive. Secondly, the rule cannot be invoked in the interests of a third person, but only if the child gains some direct benefit by it. So it was refused in *Elliot* v. *Joicey,*[34] where A's property was to be held "in trust for [B] absolutely . . . in the event of [B] leaving any issue . . . surviving." In the House of Lords' view "surviving" would not normally mean "posthumous": but, crucially, even if *pro jam nato* were applied that would benefit B's estate and not necessarily his issue. The issue would benefit only indirectly (by B's will) or not at all, if B were insolvent.

Further reading

Scottish Law Commission: Report No. 34 (1974), "Presumption of Death".
"Common Calamities and the Presumption of Death", 1963 S.L.T. (News) 101.
M. C. Meston, "Succession Rights of Posthumous Children" (1970) 15 J.L.S. 33.
"Presumption of Death", 1977 S.L.T. (News) 217.

---

[28] See Meston (1970) 15 J.L.S. 33.
[29] Bankton, *Inst.*, I. ii. 7.
[30] Erskine, *Inst.*, III. viii. 76.
[31] See Scot. Law Com. Report No. 30 (Cmnd. 5371), "Liability for Antenatal Injury."
[32] *Jervey* v. *Watt* (1762) Mor. 8170.
[33] 1950 S.C. 117.
[34] 1935 S.C. (H.L.) 57.

CHAPTER 2

ENTITLEMENT TO INHERIT

INTRODUCTION

2.1 Many legal systems recognise various factors which debar a person from inheriting on intestacy or under an otherwise valid will. Commonly someone who witnesses[1] or writes out[2] a will—or his spouse—may not take benefits under it. That point, where relevant in Scotland, makes the entire will formally invalid.[3] Otherwise Scots law debars only the "unworthy heir." Its former discrimination against adopted and illegitimate children, tending to recognise only legitimate blood-relationships, has now largely been removed by statute.

THE UNWORTHY HEIR

1. General

2.2 Civil law systems identify various circumstances personal to a beneficiary which make him unworthy to inherit; common law systems treat this question in terms of public policy. South African law, for instance, has several types of unworthiness, such as adultery, concealing a will, or unlawful killing. Whatever the early Scots rules (such as barring inheritance by wayward fornicating daughters[4]), the present Scots law derives largely from three overlapping sources: the Parricide Act 1594, English rules of public policy, and the Forfeiture Act 1982.

2. The Parricide Act 1594

2.3 "... Quhatsumeuir he be that hes slayne or sall heireftir slay his father or mother guidschir or guddame and hes bene alreddie or salbe heireftir convict be ane assyise The commitaris of the said cryme and his posteritie in linea recta salbe disheresit in all tyme heireftir fra thair landis heretages takis possessionis and the samyn sall apertene to the nixt collaterall and narrest of blude quha vtherwayes micht succeid falyeing of the richt lyne."

---

[1] England: Wills Act 1837, s. 15.
[2] South Africa: see Corbett *et al.*, *The Law of Succession in South Africa*, p. 74.
[3] Only in the case of notarial execution of a will: see para. 6.21.
[4] *Regiam Majestatem*, II. 49.

The precise scope of the Act is unclear,[5] but is so limited that the Act has never actually been successfully used to disinherit anyone. Conviction of murder is required: so in *Oliphant* v. *Oliphant*,[6] where a man killed his mother but escaped and was legally declared fugitive, the Act did not apply. Succession to moveables is apparently not affected. Only killing of parents or grandparents is covered: not spouses. Finally, the Act disinherited the murderer and his descendants: but the analogous concept in treason cases of "corruption of the blood" has since been abolished,[7] and that may restrict the Act to disinheriting the murderer himself. His own children would then inherit as if he had predeceased the victim.

3. Public policy

2.4 English law has evolved principles of public policy to prevent criminals inheriting or taking other benefits from their victims. The modern rule, since adopted by Scots law, is relatively recent: prior to the Forfeiture Act 1870 the property of convicted felons was forfeited to the Crown.

(a) The scope of the rule

2.5 To what crimes does the rule apply? The principle has been variously stated. In the classic case of *Cleaver* v. *Mutual Reserve Fund Life Association*[8] it was said that "no system of jurisprudence [will enforce] rights directly resulting to the person asserting them from the crime of that person." In that case a woman, entitled under the Married Women's Property Act 1882 to the proceeds of life assurance taken out by her husband in her favour, murdered him. She was debarred from taking the proceeds; they thus formed part of the husband's estate and passed to their children. This broad rule would not normally cover crimes committed accidentally or by an insane person.

The rule is usually stated more restrictively. Lord Esher M.R. in *Cleaver* spoke simply of "the person who commits murder." The problem area is manslaughter or culpable homicide. The courts were quick to exclude the rule where drivers (even if convicted of manslaughter) claimed insurance against death caused by their reckless or careless driving.[9] But in succession cases they preferred to

---

[5] Bankton, *Inst.*, II. 331; Erskine, *Inst.*, IV. iv. 47.
[6] (1674) Mor. 3429.
[7] Criminal Justice (Scotland) Act 1949, s. 15(1).
[8] [1892] 1 Q.B. 147 *per* Fry L.J. at p. 156. See also *Re Crippen* [1911] P. 108 at p. 112.
[9] *Tinline* v. *White Cross Ins. Ass. Ltd.* [1921] 3 K.B. 327. See MacGillivray & Parkington, *Insurance Law* (6th ed.), pp. 227–236.

treat manslaughter as an absolute bar to inheritance.[10] So in *Re Giles, Deceased*[11] a woman guilty of her husband's manslaughter on grounds of diminished responsibility could not inherit: "neither the deserving of punishment nor carrying a degree of moral culpability has ever been a necessary ingredient of the crime." As regards the question of moral culpability that is still true, so provocation is disregarded, but the manslaughter test has been redefined. In *Gray* v. *Barr*[12] the Court of Appeal stressed that the crime "varies infinitely in its seriousness" and in exceptional cases will not debar:

"The logical test is whether the person seeking the indemnity was guilty of deliberate, intentional and unlawful violence or threats of violence . . . however unintended the final death of the victim may have been."

This is now the Scottish position. In *Burns* v. *Secretary of State for Social Services*[13] a woman, provoked by her husband's violence, stabbed him; she pled guilty to culpable homicide. Approving *Gray*, the Inner House held her debarred from claiming a widow's alowance: the stabbing was intentional and the provocation was irrelevant. No reference was made to the only previous Scottish decision, *Smith, Petitioner*,[14] where *Gray* was not cited and the rule was held to be absolute if there was a conviction for murder or culpable homicide.

2.6 Conviction is not essential, so the rule applies although the killer escapes or commits suicide. The killing must be proved: the standard of proof is less stringent than in criminal law, but "the more serious the allegation, the more cogent is the evidence required to . . . prove it."[15] A conviction raises a presumption of guilt in subsequent civil proceedings, which the killer must rebut;[16] but conversely the court need not accept acquittal as conclusive of innocence.[17]

(b) The effect of the rule

2.7 (1) The rule has automatic effect: a court declarator is useful but not essential. It applies, within succession, to intestacy, legal rights, wills, and rights deriving from survivorship (such as special

---

[10] *In the estate of Hall* [1914] P. 1.
[11] [1972] Ch. 544 at p. 552.
[12] [1971] 2 Q.B. 554, 569, approving [1970] 2 Q.B. 626, at p. 640; not cited in *Giles*.
[13] 1985 S.L.T. 351.
[14] 1979 S.L.T. (Sh. Ct.) 35.
[15] *Re Dellow's Will Trusts* [1964] 1 All E.R. 771.
[16] Law Reform (Miscellaneous Provisions) Act 1968, s. 22(5).
[17] As in *Gray* v. *Barr* [1971] 2 Q.B. 554.

destinations). It also prevents the killer being appointed executor[18] or taking insurance and social security benefits arising from the death.[19]

(2) The disqualification covers the killer or any person claiming through him, such as his executors or beneficiaries if he dies. Others with independent claims are unaffected. So in *Cleaver* the couple's children inherited directly from the murdered husband rather than through his guilty wife. Similarly a third party who takes insurance benefits as an assignee for value, or under a trust, has an independent claim.[20]

(3) Foreign laws generally treat the killer as predeceasing the victim[21] so that his claim passes to the person next entitled under the victim's will or intestacy. This is also so in England. In *Re Callaway*[22] S killed her mother C, her son, and herself; C had left her estate by will to S. The Crown argued that it vested in S and, she being barred from taking, went to the Crown as *bona vacantia* (ownerless property); but it was held that the legacy lapsed and it went to the heir on intestacy, S's brother.

The Scots law is presumably the same. So a destination-over (a gift to "X, or Y [*e.g.* his issue] if he predeceases") will be effective; in a class gift (*e.g.* "my children") the killer's share accresces[23] to the other members of the class; otherwise the share may fall into residue or intestacy depending on the terms of the will. But two points are unclear. Normally if X predeceases, his children may (by representation or the *conditio si institutus*) take the share to which he was entitled if he survived: arguably that cannot apply here. In survivorship destinations (title in names of "X and Y and survivor") what happens where X kills Y: does the destination pass title to Y's estate or (logically) is it ignored so that X and Y's shares pass separately to their respective heirs?[24]

(4) Does the rule prevent the killer inheriting from the victim's heir, or apply only to inheritance directly from the victim? South Africa, for instance, debars only if the heir is a close relation.[25] There is no Scots authority.

(c) Suicide

2.8   Can a suicide's estate benefit from his life assurance policy? Two quite distinct issues arise.[26]

[18] *Re Crippen* [1911] P. 108.
[19] *Burns* v. *Secretary of State for Social Services*, 1985 S.L.T. 351.
[20] MacGillivray, *op. cit.*, pp. 236 et seq.
[21] *e.g.* Ireland, Succession Act 1965, s. 120(5).
[22] [1956] 2 All E.R. 451.
[23] For accretion in class gifts see para. 10.18.
[24] See Meston, p. 21; *cf.* (1986) 31 J.L.S. 151.
[25] *Steenkamp* v. *Steenkamp* 1952 (1) S.A. 744 (T).
[26] See MacGillivray, *op. cit.*, pp. 240–244.

(1) The construction of the policy. It may explicitly or impliedly exclude suicide, *e.g.* by requiring accidental death, or cover only insane suicide. Or it may allow only an assignee for value to claim: this was the point in *Ballantyne's Trustees* v. *The Scottish Amicable Life Assurance Society*,[27] where the suicide's wife could claim because, in return for his assigning her the policy benefits, she had agreed not to claim divorce for his adultery.

(2) Public policy. This only arises if the assurance policy allows a claim for the suicide. In England suicide was a crime until 1961, and on that basis the personal representatives' claim was struck down in *Beresford* v. *Royal Insurance Society Ltd.*;[28] again an assignee for value could claim. But suicide is no longer a crime, "the principles of public policy on which the courts act change over the generations,"[29] and *Beresford* would not now be so decided. It never was a crime in Scotland, so public policy is probably irrelevant: (1) is the only issue.[30]

(d) Law reform

2.9 The Scottish Law Commission favours new rules to replace public policy and the Parricide Act.[31] These would cover murder and culpable homicide; lesser crimes resulting in two or more years' imprisonment would debar from claiming legal rights. Conviction would be essential. The criminal would be treated as predeceasing his victim, but survivorship destinations would be ignored.

4. The Forfeiture Act 1982

2.10 The Act alleviates the effect of the public policy "forfeiture rule," but not of the Parricide Act.

(1) The Act applies if a person unlawfully kills another: so suicide is excluded. It applies where that person would, but for the forfeiture rule, acquire an interest in property: either by will, legal rights, intestacy, nomination, *mortis causa* donation, special destination, or trust. Analogous regulations cover social security benefits.[31a] The Act applies only to inheritance, so excludes rights to insurance benefits or appointment as the victim's executor (sections 1, 2(3), 2(4), 4).

(2) A court may modify the effect of the forfeiture rule only if

---

[27] 1921 2 S.L.T. 75.
[28] [1938] A.C. 586.
[29] *Re Giles, Decd.* [1972] Ch. 544 at p. 552.
[30] On this view Gow, 1958 S.L.T. (News) 142 is outdated.
[31] Memorandum No. 71, paras. 2.1–2.14.
[31a] See Ogus & Barendt, *The Law of Social Security* (3rd ed.), pp. 370–372; S.I. 1982 No. 1792, 1984 No. 451.

"satisfied that, having regard to the conduct of the offender and of the deceased and to such other circumstances as appear to the court to be material, the justice of the case requires the effect of the rule to be so modified in that case" (section 2(2)). So the victim's adultery or provocation is relevant.

Apparently the court can modify but not completely exclude the rule. This was doubted in *Re K, Deceased*,[32] was not decided in *Paterson, Petitioner*,[33] but was confirmed in *Cross, Petitioner*.[34]

(3) Where "a person stands convicted of an offence of which unlawful killing is an element" the court may modify the rule only if the case is brought within three months after the conviction. Where he "stands convicted of murder" the rule may never be modified (sections 2(3), 5). These provisions will not apply if the killer dies before he can be convicted; the rule may still be modified to benefit his estate. The Scottish Law Commission tentatively suggests a six month time limit starting from the date when the succession opens to the killer.[35]

5. The Conjugal Rights (Scotland) Amendment Act 1861

2.11 This creates a type of statutory "unworthiness" for marital misconduct. All property acquired by a wife after she obtains a decree of separation *a mensa et thoro* (*i.e.* judicial separation) will pass, if she dies intestate, to her heirs and representatives as if her husband were dead (section 6). If her husband deserts her and she obtains an order to protect property which she acquires by her own industry, that has the effect of a decree of separation (sections 1, 5).[36] If the spouses start living together again the rule ceases to apply.

ADOPTED CHILDREN

1. General rules

2.12 Before 1964 adoption had no effect on the adopted child's rights of succession. He retained his rights in respect of his natural parents, and—except by specific provision by will—did not succeed to the adopter's estate.

The Succession (Scotland) Act 1964 reverses the position. In both

---

[32] [1985] 2 W.L.R. 262 at pp. 275–276.
[33] 1986 S.L.T. 121; only modification was asked for.
[34] 1987 S.L.T. 384.
[35] Memorandum No. 71, paras. 2.16–2.18.
[36] See Clive, *Husband & Wife* (2nd ed.), pp. 673–674.

testate and intestate succession (and also deeds disposing of property *inter vivos*) an adopted person is treated as the child of the adopter and of no-one else. So he will not inherit from his natural parents. To avoid doubt, "succession" explicitly includes claims to legal and prior rights (section 23(1)).

This rule does not apply to succession to those dying before September 10, 1964, nor to titles or coats of arms (sections 23(4), 37(1)). Otherwise it is general: it applies for all purposes of succession, not just between parents and issue. But the effect was that the child had *no* rights at all if the natural parent died after, but the adopter before, September 10, 1964. To remedy this, where the adopter died then and the natural parent died after August 3, 1966, a child is treated as the natural parent's child for purposes of succession to his estate.[37]

Special rules govern the child's relationship with collaterals—brothers, sisters, and their descendants. If adopted by two spouses jointly he is deemed brother of the whole blood to any child or adopted child of them both. Otherwise he is a half-brother: *e.g.* if adopted by one spouse, or by a single parent, or where one spouse had a child by a previous marriage (section 24(1)). In determining seniority between children, the child is deemed born on the day of adoption, or (purely as between children adopted on one day) on the true date of birth (section 24A).

If a child is adopted more than once, only the last adoption is relevant for succession after that date (section 24(3)). Where adoption is revoked—as may occur if an illegitimate child's parents adopt it but later legitimise it by marrying—the revocation does not affect existing rights of succession.[38]

2. Deeds

2.13 The above rules apply to deeds executed after September 10, 1964. In addition section 23(2) contains special provisions.

(1) If a deed is executed after an adoption order, references in it to the adopter's child include the adopted person, references to the natural parents' child exclude him, and references to persons related to the child are construed as if he is the adopter's child "unless the contrary intention appears."

(2) Whatever the actual date of execution (provided it is after September 10, 1964), where a provision is effective on a person's death then the deed is deemed executed on that date. So adoptions in the intervening period after actual execution are covered. Note that

[37] Law Reform (Miscellaneous Provisions) (Scotland) Act 1966, s. 5.
[38] Legitimation (Scotland) Act 1968, s. 6(2).

that date may, paradoxically, be after the testator's death: *e.g.* A's legacy to "B's children if they survive B" includes B's adopted children.

(3) References may be express or implied. This will cover the rules of accretion and the *conditio si institutus*, or references to "parents."

The meaning of section 23(2) and its relationship to the general rule (section 23(1)) have caused debate.[39] In particular, what is the effect of A's legacy to "my child B, failing whom B's issue"? "Issue" are descendants: is A's adopted grandchild included? On one view he is not: section 23(2) governs wills (but not intestacy), "issue" ordinarily includes only biological relations, and its use in a will displays a "contrary intention" to exclude the Act. Such a view, if correct, frustrates the purpose of the Act, and it has been cogently argued that "issue" impliedly covers adopted children and that "contrary intention" requires a positive exclusion of the Act. However the Law Society of Scotland feels that in view of the doubt on the point a will should ideally make explicit reference to adopted grandchildren.

ILLEGITIMATE CHILDREN[40]

1. Introduction

2.14 The trend this century has been towards the elimination of discrimination against illegitimate children. In a wider context this has been encouraged by the European Convention on Human Rights.[41] Till 1986 reform was piecemeal; even now the concept has not been abolished, and the old law is still relevant.

2. Intestate succession

2.15 At common law an illegitimate child was *filius nullius*; a stranger in blood to both his parents, with no right to inherit from anyone.[42] In 1926 mother and child were allowed to inherit from each other if either died intestate with no legitimate issue.[43]

The Law Reform (Miscellaneous Provisions) (Scotland) Act 1968 gave child and parents reciprocal rights to inherit. He could claim legitim[43a]; his issue could represent him if he died.[44] But the rights

---

[39] *e.g.* (1965) 10 J.L.S. 95; (1969) 14 J.L.S. 204; (1979–81) J.L.S. (Workshop) lxxv, 159, 182.
[40] See generally Scot. Law Com. Report No. 82 (1984).
[41] Arts. 8 and 14. See *Marckz* v. *Kingdom of Belgium* (1979–80) 2 E.H.R.R. 330.
[42] Erskine, *Inst.*, III. x. 8; *Clarke* v. *Carfin Coal Co.* (1891) 18 R. (H.L.) 63.
[43] Legitimacy Act; extended to heritage by Succession (Scotland) Act 1964.
[43a] *i.e.* legal rights; see para. 4.11.
[44] *i.e.* if he would have inherited from someone had he survived, they would inherit in his place. See para. 4.25.

went no further: they did not extend to other relations (such as brothers); the child, not being "lawful issue," could not himself represent a predeceasing parent. If the child died it was presumed (rebuttably) that his father did not survive him. Furthermore, a deceased's executors were (and still are) protected from liability if they distribute his estate without checking that he left no illegitimate children (section 7).

The Law Reform (Parent and Child) (Scotland) Act 1986 virtually abolishes the effects of illegitimacy. "The fact that a person's parents are not or have not been married to one another shall be left out of account in establishing the legal relationship between the person and any other person" (section 1(1)). The child can now inherit from anyone as if legitimate. But:

(1) The Act will not apply to succession to titles and honours (section 9(c)), or to deaths before December 8, 1986. It only affects previous Acts if it explicitly repeals or amends them; the Succession (Scotland) Act 1964, among others, is amended to delete references to illegitimacy[45] (Schedules 1, 2).

(2) The presumption of non-survivance by the child's father is abolished; the executors' protection is extended to cover all undiscovered paternal relatives of the child (Schedule 1, paragraph 10).

3. Testate succession

2.16 At common law the child could, in effect, only inherit by will if expressly named: it was strongly presumed that descriptive terms such as "children" included only legitimate people.[46] By the Law Reform Act of 1968, in construing a deed executed after November 25, 1968 to determine who is entitled to benefit under a provision in it, both legitimate and illegitimate relationships are included "unless the contrary intention appears" (section 5). The provision extends to inheritance under the *conditio si testator*, the *conditio si institutus*, and accretion,[47] but not to titles or honours or to interpretation of statutes.

Under the 1986 Act illegitimacy is irrelevant in construing deeds (section 1(2)). This is wider than the 1968 Act: it is not confined to inheritance and will, say, cover entitlement to be appointed executor. But it does not apply to deeds executed before December 8, 1986 (which the common law or 1968 Act still govern), nor to later deeds which make reference to illegitimacy. So a testator may still exclude

---

[45] In particular ss.4 and 10 A are completely deleted.
[46] *e.g. Mitchell's Trs.* v. *Cables* (1893) 1 S.L.T. 156.
[47] See paras. 7.12, 10.20, and 10.16 respectively.

illegitimate children from his will. They may always claim legitim, which no will can defeat.[48]

Further reading

B. Davis, "Ex Maleficio non Oritur Actio?", 1969 S.L.T. (News) 49.
J. A. M. Inglis, "Succession and Special Destinations" (1986) 31 J.L.S. 151.
"Succession and Public Policy" (1986) 31 J.L.S. 246.
M. C. Meston, *The Succession (Scotland) Act 1964* (3rd ed.), Chap. 7.
A. J. McDonald, "Adopted Persons" (1965) 10 J.L.S. 95.
"Issue and Adopted Children" (1979–81) J.L.S. (Workshop) lxxv, 159, 165, 172, 182, 191, 206.
M. C. Meston, "Bastards in the Law of Succession", 1966 S.L.T. (News) 197.
M. C. Meston, "Illegitimacy in Succession" (1986) 31 J.L.S. 358.

[48] See paras. 4.11, 9.1.

CHAPTER 3

PAYMENT OF DEBTS

ORDER OF PAYMENT

1. Introduction

3.1 A deceased person's debts do not die with him. His estate remains liable for them after it passes into the hands of his executor.[1] This is the principle of "passive representation." If he objects to that liability he may of course simply decline to be executor.

He is liable for *all* the deceased's debts if he deals with the estate without obtaining confirmation of his title—"vitious intromission"—but provided he has confirmation his liability is limited to the value of the estate confirmed to.

On the same principle beneficiaries are liable, up to the value of their inheritance, for debts unpaid by the executor. Such liability is in fact rare: creditors cannot sue beneficiaries if the executor had sufficient funds when the estate was distributed and yet they failed to claim from him. *Menzies* v. *Poutz*[2] illustrates the effect of the rule where it applies: a widow was sequestrated four years after getting confirmation to her husband's estate; it then transpired he had also been bankrupt; his creditors had a preferential claim in *her* bankruptcy.

3.2 So the executor, after gathering in the deceased's property, must pay all known debts before anything—even income—goes to beneficiaries.[3] It is unnecessary (though common) to stipulate this by will. He should, by advertisement if necessary, take steps to ascertain all debts due; he may, but need not, require creditors formally to constitute debts by court decree. Having paid out all known debts he may, a year at most after the death, start paying beneficiaries.

If the executor knows or should know that the estate is absolutely insolvent, and is likely to remain so, he must within a reasonable time take steps to have a judicial factor or trustee in bankruptcy appointed. Otherwise any dealing with the estate constitutes vitious intromission and he may be liable for *all* the deceased's debts.[4]

---

[1] See McLaren on *Wills*, Vol. II, pp. 1280 et seq. and 1301; Wilson & Duncan, pp. 453–458.
[2] 1916 S.C. 143.
[3] *Heritable Securities Investment Association Ltd.* v. *Miller's Trs.* (1892) 20 R. 675.
[4] Bankruptcy (Scotland) Act 1985, s. 8(4). See McBryde, *Bankruptcy*, pp. 32–33, 41 and 236–238.

2. Time of payment

3.3 Before modern bankruptcy law emerged, creditors could enforce payment on the principle "first come, first served." Slower creditors might find the debtor's property already exhausted. The trend in modern times has been to put creditors on a more equal footing. In line with that, since 1662[5] debts intimated to the executor within six months after death ordinarily rank equally: they have equal priority. He cannot be compelled to pay within that period; if he does so he is personally liable to other creditors if the estate turns out to be insufficient to pay them as well. After the six months he may if satisfied the estate is solvent pay creditors in order as they claim, and he is not personally liable to later claimants if he has paid out all the assets in good faith to earlier ones.

Conversely, certain "privileged debts" may be paid within the six months even if other creditors cannot be paid in full. This is because those debts have a preference if the estate is declared bankrupt. The category was developed by the courts, but should now be read subject to the modern statutory rules of bankruptcy; some of the older examples are obsolete.

3. Order of payment[6]

3.4 Debts must be paid in the following order. Each class of debt must be paid in full before the next class. Within each class debts rank *pari passu* (equally),[7] so the same proportion is paid of each if they cannot all be paid in full.

(a) Expenses of sequestration

If the estate is bankrupt, the outlays and remuneration of the interim trustee and the permanent trustee (in that order) must be paid first.[7a]

(b) Deathbed and funeral expenses

3.5 These are privileged debts[8] and are payable ahead of all others, even debts secured over the deceased's general property.[9]

"Deathbed" covers medical expenses of the deceased's last illness, such as medicines and doctors' fees.[10] Funeral expenses include

---

[5] Act of Sederunt, February 28, 1662.

[6] See McBryde, *Bankruptcy*, pp. 205 *et seq.*; Wilson, *Debt*, pp. 288–290.

[7] *e.g. Peter* v. *Monro* (1749) Mor. 11852 (funeral expenses).

[7a] Bankruptcy (Scotland) Act 1985, s. 51 (1)(*a*), (*b*).

[8] *Sheddan* v. *Gibson* (1802) Mor. 11855.

[9] *Rowan* v. *Barr* (1742) Mor. 11852 (landlord's hypothec); *Drysdale* v. *Kennedy* (1835) 14 S. 159.

[10] *Sanders* v. *Hewat* (1822) 1 S. 333 (new ed. 370).

cremation.[11] Mourning clothes for the widow are also a privileged debt, which is not discharged by the widow accepting a provision by will "in satisfaction of all claims";[12] no cases refer to widowers, but mourning debts are in any event now rare and the Scottish Law Commission favours their abolition.[13]

The expenses must be reasonably incurred. In old cases, now outdated, the test was suitability to the deceased's social rank; but simple extravagance should still disallow the debt. Take *Glass* v. *Weir* where, out of a £300 estate, £8 was spent on spirits for a four-day drinking spree: the court cut this to a more sober £3.[14] The position of a gravestone is unclear. One old case suggests that it is a funeral expense if reasonably incurred.[15] The cost is now deductible for purposes of inheritance tax.[16] It is best to make specific provision by will, and essential if trustees are to make ongoing payments for its upkeep.

Reasonably incurred costs of obtaining confirmation and of executry administration rank along with funeral expenses.[17]

(c) Secured debts

3.6 A creditor holding a security over the deceased's property can enforce it at any time. He can of course sue for the balance of his debt, ranking according to the normal rules as privileged, preferred, or ordinary according to its nature.

(d) Preferred debts

3.7 Some of these were classed as privileged at common law. Various statutory preferences—such as assessed taxes and rates— were abolished by the Bankruptcy (Scotland) Act 1985. Two main types now exist[18]:

(1) Taxes and social security contributions due in respect of specified periods: e.g. P.A.Y.E., V.A.T., car tax, and betting duty. In most cases the period is 12 months immediately before death; the Inland Revenue can no longer—as before—pick the year most advantageous to it.

(2) Employees' wages for four months before the employer's

---

[11] Cremation Act 1902.
[12] *Griffiths' Trs.* v. *Griffiths*, 1912 S.C. 626.
[13] Memorandum No. 22 (1976), para. 4.19; No. 71 (1986), paras. 8.1–8.2.
[14] (1821) 1 S. 163 (new ed. 156). See now Bankruptcy (Scotland) Act 1985, s. 51(1)(c).
[15] *Moncrieff* v. *Monypenny* (1713) Mor. 3945; the point was not directly decided.
[16] Inland Revenue Statement of Practice 7/87.
[17] Bankruptcy (Scotland) Act 1985, s. 51(1)(c).
[18] Bankruptcy (Scotland) Act 1985, Sched. 3; S.I. 1986 No. 1914. As regards payment within the six months, see Wilson & Duncan, p. 454.

death, up to a maximum of £800; or money advanced (by, say, a bank) to pay wages and actually used for that purpose.

(e) Ordinary debts

3.8 There are innumerable types: debts arising from delict, quasi-contract, or contract. Expenses relating to the birth of the deceased's posthumous child form one rare example.

A spouse or child may be able to claim aliment as a debt from the estate. This has three distinct aspects:

(1) Temporary aliment after the death of the father or husband, or (probably) the wife.[19] This is strictly speaking not a privileged debt, and has no preference over ordinary creditors; but if the estate is not manifestly insolvent the executor may pay reasonable aliment within the six months without having to reimburse creditors if it later turns out insolvent.[20] The purpose is to provide support till the estate can be distributed: so it lasts for six months after the relative's death[21] and is due irrespective of the value of any legacies or inheritances. One may lose one's entitlement if one has clearly renounced it, or if one is otherwise well provided for during that period.

(2) Continuing aliment rests on a general principle that "in every case the representatives of a person deceased . . . are, out of [their] succession, liable in aliment to those whom the deceased himself was under a natural obligation to maintain."[22] Though it is sometimes termed a debt (and so has priority over legal rights[23]) it is payable *after* ordinary debts and—unlike them—cannot delay payment of legacies. The claim is primarily against beneficiaries to the extent that they are enriched by inheritance, and only against the executors while the estate is still in their hands. It is equitable: it lasts for as long as one needs support, but fails if one expressly renounces one's rights or receives a fair and adequate share of the deceased's estate.

The Scottish Law Commission considers whether the concept should be abolished, but makes no recommendations.[24]

(3) These claims are a continuation of the deceased's obligation to aliment his family. But if the estate is bankrupt unpaid aliment cannot be claimed unless it is quantified by court decree or by a legally binding obligation evidenced in writing, *and*—in cases involving spouses—they were divorced or living apart.[25]

---

[19] Married Women's Property (Scotland) Act 1920, s. 4.
[20] *Barlass* v. *Barlass's Trs.*, 1916 S.C. 741.
[21] Or, in older law, till the next term day of Whitsunday or Martinmas.
[22] Erskine, *Inst.* (3rd ed.), I.vi.58 (note by Lord Ivory). Nearly all cases involve widows or children.
[23] *Anderson* v. *Grant* (1899) 1 F. 484.
[24] Memorandum No. 71, paras. 8.2–8.6.
[25] Bankruptcy (Scotland) Act 1985, Sched. 1, para. 2(1).

INCIDENCE OF DEBTS

1. General

3.9 A creditor may demand payment of his debt from any part of the estate, whether heritable or moveable. But the type of debt determines which part of the estate must ultimately bear liability for it. The part which pays the creditor will be repaid so far as possible from the part primarily liable.

Before 1964 this involved reimbursement between those to whom the deceased's property passed: the executor (moveables) and (for heritage) the heir at law or heir of provision. Under the Succession (Scotland) Act 1964 the property now goes to the executor,[26] but the old rules governing incidence of debts were expressly preserved.[27] They now have two purposes. They allocate a debt to heritage or moveables: this is important in calculating the moveable estate available for legal rights. Secondly, a debt may be payable out of a specific item (and thus the beneficiary taking the item bears the cost) or out of the residue of the general estate.

2. Heritable and moveable debts

3.10 The basic principle is that "the personal estate is the primary fund for the payment of unsecured obligations, as the real [heritable] estate is for the payment of obligations secured on heritage or attached to it."[28] Moveable debts are paid out of moveables, heritable out of heritage. So heritable debts reduce the assets available for some prior rights, and moveable debts those available for legal rights.[29]

Ordinary debts arising from delict or contract are moveable. This includes the unpaid price of heritage under a contract of sale (conversely, a house is a heritable asset of the estate even though a real right has not yet been obtained by registration). Arrears of feu duties and rent, and obligations of warrandice in respect of land, are moveable. The rationale is that they are all normally paid out of cash funds.

A debt is heritable if declared a real burden or if secured over heritage. A standard security over a house (a mortgage) is the obvious example: it will reduce the surviving spouse's prior right in the house.[30] Quasi-contractual obligations to recompense someone for

---

[26] With exceptions, like property subject to special destinations.
[27] 1964 Act, s. 14(3).
[28] McLaren, Vol. II, p. 1305.
[29] For prior rights see para. 4.7, for legal rights para. 4.11.
[30] As defined in Succession (Scotland) Act 1964, s. 8(6)(d).

improvements to land are also heritable, as are "rights having a future tract of time" such as annuities.

3.11 Complications arise if two securities exist for one debt—one moveable (such as a life assurance policy assigned in security to the lender) and one heritable (a standard security). In that case the debt must be deducted from heritage and moveables in proportion to the two securities' respective values. If two borrowers have taken out a joint mortgage and joint policy there must also be an apportionment between them. Now in reality the policy pays off the whole loan. Legal rights are then due out of the proceeds. The effect is that the sum subject to legal rights (policy less appropriate proportion of loan) exceeds the cash actually available to pay them (policy less whole loan) and cash must be found from elsewhere in the estate to compensate.

3.12 Where a debt is secured over a particular asset—heritable or moveable—whoever inherits the asset takes *cum onere* (subject to the debt). He must pay the debt if he wants the asset. Take *Stewart* v. *Stewart*:[31] an insurance policy had been assigned to a bank in security for a loan; the legatee only took the policy after repayment of the loan. The same goes for a loan secured over a house: even if an insurance policy provides funds to pay it off (as is common) the legatee must in principle reimburse the estate.[32]

3. Provisions in wills

3.13 A well-drafted will may specify what assets debts should be paid out of. It may thus alter the normal rules of incidence, by (say) passing certain items to beneficiaries "free of debts" or instructing that debts be paid out of the residue or some other part of the estate. The courts have evolved various rules to decide the effect of such provisions. The question is to ascertain the testator's intention as expressed in the will: the mere fact that executors for convenience pay debts out of particular assets will not itself alter their ultimate incidence.

(1) There must be express words or clear implication:

> "The heritable and the moveable succession must respectively bear the debts and burdens appropriate to each, unless the testator in his settlement gives express directions to the contrary, or gives directions with reference to the disposal of his means and estate which by clear and necessary implication plainly shew

---

[31] (1891) 19 R. 310.
[32] For the effect of mortgages and insurance policies see Gretton (1987) 32 J.L.S. 303, (1988) 33 J.L.S. 141; Dalgleish (1987) 32 J.L.S. 423.

that a particular . . . debt is to be paid out of that part of his succession upon which it would not fall but for these directions."[33]

Several of the reported cases concern annuities, which under normal rules are paid out of heritage. In *Breadalbane's Trustees* v. *Duke of Buckingham*[34]—one of a string of cases which helped impoverish the vast Breadalbane estates—trustees were to pay the "whole free proceeds" of certain lands; those lands were unaffected by the annuity, which thus was a burden on the other heritage. But one may, as in *Gordon* v. *Scott*,[35] implicitly or expressly instruct annuities to be paid out of the residue of the moveable estate.

(2) If the will expressly states that debts are to be paid out of a particular asset, the rest of the estate is freed of liability. The legatee to whom the asset goes must pay the debt. If a will directs debts to be paid from the residue of the estate, the other assets bear the burden only to the extent that the residue is insufficient for full payment.

(3) Wills frequently contain a general direction to executors to "pay all my just and lawful debts". That by itself does not alter their ordinary incidence: it merely makes explicit the executors' legal duty. So where a debt is secured over heritable assets which are left in a legacy, the direction does not free the legatee of liability to pay. The same rule governs moveables, but has been doubted.[36] More is required in order to transfer liability to the general estate: "express directions are not essential, but the inference must be irresistible and the intention clear beyond all doubt."[37]

4. Inheritance tax

3.14 Inheritance tax is a debt of the estate. It is chargeable on the value of the deceased's estate immediately before his death after deducting his debts and funeral expenses. Executor and beneficiaries are both liable to account for the tax attributable to the estate (respectively) confirmed to or inherited; the executor is liable first because he must account to the Capital Taxes Office for the tax before he can obtain confirmation, normally doing both through the standard Form A3 inventory. A will cannot alter the rules of accountability. The incidence of inheritance tax on particular assets is a separate issue: that can be altered by will.

---

[33] *Gordon* v. *Scott* (1873) 11 M. 334: Lord Kincairney at p. 337.
[34] (1842) 4 D. 1259.
[35] *Supra.* Contrast *Smith's Trs.* v. *Smith*, 1912 1 S.L.T. 484 where the heritable estate bore the burden.
[36] By Lord Dunedin in *Reid's Trs.* v. *Dawson*, 1915 S.C. (H.L.) 47 at p. 50; *cf. Stewart* v. *Stewart* (1891) 19 R. 310. See also *Brand* v. *Scott's Trs.* (1892) 19 R. 768.
[37] *Muir's Trs.* v. *Muir*, 1916 1 S.L.T. 372.

Subject to any contrary intention shown in the deceased's will, inheritance tax attributable to the deceased's United Kingdom property which vests in his executors (excluding trust property) is a testamentary expense. Thus it will normally fall on the residue of his estate. Where it is *not* a testamentary expense it must "where occasion requires" be repaid to the executor by the beneficiary who takes the assets to which the tax is attributable.[38]

These rules do not distinguish between heritable and moveable property. It was originally thought that specific legacies of heritage—but not moveables—bore their own tax, so that the legatee must reimburse the executor for the *pro rata* share of tax attributable to that asset. That had been the rule for estate duty. But it was decided in *Cowie's Trustees, Petitioners*[39] that inheritance tax falls on the general estate rather than the specific asset: only if the testator by will says otherwise must the legatee bear the tax.

The testator may expressly leave a legacy "free of tax." Tax must of course be paid in respect of it (unless it is exempt, such as a gift to a spouse) but it is paid not by the beneficiary but by the executor out of the residue. Special rules dictate how the appropriate amount of tax is calculated.[40] A share of the residue may be left "free of tax," but not the whole residue—as there then would be nothing to pay tax from. "Free of tax" provisions are interpreted as referring to tax payable only in respect of the testator's own death, and not future tax charges (*e.g.* on a liferenter's death).

5. Special destinations

3.15 A special destination is a provision in a property title stating who takes it on an owner's death. In the usual survivorship destination (property owned in the names of "A and B and the survivor") a deceased's share passes automatically to the survivor when he dies; it does not vest in the executor. Under other special destinations the deceased's share vests in the executor purely to enable it to be conveyed to the person entitled under the destination.[41] Because (unlike other assets) the property does not vest in the executor for the purpose of paying the deceased owner's debts, it was decided in *Barclays Bank Ltd.* v. *McGreish*[42] that the successor takes it free of debts: therefore the creditor cannot sue him.

The decision has been heavily criticised.[43] It is irrelevant whether

---

[38] IHTA 1984, s. 200 (accountability), s. 211 (incidence).
[39] 1982 S.L.T. 326; *sub nom. In Re Dougal* [1981] S.T.C. 514.
[40] See *Capital Taxes Encyclopaedia*, paras. B.6.01–B.6.21.
[41] Succession (Scotland) Act 1964, s. 18(2).
[42] 1983 S.L.T. 344.
[43] *e.g.* Morton, 1984 S.L.T. (News) 133.

the property passes via the executor: it is part of the deceased's estate albeit it devolves automatically rather than by will. The successor is an "heir of provision" and—just as before 1964—creditors should be able to sue him to the value of his inheritance. On that interpretation *McGreish* wrongly alters the existing law.

Further reading

Elder, *Forms of Wills* (1947), pp. 20–21, 46–47, 56–57.

McLaren, Vol. I, pp. 126–129, Vol. II, pp. 1280–1329.

Meston, Chap. 3, *passim*.

Wilson & Duncan, pp. 452–459.

Special Destinations: see 1984 S.L.T. (News) 133, 180, 299; (1984) 29 J.L.S. 154.

CHAPTER 4

INTESTATE SUCCESSION

BACKGROUND

4.1 A person dies intestate if he does not dispose of his property by will. In any society the rules of intestate succession are of great importance. They may govern the bulk of deaths—perhaps two-thirds of Scots people die intestate. They may, depending how equitable they are, influence whether people make wills or not. Furthermore they embody broad principles as to how a society considers property should be disposed of on death. It might, for instance, revert to the state; it might go to the deceased's dependants. It may or may not be permissible to opt out of these rules entirely and make a will disposing of one's property in a different way.

The modern Scots law is contained in the Succession (Scotland) Act 1964, which radically altered the old rules. But the Act is not a comprehensive code, and one important aspect of intestate succession—the protected "legal rights" of spouse and children—derives not from it but from the old common law.

4.2 The pre-1964 law had two striking features.

(1) *Heritable and moveable property.* Different rules governed their disposal. Moveables passed to the executor for distribution to the beneficiaries; heritage passed directly to the person entitled to succeed, the heir-at-law. In each case the order of succession was, broadly: descendants; if none, collaterals (such as brothers); if none, *paternal* ascendants (father, grandfather, and so on).[1] Inheritance depended on blood relationship: except in legal rights—discussed below—the spouse was traditionally excluded. If no blood relation existed, the Crown succeeded as *ultimus haeres.*[2]

Beyond that there were two main differences, due to the rules for heritage deriving from feudal society: their rationale was to transfer the property undivided to a male heir. First, heritage involved primogeniture: the oldest male heir took everything. Moveables were divided equally among a class of people: *e.g.* children. Second, and more important today, was "representation." If an heir died before the intestate person, his own heirs "represented" him: they stood in his shoes and inherited in his place. Representation of all heirs was infinite in the case of heritage: a great-grandchild, say, could take

---

[1] This greatly over-simplifies the scheme. See Currie, p. 102.
[2] *i.e.* literally "last heir".

under it. Representation was more limited for moveables, and non-existent for legal rights.

(2) *Legal rights.* Scots law recognised various protected rights of inheritance known as "legal rights." Those affecting heritage gave a surviving spouse or child income arising from the property: these were "terce" (for the widow) and "courtesy" (for the widower). They were abolished in 1964. Those affecting moveables, *ius relictae* (for the widow), *ius relicti* (for widower) and legitim (for children), are discussed later in this chapter.

Reform was long overdue. In 1911 the surviving spouse was given a limited protected right to inherit, over and above legal rights. The proposals of the Mackintosh Committee in 1950 led ultimately to the Succession (Scotland) Act 1964.

THE SCOPE OF THE ACT

1. General policy

4.3 The Act sets out to improve the position of the surviving spouse: it gives her *prior rights* to the intestate estate.[3] It preserves the stress on blood relationship, but extends that to relations on the mother's side. As amended, it now gives adopted and illegitimate children virtually the same rights as others. Finally, it applies the same legal *machinery* to heritage and moveables—both normally pass through the executor—and gives much the same *rights* to inherit, with one unfortunate exception: legal rights only apply to moveables.[4]

The Act is not retrospective, and applies to deaths on or after September 10, 1964. It does not apply to titles, coats of arms, and honours; these remain governed by the old law. Until 1968 it did not apply to crofting tenancies.[5]

2. Intestate estate

4.4 Three definitions should be borne in mind.

(1) The "estate" is "the whole estate, whether heritable or moveable ... [or both] belonging to the deceased at the time of his death or over which [he] had a power of appointment ... [and] the interest of a tenant under a tenancy which was not expressed to expire on his death." Special rules govern powers of appointment and special destinations.[6]

---

[3] For fuller discussion see below at para. 4.7.
[4] s. 1. See chap. 2, *supra*; chap. 13, *infra*.
[5] s. 37 (1) (*a*), (*d*), (*e*), 37 (2).
[6] s. 36 (2).

(2) One dies intestate by "leaving undisposed of by testamentary disposition the whole or any part of" one's estate, and the "intestate estate" is initially that undisposed-of part.[7]

(3) A testamentary disposition includes any deed taking effect on the intestate's death "whereby any part of his estate is disposed of or under which a succession thereto arises."[8]

The effect, taking the rules together, is as follows.

(i) The Act applies to partial intestacy, where a will (intentionally or not) validly disposes of only part of the estate. It ignores the part which is left by will, except that the cash prior right is set off against legacies. But one can claim legal rights out of testate and intestate estate quite independently of the Act: a will cannot defeat them.

(ii) A special destination is a clause in the title to property, such as a house, governing its passage on death. If the clause deals with the event of the intestate's death, this is not "intestate estate"—whoever put the clause in the title. The reason is that "disposal" is not restricted to actions by the intestate person: it covers instructions made by earlier owners. All this assumes the destination had not been evacuated, *i.e.* revoked: if it had, it passes on death according to the ordinary rules of succession.

(iii) A power of appointment is a provision in a will authorising someone else, the donee of the power, to dispose of one's own property in a certain way. In effect one to some extent delegates one's will-making power. If on the donee's death the power is unexercised and passes to someone else, then (in the case of heritage) the property falls outwith the donee's estate. Otherwise it falls under his estate, but is not intestate estate.

(iv) A *mortis causa* lifetime gift,[9] though not a will, is a testamentary disposition for the purposes of the Act.

3. Artificial intestacy

4.5 Intestacy can come about after the deceased's death even though he left a will. That may happen by accident or deliberately.

A legacy may be ineffective for some reason. It may be so imprecise that the beneficiary cannot be identified: it then lapses for uncertainty. It may be contrary to public policy. The legatee may have died. The will should ideally say what is to happen to the item on that event. Normally it makes specific provision for disposal of the "residue," the remainder of the estate after payment of debts and legacies: the item should then fall into the residue. But if it does not—there is no

---

[7] s. 36 (1).
[8] s. 36 (1).
[9] See para. 5.13.

residue clause—the item is undisposed of by the will. It then falls into intestacy and the rules in the 1964 Act apply.

Similarly the legacy may be intrinsically valid but lapse because the legatee does not take it. He may simply disclaim it. If he claims legal rights he cannot take a benefit under the will: he must choose between them. That is "approbate and reprobate."[10] Again in each case intestacy results if the will names no-one else to inherit on that event.

The odd effect is shown in *Kerr, Petitioner*.[11] A widow was left all her husband's fairly small estate; there was no other provision in the will. She would have been better off under intestacy. The reason was that if she took under the will, she could not claim prior rights (it not being intestate estate) or legal rights (approbate and reprobate forbade her) but her children could claim legal rights (as indefeasible by will): so she would not in fact get the whole estate. If she took under intestacy, she could claim prior rights; those have preference over legal rights and in her case would use up the whole estate. So a will cannot defeat legal rights, but intestacy can to the extent of prior rights. She disclaimed her benefit under the will, got prior rights, and took the whole estate; the children got nothing.

Kerr will not always be useful. The size of prior rights depends on the types of assets in the estate—house, furniture, and cash. If the estate is large, there is a surplus over prior rights and there may be no cash benefit in disclaiming the will. If the will contains a residue clause, or a "destination-over" whereby someone else inherits if the widow disclaims, there is no intestacy.

One course, under current law, is to make a simple will as in *Kerr*. The widow can decide herself in due course whether she is best taking the legacy or prior rights.[12]

4. Order of dividing the estate[12a]

4.6 As a result of the Act there are six stages in distributing an intestate person's estate. They must be carried out in a set order. Because some rights are exigible from heritage and others from moveables, the deceased's heritage and moveables must be quantified separately until after stage (5):

   (1) Payment of debts;
   (2) Prior rights: right to dwelling-house (section 8(1));
   (3) Prior rights: furniture and plenishings (section 8(3));
   (4) Prior rights: right to cash (section 9);

---

[10] See para. 9.3.
[11] 1968 S.L.T. (Sh. Ct.) 61.
[12] For such post-death rearrangements and their tax effects see para. 5.23.
[12a] For examples see Meston, App. 2; Hastings, *Expenses*, App. 3.

(5) Legal rights;
(6) Free estate (section 2).

Prior Rights[13]

4.7 Prior rights are an innovation of the Act, though under the Intestate Husband's Estate (Scotland) Acts 1911 to 1959 a spouse had a more limited right of succession where no children survived. They apply in favour of a surviving spouse, but only on intestacy (unlike legal rights). They prescribe after 20 years:[14] they cease to be legally enforceable.

1. Dwelling-house

4.8 The surviving spouse has a right to the deceased's dwelling-house or, depending on its value, cash in lieu. Four questions must be asked:

(1) Had the deceased a "relevant interest" in the dwelling-house in question? He must have been owner or tenant. Rent Act tenancies are excluded (they have similar parallel rules). If the tenancy was worded to end with the death, there is no interest for the spouse to inherit.[15]

"Dwelling-house" includes a part of a building occupied as a separate dwelling: *e.g.* a flat. It also includes garden and amenity ground attached to the house itself, so the spouse gets that too.

(2) Was the surviving spouse ordinarily resident in the house at the date of the death? Where the deceased lived is immaterial. If the spouse was ordinarily resident in two such houses (*e.g.* town house and country cottage) she must choose one only, but has six months after the death to do so.

(3) What was the value of the deceased's interest? If over £65,000[16] the spouse will receive that amount in cash instead. If the value is disputed, it is to be fixed by arbitration by one arbiter chosen by agreement or by the sheriff for the area where the deceased was domiciled at his death or (if that was abroad or unknown) for Edinburgh.

The interest is valued under deduction of heritable debts secured over it: *i.e.* mortgages. So the spouse gets the house less the amount of the mortgage, while any surplus insurance proceeds which pay it off on death are not hers but are an asset of the estate. In effect she may have to reimburse the estate if she wants the house at its full value.

---

[13] See generally Clive, *Husband & Wife* (2nd ed.), pp. 679 et seq.
[14] Prescription and Limitation (Scotland) Act 1973, s. 7 and Sched. 1, para. 2 (*f*).
[15] See also s. 36(2).
[16] Set by S.I. 1988 No. 633, under s. 8(1).

(4) Is the interest, though worth under £65,000, an exception to the rule? If so the spouse gets cash to the value of the interest.

There are two such exceptions: where the dwelling-house forms part of property that the deceased tenanted; and where it forms part or all of property used by the deceased to carry on a business, and the value of the estate as a whole would be likely to be substantially diminished by disposing of the house separately from the other business assets.

2. Furniture and plenishings

4.9 This right applies where the estate includes the furniture and plenishings of a house where the spouse was ordinarily resident at the date of death. The spouse is entitled to receive them or, if they total over £12,000,[17] items coming in total to that sum.

Again arbitration is possible. If there is more than one such house the spouse has six months to choose from which house to take the contents: she cannot pick and choose from both. This election is quite separate from that as respects the dwelling-house under section 8 (1): the contents can be from a different house; indeed (by contrast with the former election) the house need not itself be part of the deceased's intestate estate, provided the contents themselves are.

Furniture and plenishings include "garden effects, domestic animals, plate, plated articles, linen, china, glass, books, pictures, prints, articles of household use and consumable stores." That is not an exhaustive definition; it may be a nice question in some cases whether an item falls within the list. They exclude articles and animals used at the date of death for business purposes, money and securities, and heirlooms. An "heirloom," rather unhelpfully, is "any article which has associations with the intestate's family of such nature and extent that it ought to pass to some member of the family other than the surviving spouse."

3. Monetary right

4.10 The surviving spouse has the right to a sum of cash from the intestate estate (section 9). This is in addition to the rights to house and furniture, which have priority and must be dealt with first: the "intestate estate" available for purposes of section 9 is that available after satisfaction of debts and section 8 prior rights.

The sum is currently £21,000 if the deceased left surviving children and £35,000 if he did not.[18] The spouse will also receive interest on the

---

[17] S.I. 1988 No. 633.
[18] S.I. 1988 No. 633.

sum from the date of death till actual payment: the rate is fixed from time to time by the Secretary of State, and is currently 7 per cent.[19] If the spouse is entitled to receive a legacy from the deceased's estate, that must be set off against the cash sum (unless the legacy is of a "section 8-type" dwelling-house or of furniture and plenishings in it). That contrasts with the section 8 prior rights: house and furniture prior rights need not be set off against corresponding legacies.

Note that "legacy" is widely drawn to cover, say, special destinations and *mortis causa* gifts: "any payment or benefit to which a surviving spouse becomes entitled by virtue of any testamentary disposition." The set-off is calculated on the value at the date of death.

All the three prior rights are independent of each other; they are not simply aspects of a cash fund. So what the spouse gets depends very much on precisely what mix of assets was in the estate.

If any surplus estate is left after payment of prior rights, the next stage is to calculate legal rights due out of the moveable property.

LEGAL RIGHTS

1. Nature of legal rights

4.11 Legal rights are a distinctive feature of Scots law. They are probably a relic of an old form of "community of property" within the family: a person could not dispose of his property on his death just as he liked; his spouse and children had some claim on it. Freedom of testation over part of the estate—the "dead's part"—was probably a later innovation. Such rules were once more widespread, and still exist in an updated form in many Civilian legal systems. English law, by contrast, moved long ago to allow complete freedom of testation, and has only recently reintroduced a limited form of family protection.[20]

As such, legal rights are more like debts than ordinary rights of succession.[21] They are paid *after* ordinary debts, but *before* ordinary rights of succession. They apply in both testacy and intestacy, and cannot be defeated by will: so they protect the family against disinheritance. If the will cuts them out they can claim legal rights instead; the provisions in the will are abated—reduced—to the extent necessary to make property available to pay legal rights. Even if they are left legacies they can *elect* for legal rights instead; in that case they

---

[19] Law Reform (Miscellaneous Provisions) (Scotland) Act 1980, s. 4; S.I. 1981 No. 805.

[20] Wills Act 1837; Inheritance (Provision for Family and Dependants) Act 1975.

[21] *Naismith* v. *Boyes* (1899) 1 F. (H.L.) 79.

lose the legacies. The rights are automatic: they need no court application. Spouse and children are thus far better protected than in England, where discretionary payments require application to the courts.

The property available for legal rights depends on whether the deceased left a surviving spouse, or children, or both. *Ius relictae* gives the widow one-third of the moveable estate (if descendants survive) and one-half otherwise; similarly *ius relicti* for the widower. Legitim (the "bairns' part") gives children (and their offspring by representation if they die first) one-third of the moveable estate in aggregate, or one-half if there is no surviving spouse. The remaining one-third or one-half is the "dead's part": he can make a will over that without fear of challenge from spouse or children, and if he does not it becomes the "free estate" for distribution under the rules of intestacy.

In principle the claimant's right is to cash, not to particular assets from the estate. The executor can hand over assets, but failing agreement among all concerned he can sell and transfer the proceeds. But if the assets fetch more than their death value the rights must be revalued[22] and capital gains tax may be due.[23]

2. Heritable and moveable property

4.12 Legal rights are exigible only from moveable property. For that reason heritable and moveable assets and debts of the estate must be segregated on paper at the stage of paying debts and distributing prior rights.

(a) Types of property[24]

4.13 Usually it is obvious whether an item is heritable or moveable. Some types of property have special rules, and others are, by a quirk of history, legal chamaeleons—heritable for one purpose and moveable for another. The main examples are:

(1) Heritable securities: such as a standard security over a house, *i.e.* a mortgage. Their treatment depends on whether one is dealing with the estate of the creditor or the debtor. As regards the creditor they are moveable for most purposes, except—to be perverse—(a) taxation, which may affect the incidence of IHT; and (b) legal rights. So investments in heritable securities are not subject to legal rights.[25]

---

[22] Allan (1988) 33 J.L.S. 130; see para. 4.19.
[23] Scobbie (1987) 32 J.L.S. 341; see para. 12.29.
[24] See Meston, pp. 45–47. For legacies see para. 10.25, *infra*.
[25] Titles to Land Consolidation (Scotland) Act 1868, s. 117, as amended by Succession (Scotland) Act 1964, Sched. 3.

More normally one is dealing with the estate of the debtor: the person who has taken out the mortgage. Heritable debts are in principle set against heritable assets, unless (in testacy) the will alters their incidence. If the lenders also had a life assurance policy (covering the sum due) assigned to them in security of the same debt, one must calculate what proportion it bears to the total amount of the two securities: that proportion of the *debt* is treated as moveable, the rest being a heritable debt. The policy security thus reduces the estate subject to legal rights.

(2) If the deceased had sold heritage but not received the price, the right to the price is moveable under the doctrine of *conversion*. If he has bought but not paid, the asset is heritable but the debt (the price) is moveable.

(3) Suppose the deceased had, when he died, a vested right under someone else's will. That right is an asset of his estate. In the case of a specific legacy, if the item itself was moveable so is his right to it. With general legacies the legatee usually only has a right to cash, which is moveable whatever the deceased's original property was.

(b) The effect of prior rights

4.14 The prior right to a house is plainly deducted from heritage; that to furniture, from moveables. When cash is paid in lieu of the house, it seems that should also be taken off heritage.

If the monetary provision were all taken out of moveables, that would deplete the legitim fund and would be unfair on the children. So it is deducted from heritable and moveable assets in the same proportions that they form of the estate at that stage. Note that that is purely a paper calculation so that one can value what is available for legal rights. In practice the monetary right may be satisfied by giving the spouse heritable assets: that is a matter of choice and is immaterial for calculating legal rights.

3. Entitlement to legal rights

(a) Representation

4.15 Suppose a child was entitled to legitim but died before his parent leaving a grandchild. Before 1964 the child's legal rights would simply have been extinguished. The 1964 Act allows the grandchild to "represent" the child: to step into his shoes and inherit his claim. So section 11(1), as amended, provides:

> "Where a person dies predeceased by a child who has left issue who survive the deceased, and the child would, if he had survived

the deceased, have been entitled ... to legitim out of the deceased's estate, such issue shall have the like right to legitim as the child would have had if he had survived the deceased."

This originally applied only to legitimate children, but the distinction has now been completely abolished in intestacy.[26] The idea is analogous to the *conditio si institutus sine liberis decesserit* in wills. But there is no representation under *ius relictae* or *relicti*: if there were, a stepchild of the deceased, unrelated to him by blood, could claim; and that would run contrary to the whole ethos of the 1964 Act.

4.16 The problem then is how to divide legitim if there are several claimants. Suppose A left two children B and C; B survives and has a grandchild D; C has died leaving two grandchildren E and F. There are two possible modes of dividing the legitim fund. One is *per capita* division: equal shares of one-third each. The other is *per stirpes* division. A *stirps* is a branch of a family tree; *per stirpes* division would divide the fund at the level of B and C so that B takes half and E and F take a quarter each. (The problem also arises in wills, where the question is often where the will places the head of the *stirps*.)

Section 11(1) by itself suggests *per stirpes* division. In fact it is governed by section 11(2) which orders *per capita* division in some cases. The net effect is as follows:

(1) If all the descendants have the same degree of relationship to the deceased, division is equal—*per capita*. So (above) if B and C both die, D, E and F each get a third.

(2) Otherwise division is at the level of the nearest surviving relation to the deceased—*per stirpes*. So if B is alive, he takes half and E and F take a quarter each. D gets nothing because representation only operates on B's death.

(b) Date of calculation and payment

4.17 The existence of legal rights is ascertained at the date of death. Spouse or children then alive acquire a vested right, which passes to their executors if they die before payment. Several factors can delay payment. Debts take some time to be paid; claimants may claim late. A child cannot make a valid binding election till aged 18, and the executors will need to retain funds to cover a possible election at that point.

Interest accrues from death to the date of payment,[27] unless

---

[26] Law Reform (Parent and Child) (Scotland) Act 1986, s. 2.
[27] *Kearon* v. *Thomson's Trs.*, 1949 S.C. 287.

(perhaps) the delay was the claimant's fault.[28] The rate is not fixed: it is what the sum earned or could have earned by prudent management.

4.18 Similarly the estate available for payment is that at the date of death, after deducting moveable debts, IHT, funeral costs and executry expenses to obtain confirmation and realise assets.[29] Later insurance or pension payments made directly to a widow or child (as opposed to the executors) are not part of the estate: the recipient's claim derives from the policy, not from legal rights.

There are two moot points.

(1) A dies; B, a legatee, elects for a legacy instead of legal rights. Later another legatee dies before his legacy vests: that legacy lapses and the asset falls into intestacy. Legal rights are now due from it if it was part of the estate at A's death;[30] B's election affects only the *testate* estate.

(2) Income from the estate was accumulated as ordered by a testamentary trust. The accumulation later becomes illegal and any further income falls into intestacy. The income was not part of the death estate, so is probably not subject to legal rights; but the caselaw is undecided.[31]

4.19 At what date are legal rights valued? In principle it is the date of death, so one uses the figures inserted for IHT and confirmation; but *Alexander* v. *Alexander's Trustees*[32] illustrates an exception. A widow and child wanted to claim legal rights in place of legacies; the assets had been sold soon after the death at a lower value than that estimated for tax purposes. The court held that the realised and not the estimated value is used if executors sell assets in due course without delay. On the other hand later profits or losses resulting from the executors' administration have no effect on the valuation for legal rights.

(c) Collation inter liberos

4.20 The purpose of collation is to ensure equality in the distribution of the legitim fund among claimants. If one claimant has received advances from the deceased during his life, other claimants can require the advances to be notionally added to the fund. So it applies

---

[28] *Wick* v. *Wick* (1898) 1 F. 199.
[29] *Russell* v. *Att. Gen.*, 1917 S.C. 28.
[30] *Naismith* v. *Boyes* (1899) 1 F. (H.L.) 79.
[31] *cf. Moon's Trs.* v. *Moon* (1899) 2 F. 201, *Wilson's Trs.* v. *Glasgow Royal Infirmary*, 1917 S.C. 527. See Wilson & Duncan, p. 117.
[32] 1954 S.C. 436; *Gilchrist* v. *Gilchrist's Trs.* (1889) 16 R. 1118.

only when there is more than one claimant: one cannot insist on non-claimants collating and so increase the legitim fund.[33]

Not all advances need be collated. An advance of heritable property is irrelevant. An advance in discharge of the natural duty to maintain and educate the recipient need not be collated;[34] similarly remuneration under a contract. Nor need a loan by the deceased (that will be an asset of the estate anyway) or one made on the express basis of being in addition to legitim. But advances in order to set the recipient up in the world—say, to furnish a home of his own—or in business must be collated.

The method is to add the advance to the fund (on paper); divide equally among claimants; and deduct the advance from the recipient's resulting share. If that gives him a minus quantity he need not actually repay anything; he simply gets no legitim. Envisage four claimants A, B, C, and D: £50,000 is available; A had an advance of £10,000. The legitim fund is £60,000: A gets £5,000 and the others £15,000 each.

4.21 The 1964 Act, in conjunction with representation, allows collation of advances to a predeceasing child who is being represented (section 11(3)). The representer must collate an "appropriate proportion" of such advances. The problem is that the representer's *per capita* share of legitim may not be the same as the child's would have been, and that the Act does not define "appropriate proportion." The Act gives no clear answer.[35]

4. Extinction of legal rights

(a) Discharge during deceased's lifetime

4.22 Before 1964 it was possible for parents to discharge their children's legal rights by means of an antenuptial marriage contract. *Callander* v. *Callander's Executor*[36] shows just how inequitable this could be. The *quid pro quo* in the marriage contract was to set up a trust fund whose income would go to the children. Many years later the trust was wound up by a deed. A son argued that as a result his legitim should revive: the Lords found no support for that in the words of the deed.

Since the 1964 Act only the person entitled to legitim can discharge it. That was always so with spouses. But pre-1964 discharges remain in force (section 12).

[33] *Coats' Trs.* v. *Coats*, 1914 S.C. 744.
[34] Erskine, *Inst.*, III. ix. 24.
[35] Meston at 1967 S.L.T. (News) 195 suggests solutions.
[36] 1972 S.C. (H.L.) 70.

The effect is that the estate available for legal rights is divided between claimants as if the person giving the discharge had died before the deceased.

(b) Renunciation after deceased's death [37]

4.23 The effect is that legal rights are calculated as if the discharger was a claimant, but his share then falls into the free intestate estate. So renunciation, unlike pre-death discharge, does not increase the other claimants' shares.

A child under 18 cannot make a binding discharge or renunciation. The executors must retain sufficient funds in case he decides to claim at that age. But in calculating legitim for IHT purposes they can make a provisional election within two years after the death; failing that IHT is assessed as if legitim was claimed; but whichever they choose the assessment can be reopened to reflect what the child decides at 18 (or, at latest, before he is 20).[38]

(c) Prescription

4.24 Legal rights, like prior rights, prescribe—lapse—if not claimed in 20 years after becoming enforceable. That refers to the date of death, the claimant reaching 18, or intestacy arising, as appropriate.[39]

THE FREE ESTATE

4.25 The free estate is what is left after debts have been paid and prior and legal rights satisfied. If the deceased left no surviving spouse or children, it comprises the whole estate.

The estate is distributed in the order laid down in section 2(1). One simply goes through each successive class of relations till one finds someone entitled to inherit. One must exhaust each category of relative before going on to the next. There is no limit except the practicality of tracing a genealogical link (legitimate or not): anyone, however distant, may inherit.

Each category in section 2(1) is read subject to sections 5 and 6 which provide for infinite representation of a deceased beneficiary, and for division *per capita* and *per stirpes* in that process. For instance (in (3) below) nephews and nieces, and their own descendants, have preference over (4); (6) gives cousins preference over (7). Sections 5

[37] See Election at para. 9.3.
[38] IHTA 1984, s. 147. The Inland Revenue *may* allow a later decision.
[39] Prescription and Limitation (Scotland) Act 1973, s. 7, Sched. 1, para. 2 (*f*).

and 6 apply to all beneficiaries except the deceased's parents and spouse: this will (for instance) prevent someone inheriting who is a child of one's spouse but is not related to oneself—*i.e.* a stepchild. The law still stresses a blood tie with the deceased person. The "parent" exception stops one's half brother (or sister) taking *that parent's* share by representation; he/she can (as discussed below) in some cases inherit a share in his/her *own* right as a collateral.

4.26 The order of succession (subject to representation) is:
(1) children;
(2) parents *and* brothers or sisters (if someone survives from both classes): each class takes half the estate;
(3) brothers or sisters (if no parents alive);
(4) parents (if no brothers or sisters alive);
(5) spouse;
(6) uncles and aunts, both maternal and paternal;
(7) grandparents;
(8) grandparents' brothers or sisters; and so on.

Those in (3), (6) and (8) are examples of *collaterals*: brothers and sisters of the intestate or of an ancestor. They are classified as being of the whole blood (sharing both parents with the intestate or ancestor) or half blood (sharing one). The first class has preference over the second; but among the second it is immaterial whether the parent was their mother or father (section 3).

4.27 If no relation is found, the estate goes to the Crown as *ultimus haeres*. The Queen's and Lord Treasurer's Remembrancer, an official who is now the same person as the Crown Agent, takes possession of the estate without obtaining confirmation. He will advertise for possible relatives, but anyone who knows of one must tell him. He will then pay the debts and the balance goes to the Treasury. But unrelated people who apply for money from the funds may be paid at his discretion. At one time these were often illegitimate relations (who then had no right to inherit); now it may be someone like a housekeeper who has a moral claim.[40]

LAW REFORM

4.28 The Scottish Law Commission consider numerous possible changes to intestate succession and legal rights.[41] Among the possibilities canvassed are:
(1) to replace *prior rights*, as currently constituted, with either a fixed cash proportion of the estate, or alternatively a "slicing"

---

[40] See Wilson & Duncan, p. 417; Currie, p. 114.
[41] Memorandum No. 69 (1986).

system: 100 per cent of the first £x,000, 80 per cent of the next £x,000, and so on;

(2) as regards *legal rights*:

   (i) to restrict them to cases of partial intestacy. In total intestacy the rules for the free estate should protect the family well enough;

  (ii) to replace the present automatic entitlement with discretionary provision on application to the courts. This would bring Scots law much closer to the English ethos of family provision;

 (iii) to extend that provision to others such as cohabitees and children who, though unrelated, were accepted into the family;

 (iv) to abolish collation.

Further reading

Meston, *The Succession (Scotland) Act 1964*, Chaps. 4–6.
Clive, *Husband and Wife* (2nd ed.), pp. 679–699.
Meston, "Collation of Advances by Ancestors," 1967 S.L.T. (News) 195.
N. R. Allan, "Legal Rights" (1988) 33 J.L.S. 130.

CHAPTER 5

WILL SUBSTITUTES

5.1 Scots law recognises a number of methods whereby, without making a will, one may provide for succession on death. Various types of lifetime deed may contain provisions which have a testamentary effect.

SPECIAL DESTINATIONS

1. Types of special destination

(a) General

5.2 The purpose of a destination is to regulate the order in which people own property. The type found in wills is the destination-over, which provides for a substitute beneficiary to succeed either after an original institute or in his place if he fails for some reason to inherit.[1] The special destination, by contrast, occurs in documents of title which regulate the ownership of property during the maker's lifetime and also its inheritance on his death. It is thus not a testamentary writing but it has a testamentary effect: it supersedes the rules of intestate succession without the need to make a will. It may relate to moveables or, more commonly, heritage.

The usual type is a survivorship destination: property is taken in the name of "A and B and the survivor of them"; this frequently occurs when spouses buy their matrimonial home. It is loosely analogous to the English "joint tenancy." Rarer types specify named individuals—"A then B then C"— or a class— "my male heirs."

The essence of the special destination is that it alters the ordinary rules of intestate succession; otherwise, after all, it would have little point. But for the destination each person's share would pass straight to their beneficiaries. It is "special" in that it deals with a particular item of property as opposed to the grantor's whole estate. A destination to "heirs" is not special: they would take on intestacy anyway. Judicial definitions are rare, but that in *Cormack* v. *McIldowie's Executors*[2] is important and controversial:

"I . . . regard a special destination as one in which the particular property in the deed is disponed to the particular person (or

---

[1] See Murray, pp. 138–141; *infra*, paras. 10.13, 11.13.
[2] 1975 S.C. 161, at p. 177 per Lord Justice-Clerk Wheatley.

43

persons) specifically nominated by the granter, without regard to the normal operation of the law of succession on intestacy."

That formulation apparently excludes "class" destinations, and has been challenged for that reason.[3] The case concerned an agricultural tenancy: the court feared that including "class" destinations would, absurdly, take most tenancies outwith the scope of the 1964 Act.

(b) Types of property

5.3 At one time one could not dispose of heritable property by will, but only by a *de praesenti*—immediate—lifetime conveyance. One way to circumvent this was to include in that conveyance a special destination stating to whom the property passed after the buyer's death. Its *raison d'être* vanished when wills of heritage were allowed in 1868,[4] but it is still used for convenience.

One may also find destinations in any document of title for moveable property. *Connell's Trustees* v. *Connell's Trustees*[5] illustrates their scope. That case confirmed that a bond—a document constituting a debt—may contain a destination. So may shares in companies.

Contrast a deposit receipt—a receipt for money deposited in a bank. Often the depositor includes on it names other than his own. That is convenient: it gives those named on it the right to uplift the money from the bank. But it is not a document of title: it does not prove who owns the money.[6] In principle only the depositor himself is owner. So if he puts a destination on the receipt it has no testamentary effect: the survivor can uplift the funds but must pay them on to the depositor's executor as part of his estate.[7] So in *Dinwoodie's Executrix* v. *Carruthers' Executor*[8] X and Y respectively provided £50 and £400 of a deposit; despite a survivorship destination, X as survivor only owned what he had put in, Y's executors getting the rest.

There is a further problem with share certificates. In England a simple joint holding by "A and B" implies a survivorship destination though none is expressed; in Scotland that is not so. But the English rule apparently applies to shares held by Scots in English companies. The rule has been doubted, and does not apply to Government stock, which is deemed British rather than English.[9]

---

[3] Halliday (1977) 22 J.L.S. 16; see Scot. Law Com. Memorandum No. 71, para. 3.24.
[4] Titles to Land Consolidation (Scotland) Act 1868, s. 20.
[5] (1886) 13 R. 1175.
[6] The same applies to names on a bank account.
[7] *Connell's Trs.*; *Crosbie's Trs.* v. *Wright* (1880) 7 R. 823.
[8] (1895) 23 R. 234.
[9] *Connell's Trs., supra; cf. Cunningham's Trs.* v. *Cunningham*, 1924 S.C. 581, *Colenso's Exr.* v. *Davidson*, 1930 S.L.T. 359.

(c) The effect of special destinations

5.4 Because a destination is contained in a lifetime conveyance but has testamentary effect, one should distinguish its effect during life and on death. Consider the typical case where A purchases property in the name of "A and B and the survivor."

In bare principle A, as buyer, remains full owner of that property during his lifetime; B has no rights till the destination operates on death. Merely taking title in another's name gives them no immediate rights: delivery of the document—or an equivalent act—is also essential. Failing delivery, the destination still operates on A's death because testamentary provisions need no delivery, but B has no half share while A lives:

> "The doctrine of special destination is that if (1) anyone takes the documentary title to property or securities (including shares), which he has acquired in his own right or out of his own means, in favour of some other person (either solely or jointly with himself . . .), and (2) if such title remains in the possession of the acquirer undelivered to such other person during the acquirer's lifetime, then such title is held to constitute a valid nomination of such other person as successor of the acquirer in [that] property—to the extent of the whole, if the title is in favour of [the other] solely or as survivor."[10]

Heritage is registered in the Register of Sasines or Land Register: that is the legal equivalent of delivery, so A and B are at once common owners. Non-delivery is much more likely with documents of title to moveables: suppose A keeps them in his files till he dies? Some actions are deemed equivalent to delivery, but there is no closed list. What is needed is "a dealing with the document in such a way as to put it out of the power of the [grantor] to deal with it."[11] Confusingly, registering shares in a company register has been accepted in some cases but not others.[12]

5.5 Assuming delivery (or the equivalent), A and B are common owners of the property while they both live. Each is full owner of a *pro indiviso* share, and has an unrestricted right to dispose of it *inter vivos*; neither has any rights over the other's share. That was clear in *Steele* v. *Caldwell*,[13] where the husband put his wife out of the house and sold his half-share to strangers who took up residence: the wife could

---

[10] *Dennis* v. *Aitchison*, 1923 S.C. 819, at p. 825 *per* Lord President Clyde; affirmed 1924 S.C. (H.L.) 122.
[11] Lord President Dunedin in *Carmichael* v. *Carmichael's Exx.*, 1920 S.C. (H.L.) 195 at p. 201, where intimating an insurance policy to a beneficiary was sufficient.
[12] *Inland Revenue* v. *Wilson*, 1928 S.C. (H.L.) 42; *cf. Dennis* v. *Aitchison, supra.*
[13] 1979 S.L.T. 228.

not stop that. (The Matrimonial Homes (Family Protection) (Scotland) Act 1981 would now protect her right to occupy the house, but as regards ownership the principle remains.) Having said that, in one maverick case[14] three children A, B and C were treated as *joint* owners: the special factor was supposedly an agreement that they could use the property for life as a family home. For that reason none of them could have sold their share without the others' consent.

(d) Operation of destination on death

5.6 Before 1964 heritage passed on death directly to the person entitled to succeed: the heir-at-law or, in the case of special destinations, the heir of provision. The 1964 Act abolished the machinery of "service of heirs"; under the Act both heritage and moveables ordinarily pass to the executor for distribution to beneficiaries.

Special rules for destinations were thus necessary. In principle heritage subject to an unrevoked special destination is not part of a deceased's estate under the Act (section 36(2)(*a*)): so it does not go to the executor for ordinary distribution. But title must pass to the heir somehow. With survivorship destinations his title is automatic by virtue of survivance: nothing need be done. With other types the property vests in the executor purely for him to have it conveyed to the person entitled under the destination (section 18(2)).

2. Revocation of special destinations

(a) Revocability

5.7 We have seen that a destination can be defeated by lifetime dealings: *Steele* v. *Caldwell*. In principle one may also evacuate—revoke or defeat—it by will. One cannot of course affect other co-owners' shares by so doing.

Two factors bar revocation; both depend on who paid the purchase price of the property. First, the destination may be contractual because the two co-owners contributed equally to the price, as in *Perrett's Trustees* v. *Perrett*:[15] "each took the chance of getting the half of the other, and accordingly . . . the property stands upon its own destination and is not carried, and could not be carried, by any testament whatsoever . . . this destination could [not] have been altered except by joint consent of the spouses." Alternatively they

[14] *Munro* v. *Munro and Another*, 1972 S.L.T. (Sh. Ct.) 6.
[15] 1909 S.C. 522 at p. 527 *per* Lord President Dunedin. See also *Marshall* v. *Marshall's Exr.*, 1987 S.L.T. 49.

may contribute in kind by pooling property, as in *Shand's Trustees* v. *Shand's Trustees*.[16] Secondly, if one co-owner paid the whole price he can revoke, but the co-owner who paid none cannot: the destination is a condition of the "gift". Similarly if both co-owners had a gift from a third person, neither can revoke.[17] Inevitably the words of the conveyance are crucial evidence. They will narrate who paid the purchase price; they may, as in *Shand's Trustees*, go further and refer to an agreement. But they are not always accurate. In *Hay's Trustees* v. *Hay's Trustees*[17a] this was admitted, so extrinsic evidence was allowed to prove who actually paid the price. *Hay's Trustees* was special: in *Gordon-Rogers* v. *Thomson's Trustees*[18] there was no such admission, the words of the conveyance (as a probative deed) were conclusive, and extrinsic evidence was not allowed to contradict them.

(b) Revocation

5.8 Supposing a destination can be revoked, "evacuated": has it been? The old common law was vague, relying on presumptions in an attempt to discover the testator's intention. If the testator himself created the destination (say by having it inserted when he purchased the property) he did not revoke it by a general settlement:[19] the two were read together insofar as reconcilable. If he did not create it (because he took the property by gift from the creator, or by succession under the destination) the general settlement did revoke it. If the destination postdated the will it plainly was not revoked. (A postdated codicil to an earlier will probably had no effect unless it itself affected the destination.[20])

These presumptions could be displaced by circumstances. First, a later will might be irreconcilable with the destination. It might dispose of property which was expressly or tacitly known to be subject to the destination, as in *Hay's Trustees* or *Dennis* v. *Aitchison*[20a]. Secondly, it might revoke the destination. But the usual revocation of "all previous testamentary writings made by me" would not do: while a destination has testamentary effect, it is not in a testamentary document.[21] Other circumstances might be relevant

---

[16] 1966 S.C. 178.
[17] *Renouf's Trs.* v. *Haining*, 1919 2 S.L.T. 15; *Brown's Trs.* v. *Brown*, 1943 S.C. 488.
[17a] 1951 S.C. 329.
[18] 1988 S.L.T. 618.
[19] *i.e.* a will of his whole estate.
[20] *Thoms* v. *Thoms* (1868) 6 M. 704; *Perrett's Trs; Cunningham's Trs.* v. *Cunningham*, 1924 S.C. 581; *Murray's Exrs.* v. *Geekie*, 1929 S.C. 633.
[20a] *Supra* at n. 10.
[21] *Murray's Exrs.* v. *Geekie*, *supra* but note doubts in *Colenso's Exr.* v. *Davidson*, 1930 S.L.T. 359.

evidence of the testator's intention: for instance his actings, but not his oral statements of intention.[22]

5.9 The old law still applies to wills executed before 10 September 1964: the testator's date of death is immaterial. Under section 30 of the 1964 Act, a testamentary disposition executed on or after that date will not evacuate a special destination unless it contains a specific reference to the destination and a declared intention on the part of the testator to evacuate it. This is strictly construed:[23] implied revocation thus disappears.

5.10 Special destinations between spouses, like wills, are not revoked by divorce. Even if one spouse transfers his share to the other in a divorce settlement, the destination will still operate in his favour if the other dies before him. Evacuation should not be overlooked.

3. Law reform

5.11 Special destinations have complex and confusing rules, and their very concept is widely considered outdated. The Scottish Law Commission tentatively suggests several changes if they are not to be abolished entirely.[24] The rules for lifetime and testamentary evacuation should be harmonised, preferably by easing the prohibition on evacuation by will. The powers of spouses to evacuate should be equalised, abolishing the present rule that only the spouse who paid for the property can evacuate (as in *Brown's Trustees*).

The Commission consider class destinations (as in *Cormack*). They should be treated as special destinations, except for purposes of succession to leases under the 1964 Act: that would reverse the wider principle in *Cormack* while preserving the practical effect of the decision as regards tenancies.

At present destinations only exist if express in the title deed: Scots law does not imply them among co-owners. (Contrast the rules for joint property and joint tenancies in Scotland and England respectively.) The Commission decided against introducing automatic destinations.

NOMINATIONS[25]

5.12 A nomination is a document of a testamentary nature and is akin to a special destination. It relates to funds deposited by

---

[22] *Murray's Exrs.*; *Colenso's Exr.*

[23] *Stirling's Trs.* v. *Stirling*, 1977 S.C. 139; *Marshall* v. *Marshall's Exr.*, 1987 S.L.T. 49.

[24] Memorandum No. 71 (1986), paras. 3.9–3.40.

[25] See Currie, pp. 285 et seq.

someone, or credited to him, with certain official savings or benevolent bodies. It gives the nominee the right to those funds after the nominator's death without the need for an executor to obtain confirmation to them.

Nominations are based purely on statute, and the rules governing each individual type depend on the particular statute allowing it. The most important current types relate to friendly societies, industrial and provident societies, and trade unions. Obsolete types include National Savings Certificates and the National Savings Bank (before May 1, 1981) and the Trustee Savings Bank (before May 1, 1979); nominations made prior to those dates are still valid. The current maximum sum is £1,500;[26] there is no limit for TSB and National Savings funds.

The formalities of execution differ from those for wills. Normally they require the nominator to sign—a mark being permitted for National Savings only[27]—and to deposit the form with the society. One witness may be required, who cannot be the nominee. The nominator must be aged over 16: a concession for England (where 18 is the usual limit for wills) but more stringent than for Scots wills. However, if a document is invalid as a nomination for lack of age or formality, it may still be valid as an ordinary Scots will.

A nomination falls if the nominator marries or the nominee dies. It can only be revoked by the prescribed statutory formalities, and not by a will (though that may convert the nominee's right from being beneficial to purely administrative). The rule seems clear, though in the only two relevant cases some doubts were expressed.[28]

On the other hand, a nomination simply allows the nominee to get payment of the fund. It does not decide whether his right is beneficial (he owns the funds) or, like a deposit receipt, merely administrative (so that he must pay them over to the executor). The second is rare; a later will, while not revoking the nomination, can have this result if the relevant regulations permit it.[29]

DONATION *MORTIS CAUSA*

1. Definition and characteristics

5.13 The classic case of a *mortis causa* donation was *Morris* v. *Riddick*.[30] Morris, terminally ill, gave Riddick a deposit receipt for

---

[26] Administration of Estates (Small Payments) Act 1965, ss. 2, 6.
[27] *Morton* v. *French*, 1908 S.C. 171.
[28] *Ford's Trs.* v. *Ford*, 1940 S.C. 426; *Clarke's Exr.* v. *Macaulay*, 1961 S.L.T. 109.
[29] *Young* v. *Waterson*, 1918 S.C. 9.
[30] (1867) 5 M. 1036 at p. 1041.

£300, endorsed it in Riddick's name, and gave him a note for the bank to that effect; the gift was on the footing that he did not recover. This was not a legacy; it was held to be a donation *mortis causa* so that the sum went to Riddick and was not part of Morris's estate. Lord President Inglis defined donation *mortis causa* as:

> "a conveyance of an immoveable or incorporeal right, or a transference of moveables or money by delivery, so that the property is immediately transferred to the grantee, upon the condition that he shall hold for the granter so long as he lives, subject to his power of revocation, and, failing such revocation, then for the grantee on the death of the granter . . . if the grantee predeceases the granter the property reverts to the granter, and the qualified right of property which was vested in the grantee is extinguished by his predecease."

The *mortis causa* donation is thus a hybrid between a legacy and lifetime gift; it shares characteristics of both. Unlike a legacy it is effective at once, though conditional on death ensuing; it requires delivery, but not writing unless—as with land—the type of property demands writing for effective transfer. In that sense it is no different from an ordinary lifetime gift. Like a legacy the gift is revocable during the granter's lifetime, and the recipient's right is not complete unless he outlives the donor. For that reason the donor's creditors can still treat the item as part of his property (*e.g.* for purposes of diligence or bankruptcy). The gift is payable after legal rights but before ordinary legacies, even if as a result there is no estate available for legacies.

2. Essential requirements

5.14   Three elements are essential. They are interrelated, so strong evidence of one may make up for weak evidence of another.
  (1) The donor must act in contemplation of his death. There need not be fear of imminent death, but if there is it points the more strongly to *mortis causa* donation rather than a legacy.[31]
  (2) There must normally be delivery. Scots law in principle insists on delivery to transfer property rights—mere agreement being insufficient—with wills and sale of goods the two main exceptions to the rule. But the requirement is flexible, and less stringent for *mortis causa* than *inter vivos* donation. Inevitably deposit receipts illustrate the point. Formal delivery is unnecessary, but there must be some act sufficient to transfer ownership which the law may treat as equivalent

---

[31] *Blyth* v. *Curle* (1885) 12 R. 674; *Aiken's Exrs.* v. *Aiken*, 1937 S.C. 678.

to delivery. One equivalent is intimation to the bank. Contrast *Macpherson's Executrix* v. *Mackay*,[32] where the bank included the donee's name on the receipt, with *Gray's Trustees* v. *Murray*,[33] where the donor inserted the name himself without the bank knowing and never notified this.

(3) There must be *animus donandi*, intention to make an immediate (but revocable) gift rather than a legacy. Whenever property is handed over there is a strong presumption against donation (it might be sale or loan instead) which needs clear and unequivocal evidence to rebut.[34] In practice this may be a crucial element when, in (2), there has not been formal delivery.

Proof is the main problem since the donor's intention rarely appears explicitly in writing. "Accordingly, in almost all cases, the true quality of the donor's *animus* has to be inferred from implications drawn from his conduct, and the circumstances which surround his acts."[35] Documentary evidence is certainly important, but rarely conclusive: inserting a payee's name on a deposit receipt may suggest gift but may equally be done with pure administrative convenience in mind. But, as in *Aiken's Executors* v. *Aiken*,[36] oral evidence of the donor's actions or statements of intention may suffice if coupled with the terms of the document.

LIFE ASSURANCE

1. **General rules and joint policies**

5.15 If A takes out a life assurance policy on his own life it is normally payable to his executors and so forms part of his estate to be distributed on death according to will or intestacy. But if someone else, B (say a spouse or child) is beneficiary under the policy, then (even if A pays the premiums himself) the proceeds go direct to B and they are excluded from A's own estate. They thus escape IHT and legal rights.

A can achieve that result by taking the policy out in B's favour to start with, or by assigning it later. Often the policy is taken out jointly in order to benefit whichever of A and B survives longer: supposing A dies first then (depending on its terms) the proceeds may go (i) to his estate, (ii) directly to B, or (iii) they may be payable only to B's estate

---

[32] 1932 S.C. 505; also *Crosbie's Trs.* v. *Wright* (1880) 7 R. 823.
[33] 1970 S.L.T. 105.
[34] *Brownlee's Exr.* v. *Brownlee*, 1908 S.C. 232.
[35] *Macpherson's Exx.*, *supra*, per Lord President Clyde at pp. 513–514.
[36] 1937 S.C. 678; see also *Morris* v. *Riddick*, *supra*.

when B dies. Methods (i) and (ii) are usual to pay off a mortgage, (iii) to pay IHT on spouse B's death.

2. Policies written in trust

5.16 Alternatively a husband may take the policy in trust for spouse or children as beneficiaries. The most important example occurs under the Married Women's Policies of Assurance (Scotland) Act 1880.[37] At that time wives had limited powers to own property, and the main purpose of the Act was to give them funds which were protected from the husband's creditors. That is still the effect, though its original rationale is long gone, and the Act now applies equally in favour of husbands.

Unlike an ordinary trust, an 1880 Act policy is effective at once without the need for delivery or intimation to the beneficiary.[38] It need not refer to the Act by name, but must be written in favour of spouse and/or children. "Children" now includes illegitimate or adopted ones, but not stepchildren. The spouse who takes out the policy is deemed trustee with the usual powers under the Trusts (Scotland) Act 1921.

Beneficiaries acquire immediate irrevocable vested rights under the policy. If adult they can assign or renounce them.[39] If the wife divorces, she may be able to keep her rights. If she dies before her husband, her rights will either pass to her executors as part of her estate, pass to a child (if the policy has a destination-over to it), or revert to the husband (if they were conditional on her surviving).[40] It all depends how the policy is worded.

MARRIAGE CONTRACTS

5.17 Marriage contracts are made between a couple either before their marriage—antenuptial—or after, in order to regulate their respective property rights and those of their children and, in some cases, strangers. They were once much commoner than now. They were a way to protect a wife's property rights at a time when, on marriage, her moveable property passed by law to her husband; but now that marriage has few automatic effects on spouses' property rights[41] they are rare.

---

[37] s. 2, as amended by Married Women's Policies of Assurance (Amendment) (Scotland) Act 1980.
[38] *Allan's Trs.* v. *Inland Revenue*, 1971 S.L.T. 62.
[39] Married Women's Policies of Assurance (Amendment) (Scotland) Act 1980, s. 3(1).
[40] *Barclay's Trs.* v. *Inland Revenue*, 1975 S.L.T. 17.
[41] Married Women's Property Act 1920; Family Law (Scotland) Act 1985, ss. 24, 25.

In the normal way a marriage contract sets up a trust which provides for wife, child, or others. A provision is irrevocable if truly contractual and if the beneficiary is within the consideration of the marriage; otherwise it is purely testamentary, so revocable. So provisions in favour of spouses or their descendants are presumed irrevocable unless a power to revoke is expressly reserved. But the terms of the deed may give others a contractual and indefeasible right: as in *Mackie* v. *Gloag's Trustees*[42] in favour of children of the wife's previous marriage.

5.18 If a spouse makes a gift under a marriage contract he will probably receive nothing explicitly in return. If so it is a *gratuitous alienation* to an *associated person*; as such it can be challenged if he is sequestrated—made bankrupt—within five years. The rule applies to other gifts between spouses, but not to insurance policies under the 1880 Act.[43]

MISCELLANEOUS

5.19 Rather as a testator may bind himself irrevocably to leave property to someone, so a legatee with a vested right may bind himself to deal with the legacy in a certain way. He may, for instance, agree to re-transfer it in a way that the testator had wanted. That transfer is exempt from IHT if made within two years.[44] If he dies before he receives the legacy, his obligation can be enforced against his representatives.

5.20 One may of course make an outright gift *inter vivos*. The major consideration here is IHT.[45]

It may sometimes be difficult to distinguish between gifts and *mortis causa* donation: the test is whether the gift is irrevocable and unconditional, and evidence of the donor's intention is important.

5.21 One may make a binding promise to leave someone property on death. Proof is by writ (a document signed by the alleged promisor) or by an oath sworn by him in court. The document is effective and irrevocable once delivered, unlike a will which needs no delivery but is revocable till death. Promises and wills may be difficult to distinguish: the test is whether the words imply an immediately binding obligation.[46] In *Trotter* v. *Trotter*,[47] where the "promise" was

---

[42] (1884) 11 R. (H.L.) 10.

[43] Bankruptcy (Scotland) Act 1985, s. 34. Antenuptial marriage contracts no longer get favourable treatment: Law Reform (Husband and Wife) (Scotland) Act 1984, s. 5(1)(*b*).

[44] IHTA 1984, s. 143.

[45] See para. 12.2.

[46] See *Miller* v. *Milne's Trs.* (1859) 21 D. 377.

[47] 1916 1 S.L.T. 357.

linked to revocation of a legacy, it was deemed to be itself a legacy, and hence revocable.

5.22 One may create an *inter vivos* trust over property in favour of a beneficiary. But it is important whether or not the trust is revocable. If it is the truster still has control over the property and it is consequently available to his creditors for diligence or on bankruptcy. In that case the trust has little point as a means of inheritance: one might as well simply make a testamentary trust or a will, both of which have effect only on death.

Revocability depends on the truster's intention, discovered from the trust deed and surrounding circumstances. Two factors are crucial. Is the trust for the management of the grantor's affairs during his lifetime? If so it is revocable even if its words say it is irrevocable. Is the beneficiary given an immediate enforceable right—a *ius quaesitum*—or a mere right to succeed on the grantor's death? If a *ius quaesitum* the trust is irrevocable; otherwise not.[48]

REARRANGEMENTS AFTER DEATH

5.23 If the beneficiaries agree they can vary the division of the estate in any way they wish. So they may, by a deed of arrangement, disclaim a benefit under a will, intestacy or legal rights, or vary them and take different ones.

> "When . . . every possible beneficiary desires and consents to a particular course being adopted—all the beneficiaries being of full age and *sui juris*—and none of them being placed under any restraint or disability by the . . . deed itself—then no one has any right or interest to object."[49]

Note that, failing such agreement or a specific legacy, beneficiaries have a right only to cash and not to specific assets. The executor should then sell the assets and distribute the proceeds.

5.24 Deeds of arrangement may have tax advantages.

(1) *Inheritance tax.* Normally a disclaimer or election is a disposal for IHT purposes: so IHT would be due twice, from the deceased's estate on death and from the beneficiary on the arrangement.[50] But the variation is treated as made by the deceased, and so is exempt from IHT, *if* (i) it is made within two years after death, by the beneficiaries in writing, with no consideration received in return; *and*

---

[48] See Wilson & Duncan, *Trusts, Trustees & Executors*, pp. 131–134.
[49] *Gray* v. *Gray's Trs.* (1877) 4 R. 378, at p. 383 *per* Lord Gifford.
[50] Unless either disposal was IHT-exempt, *e.g.* to a spouse.

(ii) they make written election to the Capital Taxes Office within six months after variation. If the election means that more IHT is due from the estate—as may happen if a legacy to a spouse is redeployed to a child—the executor must also elect, and can refuse if he has insufficient estate to pay the tax. (ii) is unnecessary for simple disclaimers. Only one tax-exempt variation per item is allowed.[51]

(2) *Capital gains tax.* The same rule applies to CGT. Here election will not affect the estate (because CGT is not chargeable on death) but may benefit the beneficiary. One need not claim for both CGT and IHT—it may pay one not to—but if one does the deed must say so explicitly.[52]

There is a potential disadvantage under *income tax.* If a parent redeploys funds to his child he is treated as making a *settlement.* Until the child reaches age 18 his resulting income will be aggregated along with the parent's rather than being taxed in the child's hands. The tax bill will usually be much higher.[53]

5.25 Irrespective of tax, the deed must be valid under the general law. Three points are relevant. If a beneficiary is minor, then even if his tutor or curator consents to variation, he can have it set aside between age 18 and 22 if it reduces his rights.[54] Secondly, there may be potential unborn or minor beneficiaries with contingent rights which have not yet vested (because, for instance, they must outlive the end of a liferent). Their consent can be dispensed with by court petition,[55] and the rights can be actuarially valued and insured against. The problem can be minimised if the will provides for rights to vest at the testator's death: that also avoids the risk of partial intestacy arising if the beneficiary dies before vesting. Finally, it is no bar to variation that the beneficiary has already received or used the property—with one exception, an alimentary liferent.[56]

5.26 A testator may consciously consider the possibility of a post-death rearrangement. Classically he leaves his wife the whole estate and relies on her and other beneficiaries to sort matters out most tax-efficiently. But the risk is that beneficiaries may not agree, and that tax legislation may bar the procedure.[57] Alternatively he can set up a discretionary trust by will: there is IHT on his death but no further charge if the trustees distribute the assets within the next two years.[58]

---

[51] IHTA 1984, s. 142. For children under 18 see s. 17; para. 4.23 *supra.*
[52] CGTA 1979, s. 49.
[53] ICTA 1988, s. 663 (1).
[54] The *quadriennium utile*: see Scot. Law Com. Report No. 110 which proposes reform.
[55] Trusts (Scotland) Act 1961, s. 1.
[56] See Gloag & Henderson, para. 40.10.
[57] Possibly as early as 1990.
[58] IHTA 1984, s. 144.

In effect he achieves the flexibility of post-death rearrangement without some of the defects.

Further reading

Clive, *Husband and Wife* (2nd Ed.), pp. 326–332, 354–365 (life assurance, marriage contracts).

Currie, *Confirmation*, pp. 162–173.

McBryde, *Contract*, paras. 2.14–2.27.

D. G. Antonio, "Mortis Causa or Inter Vivos Donation?" 1954 S.L.T. (News) 121.

A. M. C. Dalgleish, "Insurance Policies in Executries", 1988 Law Soc. Scot. P.Q.L.E. 83.

G. L. Gretton, "Destinations and Leases", 1982 S.L.T. (News) 213.

G. L. Gretton, "Life Policies and the Law of Succession" (1988) 33 J.L.S. 141.

J. M. Halliday, "What Makes a Destination Special?" (1977) 22 J.L.S. 16.

M. Morton, "Special Destinations as Testamentary Instructions," 1984 S.L.T. (News) 133.

W. G., "Donation Mortis Causa", 1951 S.L.T. (News) 53.

CHAPTER 6

WILLS: FORMAL VALIDITY

6.1 Most legal systems require some formalities in making a will. The reasons are obvious. They guard against fraud: a handwritten will is difficult to forge. They ensure that the testator is fully aware of the importance of his act, and that the document is a complete and seriously-meant declaration of his testamentary intention. These points have added weight with wills as opposed to lifetime contracts, since inevitably the testator has passed away by the time his will is questioned.

The problem is to balance the need for formalities with giving effect to every serious expression of intention by the testator. On the whole Scots law takes a liberal view of formalities, by contrast at least with England where wills are normally invalid unless made before witnesses. Moreover, with the Wills Act 1963 and the admission of "international wills," the trend is towards easier recognition of wills made in countries whose formalities differ from ours.[1]

INFORMAL WILLS

6.2 Few countries allow oral or "nuncupative" wills for property of any great value: the risk of fraud is too great. English law once allowed them for moveable property, but no longer.[2] In Scotland an oral legacy is not valid for more than £8·33 (£100 Scots), and a larger oral legacy is valid up to that amount.[3]

Roman law allowed a soldier to make an informal will, the *testamentum militare*. England has an analogous statutory rule for members of the armed forces on military service and seamen at sea,[4] where it is useful because (formalities apart) it allows a will to be made at age 16 rather than 18. That age limit is not a problem in Scotland. The rule is not part of Scots law, and it is unlikely that the *testamentum militare* is either. In the only relevant modern case, *Stuart* v. *Stuart*,[5] the point was immaterial because (irrespective of

---

[1] See para. 14.18.
[2] Except for soldiers' wills: Wills Act 1837, s. 9. see generally J. G. Miller, *The Machinery of Succession*, chap. 8.
[3] Erskine, *Inst.*, III.ix.7; *Kelly* v. *Kelly* (1861) 23 D. 703.
[4] Wills Act 1837, s. 11; Wills (Soldiers and Sailors) Act 1918.
[5] 1942 S.C. 510.

formalities) there was no concluded testamentary intent: nothing but instructions for a future will.

1. Formalities and probativity

6.3 Scots law requires no particular form of words, so long as they clearly express the testator's intention. Any sort of writing—ink, typing or handwriting—will do. Even pencil writing is valid,[6] though most unwise. The problem, apart from the risk of fraudulent alteration and fading, is that pencil alterations on an ink document are taken to be mere drafts for a revised new will and do not show concluded testamentary intent.[7]

Wills may be made in three ways. They may be attested (executed before witnesses according to statutory formalities); holograph (in the testator's handwriting and signed by him); or adopted as holograph. In addition a formally valid will may validate an informal document by adopting it, and minor defects in execution may be cured by court decree under section 39 of the Conveyancing (Scotland) Act 1874.

6.4 Attested wills have one great benefit: they are probative. A probative document is one which is presumed to have been validly executed because it appears so. It proves both its own authenticity and the existence of the rights and obligations which it contains; no other evidence is necessary. Wills which are holograph or adopted as holograph are not automatically probative but "privileged": while formally valid although not attested, the grantor's handwriting and signature must be proved to be genuine. But once that initial hurdle is overcome, which occurs when the executor applies for confirmation, the distinction disappears and holograph wills then become probative.[8]

6.5 A probative will may be reduced—set aside— by an action in the Court of Session. That is not easy: strong proof is needed to challenge its apparent validity, especially where the signatures are genuine and the challenge relates to some other irregularity. *McArthur* v. *McArthur's Trustees*[9] illustrates this: someone who

---

[6] *Tait's Trs.* v. *Chiene*, 1911 S.C. 743.

[7] *Munro's Exrs.* v. *Munro* (1890) 18 R. 122.

[8] 1964 Act, s. 32; before the Act confirmation had no effect on the formal validity of wills.

[9] 1931 S.L.T. 463.

would benefit on intestacy tried to reduce a will because it was not properly witnessed. His action failed because the witnesses' evidence was contradictory and had no independent corroboration.

2. Attestation

6.6 Several "authentication statutes" prescribe how attested deeds must be executed. The main rules evolved before 1700, reaching their highpoint with the Subscription of Deeds Act 1681 and the Deeds Act 1696 which form the framework for the modern law. More recently the trend has been to lessen the formalities.[10] In most respects the law is similar for wills and *inter vivos* deeds.

In essence there are now four required formalities.

(1) The testator must subscribe the will personally on each page; if he cannot write, he can subscribe vicariously by notarial execution.[11]

(2) Two independent witnesses must see the testator sign or acknowledge his signature to them.

(3) The witnesses must sign on the last page, at the very end of the will.

(4) The witnesses must be designed—described—after their signatures, or in the testing clause.

3. Witnesses

(a) Who may act as witness?

6.7 One cannot witness a will if one is blind, insane, less than 14 years old, or cannot write. One must be "independent" and one must "know" the testator, but both tests are very flexible. One may, as in *Simsons* v. *Simsons*,[12] be related to the testator and benefit under the will; the risk is that the will is set aside if circumvention or undue influence are inferred.[13] At the other extreme, the witness need not known the testator beforehand—someone off the street is acceptable—provided they are properly introduced. As the witness's role is purely to speak to the validity of the testator's signature, he need not know the contents of the will.

(b) When should witnesses sign?

6.8 They should sign as quickly as possible, preferably (though not

---

[10] Conveyancing (Scotland) Act 1874, ss. 38, 39.
[11] See para. 6.21.
[12] (1883) 10 R. 1247.
[13] *Cf.* England where the legacy fails: Wills Act 1837, s. 15.

absolutely essentially) together and at once, and certainly before the testator dies. The classic authority is now *Walker* v. *Whitwell*,[14] which in laying down that formulation cast doubt on earlier laxer decisions where a gap of some four months was accepted.[15] In *Walker* the testatrix dictated her will to her son, who saw her sign; a second witness signed before she died six days later, but he himself only signed afterwards. The Court of Session thought that acceptable, especially considering that the son knew the contents of the will. The House of Lords disagreed. Testator's and witnesses' signatures (they said) are essential formalities which form a continuous process; the witnesses sign with the testator's consent, which obviously lapses on death.

4. Completing the testing clause

6.9 The testing clause is the last clause of an attested deed. It narrates the circumstances of its execution and designs the witnesses (usually by their occupation and address). Place and date of execution, though not essential, should be stated. An attested will is dated when the testator acknowledges his signature rather than when he signed.[16] The date may be important where revocation by a later will is alleged, or where the testator was *incapax* when the will was made.[17]

The clause should describe any material—significant—alterations made in the will before signature, such as words scored out or written on erasures. (Those should themselves be signed or initialled or they will be treated *pro non scripto* and ignored.) It also mentions differences between the testator or witnesses' names in the will and their actual signature. But it cannot itself alter the will. That is because it is left blank till after signature: it can be filled in, even after the testator's death, at any time before the will is registered for preservation or relied on in pleadings in a court action.[18] This point should be checked before sending a will to the Books of Council and Session for registration after the testator's death.

The witnesses' and testator's signatures come after the testing clause, but should be on the same page as the last words of the body of the will. It is sensible to leave enough space to fit the clause in so that it does not spill over onto another page.

[14] 1914 S.C. 560, revd. 1916 S.C. (H.L.) 75.
[15] *Stewart* v. *Burns* (1877) 4 R. 427.
[16] *Tait's Trs.* v. *Chiene*, 1911 S.C. 743.
[17] *Waddell* v. *Waddell's Trs.* (1845) 7 D. 605.
[18] Conveyancing (Scotland) Act 1874, s. 38.

5. Defects in execution

6.10 Section 39 of the Conveyancing (Scotland) Act 1874 may save a will even if it is formally invalid: the will may be declared valid and the defect disregarded. The section only applies if the will was subscribed by the testator and "bear[s] to be attested by two witnesses subscribing." Now thanks to the defect the will is improbative—its validity is not automatically presumed—so the person relying on the will has the onus of proving that it was in fact subscribed by the grantor and attested by the witnesses. He may do so in an application to the Court of Session or (more simply) the sheriff court in whose area the deceased was domiciled, or when applying to be confirmed as executor under the will.

Some defects are so minor as not to need section 39; some are curable under it; some are too grave for that. It is a matter of degree. On the one hand section 39 was not needed where, in *Grieve's Trustees* v. *Japp's Trustees*,[19] a witness included her maiden name in her signature. On the other, it is useless where, as in *Walker* v. *Whitwell*, a witness signed after the testator died, or did not see the grantor sign.[20] But it can be used, say, where the will is not signed on every sheet,[21] or where it is too late to insert witnesses' designations in the testing clause under section 38 of the Act.[22]

HOLOGRAPH WILLS

1. Definition

6.11 A will is holograph if all essential parts are in the testator's own handwriting and it is subscribed by him.[23] Alternatively a will prepared by someone else (or typed) may be "adopted as holograph" by the testator signing and *writing* those words, or similar words, at the end—preferably, but not essentially, above his signature. No witnesses are necessary.

6.12 In rare cases typing may be valid on its own, with no writing apart from the signature. In *McBeath's Trustees* v. *McBeath*[24] the testator typed a will and typed "accepted as holograph" above his handwritten signature. The will contained a statement that he typed

---

[19] 1917 1 S.L.T. 70.
[20] *Smyth* v. *Smyth* (1876) 3 R. 573; *Forrest* v. *Low's Trs.*, 1907 S.C. 1240; 1909 S.C. (H.L.) 16.
[21] *Bisset, Petr.*, 1961 S.L.T. (Sh. Ct.) 19.
[22] *Thomson's Trs.* v. *Easson* (1878) 6 R. 141. See para. 6.9, *supra*.
[23] Erskine *Inst.*, III.ii.22.
[24] 1935 S.C. 471: a seven judge court.

it. Due to illness typing was his invariable method of preparing documents. The Court of Session, by a four to three majority, upheld the will on this reasoning: the essence of holograph is that the granter writes the document personally; the law evolved before typewriting and should reflect its invention; so what is in fact typed by the grantor must be recognised as holograph. This logic suggests that a signature might itself be typed, and some of the court were not prepared to rule it out. The main, often insuperable, hurdle would be the need to prove who typed the document and "signature."

In *Chisholm* v. *Chisholm*[25] there was no adoption as holograph or statement that the will was typed by the testator. That second point allowed Lord Guthrie to distinguish *McBeath* on its facts and hold the will invalid. That was a dubious argument: such statements were insufficient evidence of holograph in contested applications for confirmation of executors.[26] At any rate the facts in *McBeath* were so special that it is rarely likely to be followed.

6.13 Suppose a testator attempts to make an attested will but fails. Perhaps the supposed "witnesses" did not see the testator sign, or did not appear at all. The will can still be valid if it is holograph.[27]

2. Proof

6.14 A holograph will is not probative: anyone seeking to rely on it must prove that the writing and signature are genuine. A statement *in gremio*—in the body—of the will has no value, *pace Chisholm*. If the will can be forged, so can the statement.

An action of declarator is one option,[28] but the point usually arises where an executor applies for confirmation of his appointment under a holograph will. Commissary practice at one time relaxed the strict law. If an *in gremio* statement was present confirmation was granted without further proof; if absent, it was not. Granting confirmation merely ratified the executor's title to deal with the estate; the will was not deemed probative and could still be challenged.

The 1964 Act made two changes. By section 21 confirmation requires affidavits from at least two people that the handwriting and signature in the will are those of the testator. By section 32, once confirmation is granted the will is now deemed probative for all purposes, so challenge will be difficult. If the testator died before September 10, 1964 the old law applies; the Act is not retrospective.[29]

---

[25] 1949 S.C. 434.
[26] *Cranston, Petr.* (1890) 17 R. 410.
[27] *Lorimer's Exrs.* v. *Hird*, 1959 S.L.T. (Notes) 8.
[28] See Macphail, *Sheriff Court Practice*, para. 20.19.
[29] This simplifies the old law: see Currie at pp. 51–52, Meston at p. 81.

6.15 Questions of confirmation apart, a holograph will proves its own date. In the absence of contrary evidence it is deemed made on the date it bears. That is not the case with *inter vivos* deeds.[30]

3. Printed will forms

6.16 It is possible to buy printed forms on which to make a will. The testator fills in the blanks relating to legacies, name of executor and the like. In principle that is not disastrous: the document will be a perfectly valid will provided it is duly witnessed. The problem arises if the form follows English formalities or if two witnesses have not signed. If it is to be valid it must be as a holograph will.

Scots law holds a document holograph if all the essential parts are in the grantor's handwriting. It must of course be possible to deduce testamentary intent from them. The questions then are: what parts are essential; and are the printed parts to be disregarded in deciding that?

The modern law originated in *Macdonald* v. *Cuthbertson*.[31] A testator living in China made an unwitnessed will on a printed form. Read as a whole it made perfect sense, but the legacies and the words bequeathing them were printed; about the only holograph words were some names and addresses. Lord McLaren, dissenting, thought printing in this context was in effect holograph (this was later the basis for the decision in *McBeath's Trustees*). But the court held that printed words must be formal and superfluous, adding nothing of any importance to the handwritten part. If that test is met (which it was not in *Macdonald*) the will receives effect.

In *Carmichael's Executors* v. *Carmichael*[32] that test was met. All vital words were holograph, except the words of bequest which were now felt inessential; "cutting out the [printed] words . . . there is still enough to make a perfectly good and intelligible will."

Modern cases apply this rule flexibly. To decide if the will is holograph, the court reads the will as a whole to see if the sense of the document can be gathered from the holograph part. One cannot ignore the printed words. If they do not add to or contradict the holograph part the will receives effect. The "essential" holograph parts may be quite brief. So in *Bridgeford's Executor* v. *Bridgeford*[33] they identified the testator, legatee and executor, and legacies; that was enough (a printed clause revoking previous wills was ignored). By contrast, to stress that the will is read *in toto*, take *Tucker* v.

---

[30] Conveyancing (Scotland) Act 1874, s. 40.
[31] (1890) 18 R. 101.
[32] 1909 S.C. 1387, *per* Lord President Dunedin at p. 1389.
[33] 1948 S.C. 416.

Canch's Trustee[34]: there was a holograph clause revoking previous wills but there were no holograph legacies; the revocation clause could not receive effect on its own.

SIGNATURE

1. Method of signature

6.17 Both attested and privileged wills require the testator to subscribe the will. Signature shows completed testamentary intention: the testator has finally made up his mind. The rule is rigorously adhered to:

> "Subscription [is] the essential and only admissible evidence of a concluded expression of will on the part of a testator . . . the rule is inflexible—no subscription, no will."[35]

So it must be the testator's own act. To guide his hand—as opposed to merely supporting his arm above the wrist—is fatal.[36] A "rubber stamp" signature is useless, as someone else might have applied it.[37]

It must be completed, but what that means may vary according to circumstances. Did the testator try to write more and fail? If so, the will also fails.[38] But a shortened or nickname may suffice—"Connie" in *Draper* v. *Thomason*[39]—as may initials. The test should be to prove that this was the testator's normal method of signature in the circumstances, taking into account that this may be a family letter rather than legal document. Exceptionally the courts ignore that "usual practice" test, as in *Lowrie's Judicial Factor* v. *Macmillan*[40] where they wished to prevent the Crown defeating the writer's clear intention and taking as *ultimus haeres*.

Such "pet" signatures are only likely in holograph wills. They are invalid in attested wills because, by requiring proof of surrounding facts, they make the will improbative.[41] Merely omitting an initial or using a maiden name can be rectified by a reference in the testing clause.

---

[34] 1953 S.C. 270.
[35] *Foley* v. *Costello* (1904) 6 F. 365.
[36] *Noble* v. *Noble* (1875) 3 R. 74.
[37] *Stirling Stuart* v. *Stirling Crawfurd's Trs.* (1885) 12 R. 610.
[38] *Donald* v. *McGregor*, 1926 S.L.T. 103.
[39] 1954 S.C. 136; also *Rhodes* v. *Peterson*, 1972 S.L.T. 98.
[40] 1972 S.L.T. 159.
[41] But the 1874 Act, s. 39 may be used for initials on any but the last page: *Gardner* v. *Lucas* (1878) 5 R. (H.L.) 105.

2. Place of signature

6.18 The testator must *sub*scribe: signature must be at the end of the document. While the courts make a presumption against intestacy so as to give effect to the testator's wishes if at all possible, failure to subscribe is fatal. The reason is that signature must show that the testator has a completed testamentary intention—he has finally made up his mind—and signature elsewhere cannot show that.

So the testator must not sign at the top or in the margin.[42] If he signs in the middle, bequests above are valid but those added below are not.[43] One should sign on the same page as the last operative provisions of the will, or it may be impossible to infer a link between the two. So if the will is on one side of a sheet and the signature on the back, it fails. In *Baird's Trustees* v. *Baird*[44] signature and testing clause were on the back: that failed. Had the testing clause run from one side to the other that might have been valid, but is not safe practice since it means the testator signing a blank sheet.

Similarly a link like "P.T.O." may suffice. Even if the only signature is on a separate sheet that may be enough provided there is a clear connection or some form of words which "adopts" the otherwise invalid will.[45]

6.19 The testator must also sign an attested will on *every* page. Strictly speaking that is only true when there is more than one separate sheet (if one sheet is folded into pages only the last need be signed) but is always best since otherwise there may be no clear link between the various pages.[46] A holograph will, being less easily forged, need only be signed on the last page.[47]

6.20 Section 39 of the 1874 Act *may* be available to cure defective subscription; but there must be subscription of some sort. So it was allowed in *Bisset, Petitioner*,[48] where only the last page was signed, but failed in *Baird*.

NOTARIAL EXECUTION

6.21 A notary is, in modern speech, a solicitor, and a notary public is the equivalent of the English commissioner for oaths. Any solicitor

[42] *Taylor's Exxs.* v. *Thom*, 1914 S.C. 79; *Robbie* v. *Carr*, 1959 S.L.T. (Notes) 16.
[43] *McLay* v. *Farrell*, 1950 S.C. 149.
[44] 1955 S.C. 286; *cf Bogie's Exrs.* v. *Bogie*, 1953 S.L.T. (Sh. Ct.) 32.
[45] *e.g. Russell's Exr.* v. *Duke*, 1946 S.L.T. 242.
[46] *Ferguson, Petr.*, 1959 S.C. 56.
[47] *Cranston, Petr.* (1890) 17 R. 410.
[48] 1961 S.L.T. (Sh. Ct.) 19.

can be appointed one. He has the power to administer oaths for affidavits: formal sworn legal declarations which are required, say, on bankruptcy or selling a matrimonial home.

A notary public, like various other officials, can also execute a will on behalf of somone who is blind or cannot write for any reason. The procedure is optional: a blind testator can if he chooses execute a will himself,[49] though there is a grave risk of fraud or circumvention.

1. Who may act?

6.22 Notarial execution may, despite its narrow name, be by a solicitor, notary public, justice of the peace, or Church of Scotland minister or his assistant in his own parish.

A notary must be absolutely independent: he must have no personal interest in the will he executes. That "is essential to the ends of justice, to the protection of the rights of parties and to the securing of purity in a public office."[50] He is disqualified from acting if he is a legatee. Similarly if the will makes him personally executor or trustee; but if it appoints someone else, disqualification requires a connection between notary and trustee which gives the notary a likely benefit under the will. Now trustees and executors must always act gratis unless a will lets them charge for their work: so mere partnership between notary and trustee is not by itself enough.[51] Nor is a contract of employment:[52] an assistant solicitor may safely notarise though his employer is trustee. But if the will permits the trustees to appoint their partners as solicitors to the trust, the notary may then get fees through the firm, and is at once disqualified.[53]

The rule is strict. The need to make the will urgently is no excuse: after all, fraud may be easier then. Even where a will conferred a benefit and the notary made a later codicil, the codicil falls: it is treated as part of the will.[54]

The effect is drastic. The whole will falls, disinheriting all the beneficiaries. Admittedly in *Irving* v. *Snow*[55] it was suggested that the provision in favour of the notary might alone be struck down, but that was a special case: the court could not invalidate the will because it was made under English law and was therefore valid in Scotland under the Wills Act 1963, but they were loath to see the clause giving a benefit to a Scottish notary.

[49] *Duff* v. *Earl of Fife* (1823) 1 Sh. App. 498.
[50] *Ferrie* v. *Ferrie's Trs.* (1863) 1 M. 291.
[51] *McIldowie* v. *Muller*, 1982 S.L.T. 154.
[52] *Hynd's Tr.* v. *Hynd's Trs.*, 1955 S.C. (H.L.) 1 (assistant solicitor).
[53] *Finlay* v. *Finlay's Trs.*, 1948 S.C. 16.
[54] *Crawford's Trs.* v. *Glasgow Royal Infirmary*, 1955 S.C. 367.
[55] 1956 S.C. 257.

2. Procedure

6.23 Section 18 of and Schedule 1 to the Conveyancing (Scotland) Act 1924 lay down the formalities. They must be strictly observed and completed in one continuous uninterrupted act; all are vital and failure in any respect cannot be cured under section 39.[56]

Testator, notary, and two witnesses gather, and the will is read to the testator. He states he is blind or cannot write (as appropriate) and authorises the notary to sign. Immediately below the will the notary writes a docquet to this effect and signs, stating his capacity, and the witnesses sign opposite his signature. The ordinary testing clause follows all this.

INCORPORATION OF OTHER DOCUMENTS

6.24 A testator may find it convenient to make a legacy by an informal letter, say, to friends or family. He may, at the other extreme, attempt to make a formal will which ultimately turns out to be invalid. A printed will form is an obvious example. Such writings are not valid wills on their own, unless holograph in their own right, but can be validated by being adopted—ratified—by another document.

The logic behind this is that the adopting document incorporates the informal one. The latter is thus in effect a schedule to the former. The adopting document must itself be formally valid, whether attested or holograph. In addition it is essential that it unequivocally identifies the informal writing: it may do so by specific reference, or, more usually, by reference to a general class of writings: "writings signed by me" and the like.

6.25 Later writings may adopt earlier ones. One way, apart from a separate formal writing, is to append a formal note to the informal one. The best example is a docquet adopting as holograph. Alternatively it may be a codicil to a will. *Craik's Executrix* v. *Samson*[57] illustrates this: a holograph codicil was written on a will form; it referred to the will by reducing the amount of a legacy in it; it thus ratified the will as a whole. In similar vein was *Macphail's Trustees* v. *Macphail*,[58] where a codicil referred to an unsigned and undated list of legacies enclosed along with it in a sealed envelope addressed to the executors: given that the list was in fact a completed testamentary

---

[56] *Hynd's Tr.* v. *Hynd's Trs.*, 1955 S.C. (H.L.) 1, where the docquet was filled in back at the solicitor's office.
[57] 1929 S.L.T. 592.
[58] 1940 S.C. 560.

document rather than a draft, it was thus made valid insofar as it did not conflict with the codicil.

6.26 It is common for a will to state that future informal writings are to be valid. Unsigned writings can be adopted, but that is unwise. The risk of fraud apart, signature has the advantage of clarity: it shows concluded testamentary intention. In its absence a note is more likely to be a mere ineffective draft for a will: one cannot easily tell.

It is more usual to adopt writings "signed by me" or "under my hand." The limits of this device were firmly drawn in *Waterson's Trustees* v. *St Giles Boys' Club* [59] to exclude writings which are not subscribed, unless it is clear from the language that "under my hand" is to have a wider meaning.

LAW REFORM

6.27 The Scottish Law Commission proposes wide ranging changes to the law governing formal writing.[60] These relate particularly to probativity, subscription, and notarial execution.

Writing would remain essential for wills; oral wills for less than £8·33 would not be possible. Any subscribed writing would be valid, but attestation would still be an option. A writing could be probative in two ways. First, if it appears on the face of the deed to be attested by one witness, signed on each sheet (as now), and shows no sign of forgery or defective attestation; second, by being validated by court decree of authenticity which would replace section 39 of the 1874 Act.

Two types of subscription would exist: by full name as given in the will (or surname plus an initial or forename), or by short name or description. Both could be used in connection with probativity by decree, but only the first for attested deeds.

Notarial execution would only be allowed by practising solicitors. Disqualifying interest would only invalidate the will insofar as it conferred a benefit in money or money's worth on the notary directly or indirectly. The actual procedure would be slightly revised.

In addition the Commission considers separately whether to give the courts a dispensing power to hold a will valid despite formal invalidity. It comes to no firm conclusion.[61]

---

[59] 1943 S.C. 369.
[60] Report No. 112, *Requirements of Writing* (1988).
[61] Memorandum No. 70 (1986), paras. 2.1–2.19.

Further reading

Currie, *Confirmation,* Chap. 3.
Halliday, *Conveyancing,* Vol. I, Chap. 2.
A. G. M. Duncan, "The Limits of Disqualifying Interest", 1979 S.L.T. (News) 173.
G. L. Gretton, "What is a Probative Writ?" (1985) 30 J.L.S. 308.
K. G. C. Reid, "Execution of Deeds" (1987) 32 J.L.S. 148.

CHAPTER 7

REVOCATION OF WILLS

REVOCABILITY

1. General

7.1   A will is "ambulatory": that is, it operates from the testator's death and is ineffective till then.[1] Even including a declaration of irrevocability in the will does not prevent revocation.

For the same reason wills are treated as an exception to the normal rule that a deed is irrevocable once delivered by the grantor to the grantee or someone on the grantee's behalf. With *inter vivos* deeds the rationale is that the grantor, by his act of putting the deed out of his physical control, shows his intention to be bound by it; that logic does not apply to a will which by its nature cannot take effect till death.[2]

7.2   That said, a testator may incur a binding obligation to leave property to someone on death. Revocation will need the recipient's consent, though he cannot stop the testator disposing of the asset to someone else while alive.

The simplest case involves an onerous contract between donor and donee: both parties undertake obligations. So in *Paterson* v. *Paterson*[3] a mother agreed to make an irrevocable settlement of her property in her son's favour, while in return he lent her money and paid her rent; her later will broke the agreement, and so the court set it aside. Alternatively there may be a unilateral promise, binding immediately albeit only payable by the estate after the promisor's death. Yet again, a person may have a *ius quaesitum tertio*, an irrevocable third party right, under a contract between two other people: the classic example is a child under a marriage contract.[4] In all these cases the donee's right is a debt of the grantor's estate and hence payable ahead of mere legacies; again unlike a legacy, it will pass to the donee's heirs if he dies before the grantor.

2. Mutual wills

7.3   Suppose X and Y make a will contained in one document, each leaving his or her property to the other and (perhaps) thereafter to

---

[1] Erskine, *Inst.*, III.ix.5.

[2] *Clark's Exr.* v. *Clark*, 1943 S.C. 216.

[3] (1893) 20 R. 484.

[4] *Fernie* v. *Colquhoun's Trs.* (1854) 17 D. 233; *Carmichael* v. *Carmichael's Exx.*, 1920 S.C. (H.L.) 195.

their child or some stranger. That is a mutual will. Either can still dispose of his own assets while alive. The question is whether he can revoke the will, whether before or after the other dies. In bare principle he can revoke: the "will" is treated as two wills in one document. But he cannot if it is contractual: an express or implicit agreement (and hence irrevocable) that each shall dispose of his or her property as stated in the will.

The issue can arise while both are alive, but usually when Y has died and the survivor X wishes to revoke a provision in favour of a child. The terms of the will are crucial. A clause governing the power to revoke is obviously important (though not conclusive): if the spouses must both jointly revoke, the survivor cannot do so by himself.[5] Reciprocity of legacies also points to contract. Beyond that, much depends on what right Y was given in X's property. Often he has a liferent and the child is given the fee: that suggests irrevocability. If he has the fee, revocability is usual[6]—but not always: the will may still expressly prevent revocation.[7]

The Scottish Law Commission decided against reform on the ground that mutual wills are so complicated already that few people make them.[8]

<h2 style="text-align:center">METHODS</h2>

1. Destruction

7.4 Destruction of a will must be *animo et facto*: there must be an intention to revoke, *animus revocandi*, and a physical act of destruction.

Apart from the obvious case of physical destruction of the original will by the testator, a special point arises. What constitutes destruction? In rare cases symbolic destruction is sufficient. In *Nasmyth v. Hare's Trustees*[9] the testator cut off the seal attached to the end of the document. This was an effective revocation despite the fact that it was still a valid holograph document. The reason was that while sealing normally is irrelevant to formal validity, in this case the testator had chosen to include this extra solemnity of execution; so his action was taken as symbolic of revocation. Also unusual was *Thomson's Trustees v. Bowhill Baptist Church*[10] where there was very clear

---

[5] *Corrance's Trs.* v. *Glen* (1903) 5 F. 777.
[6] *Hanlon's Exr.* v. *Baird*, 1945 S.L.T. 304.
[7] *Duthie* v. *Keir's Exr.*, 1930 S.C. 645.
[8] Memorandum No. 71 (1986), paras. 4.32–4.40.
[9] (1821) 1 Sh. App. 65.
[10] 1956 S.L.T. 302.

evidence of intention to revoke certain clauses: they were scored out, then physically cut out, the testator had signed near the gap, and had signed a written explanation above and below them; while this was only a copy of the original will, in the circumstances the actions constituted destruction.

The act must be carried out by the testator himself or on his authority. In *Cullen's Executor* v. *Elphinstone*[11] a widow instructed her solicitors to prepare a new will, which they executed notarially since she was blind; uninstructed, they destroyed the old will; their act was legally ineffective. But conversely, will mere authorisation of destruction suffice? *Bruce's Judicial Factor* v. *Lord Advocate*[12] makes clear that merely instructing a new will to be made does not authorise destroying the old; on the other hand, it was suggested tentatively that if the solicitor there had been ordered to destroy but had failed to, that might be regarded as constructive cancellation.

Destruction by accident, in anger, or while drunk or insane does not revoke. *Animus revocandi* is absent. The problem is proving intention or lack of it. For example, in *Laing* v. *Bruce*[13] the pursuers claimed that a will had been in the hands of the deceased before her death and was not found afterwards, and that at that time the deceased was insane. They could not prove her insanity; had they been able to they could have had the will "set up" again as unrevoked.

It may be known that the testator had a will in his possession at the time of his death which cannot subsequently be found. There is then a legal presumption that he destroyed it *animo revocandi*, which can however be rebutted by evidence to the contrary.[14]

7.5 If a will is lost or destroyed the remedy is an action to "prove the tenor" to set it up again.[15] The problem is one of evidence, both of the terms of the document and of the absence of *animus*. A draft or copy is the best proof of the terms. To establish the *casus amissionis*—how the document went missing—requires very clear evidence in the case of a revocable document such as a will. "*Casus amissionis* means not only that the writing has actually been destroyed or lost, but that its destruction or loss took place in such a manner as implied no extinction of the right of which it was the evidence."[16] It is only natural, after all, that the testator may have changed his mind without telling anyone. So in *Clyde* v. *Clyde*,[17] the facts were

---

[11] 1948 S.C. 662.
[12] 1969 S.C. 296.
[13] (1838) 1 D. 59.
[14] *Bonthrone* v. *Ireland* (1883) 10 R. 779; *Laing, supra.*
[15] See Walkers, *Evidence*, pp. 59, 249–250.
[16] *Winchester* v. *Smith* (1863) 1 M. 685.
[17] 1958 S.C. 343.

insufficient to rebut the presumption of destruction *animo revocandi*: the testator had made a formal will in his nephew's favour; 12 years later, seven years before his death, he had his solicitors return it to him; there was no evidence of ill-feeling or intention to alter it, but no-one else had access to where he kept it.

2. Deletions and alterations

7.6 A will may have been altered before its formal execution or afterwards. Both situations are discussed here, but one should bear in mind that the guiding rules are different. If before, the question is purely one of authentication: did the changes take effect as part of the original deed? If later, it is one of revocation also.[18] The distinction mainly affects attested wills, and is less important in holograph ones.

(a) Attested wills

7.7 The ordinary rules for execution apply to alterations made at or before the time of execution. Unauthenticated alterations may invalidate the whole deed if they affect an essential part such as the names of legatees. However, section 39 of the Conveyancing (Scotland) Act 1874 can be used to cure the informality of execution: this was done for unauthenticated interlineations in *Elliot's Executors*.[19] In *Syme's Executors* v. *Cherrie*[20] it was said that a declaration in the testing clause might also work.

Note, too, that the testing clause cannot alter the provisions in the main body of the will in any way (for the obvious reason that it is added after execution) and any such attempted additions are ignored. Thus in *Smith* v. *Chambers' Trustees*[21] the testing clause could not declare legacies to be "alimentary."

7.8 Subsequent alterations raise the question of *animus revocandi*. The classic statement of the required authentication was made by Lord McLaren in *Pattison's Trustees* v. *University of Edinburgh*.[22] He required four elements:

> "(1) If a will or codicil is found with the signature cancelled, or with lines drawn through the dispositive or other essential clause of the instrument, then, on proof that the cancellation

---

[18] But *cf. Syme's Exrs.* v. *Cherrie*, 1986 S.L.T. 161 where this distinction was ignored. See Halliday, *Conveyancing*, Vol. I, pp. 89–91; Reid, 1986 S.L.T. (News) 129.

[19] 1939 S.L.T. 69.

[20] 1986 S.L.T. 161.

[21] (1878) 5 R. (H.L.) 151.

[22] (1888) 16 R. 73.

was done by the testator himself, or by his order, with the intention of revoking the will, the will is to be held revoked; otherwise it is to be treated as a subsisting will."

Intention is crucial. In *Fotheringham's Trustee* v. *Reid*[23] it was absent: a woman deleted her married name simply intending to revert to her maiden name.

"(2) If a will or codicil is found with one or more of the legacies or particular provisions scored out . . . this raises no case for inquiry as to the testator's intention to revoke the instrument in whole, but [it does] as to the intention to revoke the particular provision; . . . the provision [is not] revoked unless [there is] evidence that the scoring was done by the testator himself or by his direction with the intention of revoking the clause. If the deletion were authenticated by the testator's initials, recognisable as his handwriting, [that is] sufficient proof that the deletion was the act of the testator, the full signature being only necessary to an act of positive disposition or bequest."

"(3) If a will or codicil is found with marginal or interlineal additions, apparently in the testator's handwriting . . . these [are] not part of the instrument, except in so far as they are authenticated by the signature or initials of the testator."

"(4) When the will or codicil contains words scored out and others inserted in their place, . . . the cancellation of the words in the original writing is conditional on the substituted words taking effect. Accordingly, if the substituted words are rejected on the ground that they are unsigned, the deletion is also to be rejected, and the will ought to be read in its original form."

(b) Holograph wills

7.9 The authentication rules are much laxer because fraud is less likely. In *Robertson* v. *Ogilvie's Trustees*[24] three out of seven trustees' names were written on erasures; provided the words were holograph of the testator (as was proved) the deed was valid. Even unauthenticated deletions may be given effect. In *Milne's Executor* v. *Waugh*[25] four holograph testamentary writings, all signed, were found after the testator's death in a sealed envelope; some bequests were scored out in ink. It could be inferred from the circumstances that the testator

[23] 1936 S.C. 831.
[24] (1844) 7 D. 236.
[25] 1913 S.C. 203.

made the deletions *animo revocandi*. But the courts are rightly chary of this method and need very clear proof.[26]

3. Revocation by later will

7.10 A will often expressly revokes all previous testamentary writings. The effect of such a provision depends on how the court construes it in an effort to discover the testator's intention. It may not always revoke all previous bequests. "Testamentary writings" has a wider meaning than "wills", and in *Clark's Executor* v. *Clark*[27] a revocation of "all wills previously executed by me" did not revoke a specific legacy of a stamp collection previously delivered to a legatee. In *Gordon's Executor* v. *McQueen*[28] a revocation of "two wills which are recorded in the Books of Council and Session in Edinburgh" was ineffective to revoke the testator's only previous will which did not meet that description. A revocation clause should either refer to "testamentary writings" or, if not a blanket revocation, accurately identify the will being revoked.

Revoking a will also revokes any ancillary documents, such as a codicil or an informal writing which derived its validity from it.

7.11 A will may also be revoked by implication. Again the point came up in *Clark's Executor* regarding the stamp collection. "As a general rule a later settlement of the *universitas* of the granter's estate will be held impliedly to revoke the provisions of an earlier settlement on the ground that the two deeds are inconsistent and cannot stand together. But there is no presumption that a general disposition revokes a former bequest of a specific subject."

By way of example, the testator in *Duthie's Executors* v. *Taylor*[29] conveyed her whole means and estate to testamentary trustees. That by itself might point to a universal settlement; but the will then directed various legacies and did not dispose of the residue of the estate. Looking at the testator's whole scheme it was not a universal settlement, and legacies in an earlier will stood except insofar as inconsistent with it.

Universal settlements apart, the rule is that revocation by implication occurs only where there is necessary inconsistency. Insofar as two wills are not inconsistent they are read together. For instance, in *Stewart* v. *MacLaren*[30] the testator had, in a third codicil to a will, confirmed various provisions in the will and first codicil but made no

---

[26] *Allan's Exx.* v. *Allan*, 1920 S.C. 732.
[27] 1943 S.C. 216.
[28] 1907 S.C. 373.
[29] 1986 S.L.T. 142.
[30] 1920 S.C. (H.L.) 148.

reference to the second codicil. The second codicil was held not to be revoked: "the words of revocation must be clear . . . you cannot speculate one way or the other." This principle was well stated in *Stoddart* v. *Grant*[31] where it was said that "it is a well-established principle of the law of Scotland that where a person deceased has left various writings, probative in themselves, for disposing of his or her property, they are to be understood as constituting one testamentary settlement in so far as they have not been revoked and are not inconsistent with each other."

Where implied revocation is alleged, the onus of proof is of course on the person alleging it. This was stressed in *Mitchell's Administratrix* v. *Edinburgh Royal Infirmary*[32] where, in a codicil, one provision suggested revocation of certain legacies while the other was against it. The facts were neutral; the legacies stood.

4. The *conditio si testator sine liberis decesserit*

7.12 In Scots law, unlike English, a will is not revoked if the testator later gets married or divorced. However it may be revoked by the subsequent birth of a child to the testator if it is a universal settlement and it makes no provision for the child. This is the *conditio si testator sine liberis decesserit*.

The rule applies in favour of any child born after the date of the will. The basis of the doctrine is generally taken to be a (fictitious) equitable presumption that the testator would have provided for later-born children if he had thought about them. It therefore only applies if the will made *no* such provision, however small.

The presumption can be rebutted by proof that the omission was deliberate: the testator meant not to make provision for the child in the will. But rebuttal is not easy. Evidence of a conscious and positive decision by the testator is probably necessary. It is not rebutted by mere passage of time between the child's birth and the testator's death: in *Milligan's Judicial Factor* v. *Milligan*[33] 10 years passed but that was not sufficient. One can contrast *Stuart-Gordon* v. *Stuart-Gordon*[34] where the testatrix died shortly after her daughter was born: it was proved that when considering her legacies in view of her bad health, and knowing the daughter was well provided for anyway, she had decided to omit her.

7.13 The *conditio* is not automatic. Only the child itself can invoke it and bring an action to reduce the will; he need not if he so chooses. If

[31] (1852) 1 Macq. 163.
[32] 1928 S.C. 47.
[33] 1910 S.C. 58.
[34] (1899) 1 F. 1005.

he dies his representatives cannot raise the action in his place for the benefit of his estate; nor can another disappointed legatee. Even so a practical problem can occur: an executor appointed under that will may be refused confirmation unless he rebuts the *conditio*, on the grounds that the will is presumed invalid.[35]

Unlike a simple legitim claim, the *conditio* revokes the will entirely. The child can then take legitim under intestacy. The child may be better just claiming legitim, without the *conditio*, because by avoiding intestacy he prevents prior rights defeating his claim.

5. Conditional revocation

7.14 English law clearly recognises the doctrine of *dependent relative revocation* that, when a revocation is linked to a new will or legacy, it is dependent on the legacy taking effect. Very few Scots cases admit to its existence here, and then without referring to it by name. *Gemmell's Executor* v. *Stirling*,[36] for instance, stressed that the test is that the revocation is coupled with the legacy in some way; they are interdependent. Lord McLaren in *Pattison's Trustees*[37] regarded deletions as invalid unless the new substituted words took effect.[38]

6. Revival of the revoking will

7.15 On one view revocation does not bury a will: it puts it in suspended animation. It can in some cases be revived. Suppose a testator makes a will, will no. 2, which revokes an earlier will, will no. 1. At a later date will no. 2 is itself revoked. The testator dies without a further valid will. Does will no. 1 revive by virtue of revocation of the will which revoked it?

In some cases there is no problem. Often will no. 2 is revoked by a method which also ensures will no. 1 remains dead. That may be the *conditio si testator*, or an express revocation of all previous wills. The problem arises when the final revocation is specific to will no. 2. For instance, will no. 1 contains provision for future children while will no. 2 does not: a child is then born. In that case the *conditio* revokes will no. 2 but has no effect on will no. 1.

The case law is inconsistent. In *Elder's Trustees* v. *Elder*[39] will no. 1 was expressly revoked by will no. 2, which was itself revoked by the operation of the *conditio*. The court held that will no. 1 did not revive:

---

[35] Currie, p. 80.
[36] 1923 S.L.T. 384.
[37] (1888) 16 R. 73 at p. 77.
[38] *MacRorie's Exrs.* v. *McLaren*, 1982 S.L.T. 295 (the Outer House judgment, reversed on appeal at 1984 S.L.T. 271 on other grounds) took a similar line on implied revocation.
[39] (1895) 22 R. 505.

while the law presumes that a will which makes no provision for future children is revoked on the birth of a child, there is no presumption that a prior will which has been *expressly* revoked by the later will is restored (even if it makes provision for them). By contrast, in *Nicolson* v. *Nicolson's Tutrix*[40] will no. 1 was merely impliedly revoked because will no. 2 was a universal settlement; on that ground the court refused to follow *Elder* and held that will no. 1 revived.

The most recent case, *Scott's Judicial Factor* v. *Johnston*,[41] also upheld will no. 1. The court appear to have taken the rule as settled, whereas it is still open to doubt. The practical advice given in *Scott* is to make certain that when will no. 2 is made, the testator is asked to ensure that will no. 1 is physically destroyed—either by him or his solicitor acting on his instructions. That way one can be certain that it will not revive.

7. Law reform

7.16 Among the reforms tentatively favoured by the Scottish Law Commission are the following:[42]

(1) Unless a will states the opposite it should be revoked by marriage.

(2) With the same proviso, divorce should revoke legacies in favour of the ex-spouse, and also her appointment by the will as an executor.

(3) The *conditio si testator* should be abolished.

(4) If conditional revocation exists it should not be an absolute rule, as *Pattison's Trustees* hints: the test should always be the testator's intention in the particular circumstances.

(5) There could be a rule that an expressly revoked will does not revive; it could apply to implied revocation too.

Further reading

M. C. Meston, "Revival by Revocation of the Revoking Will," 1976 S.L.T. (News) 153.

M. C. Meston, "Dependent Relative Revocation in Scots Law," 1977 S.L.T. (News) 77.

M. C. Meston, "The *Conditiones Si Sine Liberis*" (1981) 26 J.L.S. (Workshop) 203.

"Wills and the Testator's *Animus Revocandi*," 1984 S.L.G. 90.

K. G. C. Reid, "Execution or Revocation?" 1986 S.L.T. (News) 129.

---

[40] 1922 S.L.T. 473. But *cf. Bruce's J.F.* v. *Lord Advocate*, 1969 S.C. 296.
[41] 1971 S.L.T. (Notes) 41.
[42] Memorandum No. 70 (1986), Pts. V and VI.

CHAPTER 8

WILLS: ESSENTIAL VALIDITY

8.1 The term "will" is self-explanatory. A will is a declaration of what a person wills to be done with his or her estate after his or her death.[1] So, as with any legal act, he must know what he is doing. Legal capacity to undertake an act requires the ability to understand its nature and effects.[2] If that is absent, the person cannot make a will. Similarly, he must actually have made up his mind to make a will. Mere jottings for a possible future will are not enough. In legal terminology, the testator must have both testamentary capacity and concluded testamentary intent.

The underlying concept is not unique to wills. It is basic to the whole law of contract. Contracts can, in principle, be set aside if consent is defective or non-existent. But by the nature of things the emphasis is different with wills. A contract gives rise to immediately enforceable legal obligations: consequently the rules of capacity aim to protect the maker from the consequences of his actions. Error is thus an important concept. After his death the need is to protect his relations' expectations to inherit. Someone may have taken advantage of the testator's declining mental strength. So the stress is on circumvention and related doctrines.

CAPACITY TO MAKE A WILL

1. Age

8.2 Scots law regards pupils, boys under 14 and girls under 12 years of age, as not having the "use of reason." Consequently they cannot make wills. Minors, children between 12 or 14 and 18, had before 1964 no power to make a will of heritable property, but now have unrestricted testamentary capacity.[3] That contrasts with the law of contract, where for many purposes they need the consent of their curator.[4] English law is much more restrictive: one must be 18 in order to make a will, unless one is on active military service or a seaman, when the age limit is 16.[5]

---

[1] Erskine, *Inst.*, III.ix.5.
[2] See Stair, *Inst.*, III.viii.37.
[3] Succession (Scotland) Act 1964, s. 28.
[4] Guardian: normally a parent.
[5] Wills (Soldiers and Sailors) Act 1918.

The Scottish Law Commission suggests major changes to minors' legal capacity. In general they will have none till age 16, and then limited powers till age 18. But that is for lifetime transactions; the rules for wills are not changed.[6] In practice the power is of little real use till at least age 16, at which point one can take employment and get married. For anyone younger the rules of intestate succession will cover most eventualities.

Unlike children, women have always been allowed to make a will. Their right to own property *during* a marriage was until this century quite restricted, but a will only takes effect after the marriage is ended by death and those restrictions were absent.

2. Insanity

(a) The present law

8.3 An insane person lacks the power of rational thought, and so cannot test. The law presumes a person to be sane, so the onus is on whoever challenges a will to prove insanity. If a testator was the subject of an order under the Mental Health Acts, one can presume his insanity: but the presumption can be rebutted. The question is always whether, at the time of the will, the testator understood the nature and effect of his will. The will is valid if, as in *Nisbet's Trustees* v. *Nisbet*,[7] it can be shown that he had a lucid interval at the time he made it. Expert medical evidence is important. So too is the language of the will itself: if on its face it appears perfectly rational, that goes some way towards showing sanity.

8.4 The testator may only be partially insane: he may suffer from insane delusions. Perhaps he thinks his family are persecuting him. Many people may occasionally have such delusions but are quite capable of disposing of their estate rationally. There is every incentive for relatives offended by a will to allege delusions: how could any sane person not have left them better provided for? The courts look askance at such claims. The rules of insanity are not to protect relations against disinheritance; that is the function of legal rights.[8]

So delusions need not invalidate a will. The basic rule is:

"The question whether there is such unsoundness of mind as renders it impossible in law to make a testamentary disposition is one of degree . . . if his act is the outcome of a delusion so irrational that it is not to be taken as that of one having

---

[6] Report No. 110 (1988), para. 3.52.
[7] (1871) 9 M. 937.
[8] See paras. 4.11, 9.1.

appreciated what he was doing sufficiently to make his action-
... that of a mind sane upon the question, the will cannot stand.
If the testator is not generally insane, the will must be shown to
have been the outcome of the special delusion . . . The delusion
must be shown to have been an actual and compelling
influence."[9]

Thus even suicidal depression may be disregarded if it did not
affect the will.[10]

Morrison v. *Maclean's Trustees*[11] shows the limits of the rule. The
testator was given to obscene and rambling conversation. He spoke
of having "no relations." He said he had been fed when young from
an eagle's nest (indeed it seems he had). The court, reluctant to judge
its fellow man, stressed two points. First, delusions must be baseless,
such as no sane person could possibly believe. Second, "no amount of
moral depravity will afford any direct evidence of impaired intellect."
His will might be objectionable to some, but it was rational. So it was
valid.

8.5 On the same logic, someone who is so intoxicated or drugged as
to lose the power of rational thought cannot make a will.[12]

(b) Law reform

8.6 In England, unlike Scotland, the courts have traditionally had
wide protective powers over people who cannot look after their own
affairs. For instance, disputes as to parental rights may be resolved by
making a child a ward of court. Similarly the Court of Protection has
power to make an *inter vivos* settlement or a will for someone of
unsound mind.[13] This allows a legacy to be made to, say, children or
housekeepers, and for tax-avoidance schemes.

Analogous ideas have been much argued in Scotland. Some say the
incapax's curator bonis, the person appointed by the court to
administer his affairs, should be able to ask it to make a will. In the
latest discussion the Commission comes to no firm view.[14]

The problem really resolves into one of principle and practice. It is
a basic doctrine that a will reflects the testator's own personal
intention. He cannot in theory delegate his will-making power to
anyone else, though he can instruct his trustees to select a beneficiary
from a class clearly identified by him in his will. To allow such

---

[9] *Sivewright* v. *Sivewright's Trs.*, 1920 S.C. (H.L.) 63.
[10] *Smith* v. *Smith's Trs.*, 1972 S.L.T. (Notes) 81; *Ballantyne* v. *Evans* (1886) 13 R. 652.
[11] (1862) 24 D. 625.
[12] *Laidlaw* v. *Laidlaw* (1870) 8 M. 882.
[13] Administration of Justice Act 1969, s. 17.
[14] Memorandum No. 70 (1986), paras. 4.1–4.5.

delegation if he is insane conflicts with that principle. Moreover the rule has its logic. The *curator bonis* will be caught in the crossfire of pressure from self-seeking relatives. How can he know what the *incapax* would want? The tax aspect, minimal under capital transfer tax, is again important now that IHT covers only gifts made within seven years of death. Otherwise Scots law solves the problem better than English. In many cases the family's legal rights will give them adequate protection. They need not rely on a will, and they can inherit despite it if it cuts them out.

3. Facility and circumvention

8.7 An old person may suffer a degree of mental deterioration which, without amounting to insanity, leaves him easily imposed on by others. Someone may—maliciously or not—take advantage of this to persuade him to make a will in their favour. That is the essence of facility and circumvention.

Three elements are necessary: facility, the weakened mental state; circumvention, "getting round" the testator; and lesion, harm to his interests. The question to be asked is:

> "whether . . . the pursuer was weak and facile in mind, and easily imposed on; and whether the defender . . . taking advantage of the pursuer's facility and weakness did, by fraud or circumvention, procure the deed . . . to the lesion of the pursuer?"[15]

The three elements are inseparable, interrelated, and counterbalance each other. Plainly the more facile the testator, the easier it is to manipulate him. So the greater the evidence of facility, the less evidence that need be brought of circumvention. In effect the concept is a sliding scale, merging at one end into insanity (where the mental element is everything) and at the other [16] undue influence (where only pressure on the testator is needed).

(a) Facility

8.8 Facility is a clear enough concept: a weakening of faculties which does not amount to insanity but leaves the testator open to persuasion. Defining it is less simple. There is a large grey area where it borders at one extreme on insanity and at the other on undue

---

[15] See McBryde, *Contract*, para. 11.09 and cases cited.
[16] *Munro* v. *Strain* (1874) 1 R. 1039.

influence, and a given situation may raise any or all these issues. Many cases are on the borderline. Take *Gibson's Executor* v. *Anderson*.[17] A will was made in the defender's favour. The evidence could suggest either facility or insanity. They differed only in degree: "if the evidence might have warranted the conclusion that the mind of the deceased was completely incapacitated, it seems the shortest and easiest step from that to the conclusion that the deceased was facile in disposition." On the other hand facility differed from mere pliancy—lack of mental fibre, one might say. "Pliancy falls far shorter of facility in its legal sense than facility itself does of idiocy." The testator was "senile, silly and illiterate . . . of mental incapacity so marked as to disqualify him from framing the simplest of documents."

Facility may take different forms. "A man may be weak and facile from want of judgment or reason . . . [or] from mere nervousness and incapacity to resist solicitation . . . and therefore . . . you must endeavour to see whether there is any correspondence between the kind of facility that is proved and the kind of arts employed against him."[18] But susceptibility to persuasion is vital. One must not confuse that with mere lack of intellect or stupidity: one can be stupid but obstinate. The question is "the state of the mind morally and constitutionally": openness to machination, not simple lack of understanding.[19]

(b) Circumvention

8.9 This is essential, and can take many forms. Perhaps, as in *Wheelans* v. *Wheelans*,[20] one takes the facile person to a solicitor's office and produces a document to sign at once. The case law speaks of *fraud* and circumvention, but that means a sort of moral fraud wider than, say, in contract law: "improper practices and solicitation by interested parties" was the definition in *Morrison*.

If facility and lesion are present, only slight evidence of circumvention is needed.[21] But it can often be virtually impossible to prove specific instances of circumventing conduct. So the law has traditionally not required that: inference from the surrounding facts as a whole will do if coupled with evidence of facility.[22] In non-will cases the courts may insist on detailed averments of deceit or dishonesty,[23]

[17] 1925 S.C. 774 *per* Lord Blackburn.
[18] *Morrison* v. *Maclean's Trs.*, *supra*.
[19] *Cairns* v. *Marianski* (1850) 12 D. 1286.
[20] 1986 S.L.T. 164.
[21] Erskine, *Inst.*, IV.i.27.
[22] *West's Trs.* v. *West*, 1980 S.L.T. 6.
[23] *McDougal* v. *McDougal's Trs.*, 1931 S.C. 102.

but even there that is not always required if the grantor is now dead or *incapax*.[24]

4. Undue influence

8.10 Suppose that a solicitor prepares a will for a client. It contains a legacy in his favour. The client is not encouraged to obtain independent legal advice. Here there is a relationship of trust between testator and adviser; there must be a suspicion that the solicitor took advantage of his position to secure a benefit under the will. That is the essence of undue influence. If proved, the will is voidable: it can be set aside.

This is merely an aspect of a wider theory that the courts should protect people from manipulation by others in a dominating position, such as banks. It occurs also in contract law. There the English courts have suggested that the underlying doctrine is inequality of bargaining power, and that undue influence can be presumed where a transaction is manifestly disadvantageous to the weaker person.[25] Scots law does not go quite so far in that context.

Undue influence may co-exist with facility and circumvention. This happened in *Ross* v. *Gosselin's Executors*.[26] A lady died aged 90. Her will left the residue of her estate to her two nephews equally. She revised it when aged 74 and left nearly everything to one nephew, who was her solicitor. The other nephew alleged that she was eccentric and had delusions, that the solicitor looked after her affairs and induced her to give him large gifts, and that he told her the other was spendthrift. The case for circumvention was slim; delusions and eccentricity do not constitute facility (the lady may have been obstinate rather than easily-imposed on). Undue influence was more likely. Lord President Clyde distinguished the doctrines:

> "The essence of undue influence is that a person, who has assumed or undertaken a position of quasi-fiduciary responsibility in relation to the affairs of another, allows his own self-interest to deflect the advice or guidance he gives, in his own favour. On the other hand, the essence of circumvention and facility is that a person practises on the debility of another whose individuality is impaired by infirmity or age, and moulds the inclinations of the latter, to his own profit."

8.11 Three questions arise where undue influence is alleged. To

[24] *Mackay* v. *Campbell*, 1967 S.C. (H.L.) 53.
[25] *National Westminster Bank* v. *Morgan* [1985] 1 All E.R. 821 (H.L.). The literature on the subject is vast.
[26] 1926 S.C. 325.

what relationships does it apply? What actions constitute it? Finally, how must it be proved?

One cannot exhaustively define the categories of relationship in which undue influence may occur. The test has been widely phrased as a "fiduciary or quasi-fiduciary position"[27] or, more recently in *Honeyman's Executor* v. *Sharp*,[28] as "where a person, in pursuance of his profession or calling, undertakes the giving of advice to another and where, as a result, there develops a relationship between the adviser and the advised in which . . . the latter places trust and confidence in the former." That was a case of a fine art dealer. Other cases have included people in official positions—clergymen, doctors and lawyers—and parents and children. But a friend or, more intimately, a mistress[29] may be excluded. The list is not closed.

8.12 What sorts of behaviour amount to undue influence? Cases of wills have used a narrow test: there must be coercion or fraud, "coercion or compulsion overbearing the will of the testator and destroying free agency."[30] In *Weir* v. *Grace*[31] the judge cited conduct which excites terror, or a wife who prejudices her husband against his relations and stops him meeting them. In lifetime transactions the test is wider: abuse of the position of trust. The distinction has little logic. It was doubted in *Honeyman*, where the dealer gave biased advice to obtain a gift from a terminally-ill lady and also helped prepare her will. It is worth noting that precisely the same debate has occurred in relation to duress in contract, delict, and criminal law, where the theory of the "overborne will" is now discredited.[32]

With undue influence, like facility and circumvention, the actions complained of may be those of some third person. An outsider may "get at" one, not directly, but through one's spouse. Outwith the context of wills, this may happen when a bank wants the couple to grant a guarantee or mortgage: it only deals with one of them but may unduly influence the other.[33]

8.13 Normally the person alleging undue influence must prove it. But evidence of precise acts of coercion may be hard to come by. Nevertheless some situations are exceptionally suspicious: the surrounding facts may allow an inference of undue influence which demands that the trusted person provide an innocent explanation.

[27] *Forbes* v. *Forbes' Trs.*, 1957 S.C. 325.
[28] 1978 S.C. 223, *sub nom. Rodgers* v. *Sharp*, 1978 S.L.T. 977; see also *Gray* v. *Binny* (1879) 7 R. 332, *MacGilvary* v. *Martin*, 1986 S.L.T. 89.
[29] *McKechnie* v. *McKechnie's Trs.*, 1908 S.C. 93.
[30] W.H.D. Winder, 1939 S.L.T. (News) 165.
[31] (1899) 2 F. (H.L.) 30.
[32] See (1982) 98 L.Q.R. 556.
[33] *Kingsnorth Trust* v. *Bell* [1986] 1 All E.R. 423.

The classic example is the solicitor who prepares a will under which he is given some benefit: in that case (besides breaching professional ethics) the onus of proof shifts to him to give an explanation of his conduct.

5. The effect of incapacity on the will

8.14 If a will entirely lacks consent (as with insanity or nonage) or the testator's consent is defective by virtue of facility and circumvention or undue influence, the remedy is to have it reduced, *i.e.* set aside, by an action in the Court of Session.

If the action is successful the will normally falls completely. That is perhaps unjust in the sense that innocent beneficiaries suffer through one person's act of circumvention, but the rule seems clear. However, in one case partial reduction was in effect allowed. In *Horsburgh* v. *Thomson's Trustees* [34] a will was perfectly valid, but a later codicil was challenged for undue influence. The codicil was reduced but not the will, despite the fact that as a rule a codicil and will are treated as forming one composite document. The decision was sensible but unusual.

INTENTION TO TEST

1. Completed intention

8.15 A will requires no set form of words, but it must show a completed testamentary intention. The testator must intend that document to be a valid will. If he is still at the stage of deliberation, and intends it merely as jottings or instructions for a will to be made at some future time, it is ineffective. The governing test is the testator's intention.

It may be obvious that a document is a draft rather than a will. It may be headed "rough." [35] More often it is ambiguous and can be interpreted either way. In that case the court will accept extrinsic—external—evidence to supply an answer. Take *Rhodes* v. *Peterson*: [36] a woman wrote to her daughter telling her that she was going to make a formal will, but "I want you to have house and contents"; "just in case anything happens to me in the meantime this letter will establish your rightful claim." That was taken to be an immediate will and not just a reference to a future one.

[34] 1912 1 S.L.T. 73.
[35] *Sprot's Trs.* v. *Sprot*, 1909 S.C. 272.
[36] 1971 S.C. 56; and see *Jamieson's Exrs.*, 1982 S.C. 1.

The problem frequently arises where someone sends an apparently valid will to a solicitor, holograph and so formally valid, with a covering note to the effect that "I want a will made in this form." The letter casts doubt on the "will." Usually, as in *Munro* v. *Coutts*,[37] that is taken as a mere instruction for a will. Rarely it may be treated as valid. In *Maclaren's Trustees* v. *Mitchell and Brattan*[38] the decisive factor was that it was subscribed and attested.

8.16 Similarly a mere list of names or items will fail as a will unless something identifies them as legatees and legacies and the document shows completed testamentary intent; otherwise it is treated as mere jottings. Take the case of a deposit receipt with an attached list of names and amounts: a receipt itself can never be a testamentary document without some evidence that it is meant as a will. In *Cameron's Trustees* v. *Mackenzie*[39] that was lacking: "£150 to Y" was not clear enough, despite being signed. Use of legal terminology, or reference to "my last will," are helpful. But the word "will" is not always conclusive if the other factors suggest a draft, as *Colvin* v. *Hutchison*[40] shows. The list did not come to the right total: that itself was not fatal (since in a true will the sums would simply abate *pro rata* to match the correct amount of the estate) but given that it was hardly comprehensible, was signed at the side, and showed no other evidence of being meant as a will, it was invalid.

2. Error

(a) General principles

8.17 Error plays a major role in the law of contract. Contracts rest on consent; apparent consent is nullified if it arose from "essential error" as to some fact central to the contract, such as the identity of subject-matter or parties. On the other hand error is easy to allege as an afterthought, and the law today is reluctant to recognise it unless it was caused by fraud or false representations.

In theory a will can be set aside for essential error on the grounds that the testator was unaware of its nature, effect, or contents. In practice that is hardly ever necessary. Proof is difficult. There must also be fraud or circumvention: bare error is not enough. One illustration was *Munro* v. *Strain*[41] where a priest persuaded a terminally-ill old man to leave money to the church, and had the will

---

[37] (1813) 1 Dow 437.
[38] 1959 S.C. 183.
[39] 1915 S.C. 313.
[40] (1885) 12 R. 947.
[41] (1874) 1 R. 1039.

prepared for him. Facility apart, the will could be reduced for essential error. This was inferred from the surrounding circumstances: the will was not read over to the testator and he was known to have vigorously refused to make a will on those lines previously.

(b) Error in drafting

8.18 A solicitor preparing a will may have made a clerical error, and the testator may omit to check it; so the signed will, unknown to him, does not reflect his intentions. Such a will could perhaps fail for essential error.[42] In practice the courts will correct such errors, but only if they are obvious in the deed.[43]

In England such an error can now be corrected if the drafter made a clerical error or did not understand the testator's instructions.[44] In Scotland that can be done for *inter vivos* documents under section 8 of the Law Reform (Miscellaneous Provisions) (Scotland) Act 1985. The Commission suggest a rule for wills on the English model, but wider, to cover deliberate disobedience by the drafter.[45]

(c) Rules of interpretation [46]

8.19 Apart from the validity of the will as a whole, there may be questions as to a particular legacy. The courts may, by using the normal rules for interpreting wills, often correct or ignore the mistake. Where the mistake concerned a fact which was the reason for the legacy—*falsa causa*—that does not invalidate the legacy unless the legacy was conditional on the fact being correct.[47] Where a legatee or class of legatees is misdescribed—*falsa demonstratio*—the legacy still has effect if one can ascertain the legatee. If the will is ambiguous, extrinsic evidence is allowed to explain it. So the court tries to give effect to the testator's intention as contained in the will: they will not go behind it to contradict it. If ultimately these rules of construction do not identify the legacy or legatee, the legacy falls through uncertainty.

Further reading

McBryde, *Contract*, Chap. 11.
R. A. McCall Smith, "The Deluded Testator," 1973 S.L.T. (News) 61.

---

[42] *Yeatman* v. *Proctors* (1877) 5 R. 179.
[43] *Reid's Trs.* v. *Bucher*, 1929 S.C. 615.
[44] Administration of Justice Act 1982, s. 20.
[45] Memorandum No. 70, paras. 3.1–3.6.
[46] McLaren, Vol. I, pp. 367, 385.
[47] *Currie's Exrs.* v. *Currie's Trs.*, 1911 S.C. 999; *cf. Grant* v. *Grant* (1846) 8 D. 1077.

D. J. McNeil, "Making a Will for an Incapax" (1979) 24 J.L.S. 415.
W. H. D. Winder, "Undue Influence in Scots and English Law," 1939 S.L.T. (News) 165.
"Undue Influence," 1980 S.L.T. (News) 65.
"Reduction of Wills," 1963 S.L.T. (News) 53.
W. H. D. Winder: "Mistakes as to Legatees," 1953 S.L.T. (News) 149.
"Here's a How-de-doo," 1970 S.L.T. (News) 90.

CHAPTER 9

RESTRAINTS ON TESTAMENTARY FREEDOM

RESTRAINTS ON AMOUNT: LEGAL RIGHTS

1. Evasion of legal rights

9.1 Legal rights operate as a control on testation. They cannot be defeated by any testamentary disposition. Hence the testator's spouse and offspring are protected against disinheritance: they can, if not satisfied with the provision for them in the will, claim legal rights instead. They can of course choose to accept the testamentary provisions.

The will is not automatically invalid. If legal rights are claimed the will is not thereby struck down. There are two main results: the legacies in it are abated—reduced—*pro rata* to allow for the legal rights to be paid; and the person claiming legal rights forfeits all benefit under the will.

9.2 Having said that, legal rights can be evaded in four ways.

(1) They can be defeated by a genuine *inter vivos* transfer of moveable assets to a third party. The tactic succeeded in the early case of *Agnew* v. *Agnew*:[1] a father made a deed of assignation in favour of his eldest son; it reserved a liferent to himself and excluded the younger son's right to claim legitim; it was irrevocable. The court held that the father was the unlimited proprietor of his estate and so could dispose of it by deeds *inter vivos*; and the transaction was not fraudulent despite its effect.[2]

Apparently the transfer need not even be irrevocable, as long as it is not a sham and has not actually been revoked.[3] In theory the donor is allowed to reserve some benefit from the property (such as its use or income from it): but that is inadvisable because the item is then part of his estate for IHT purposes.[4]

(2) One can die intestate. If the estate is sufficiently small prior rights will exhaust it and leave nothing for legal rights to operate on: the effect is to benefit one's spouse at the children's expense. Alternatively the spouse can disclaim a benefit under the will and, unless the will makes provision for that event, create artificial intestacy.[5]

[1] (1775) Mor. 8210.
[2] See also *Lashley* v. *Hog* (1804) 4 Pat. App. 581.
[3] *Hutton's Trs.* v. *Hutton's Trs.*, 1916 S.C. 860.
[4] See para. 12.8.
[5] See para. 4.5.

(3) One can maximise the amount of heritable property in one's estate. In this connection note that a security over land (a standard security) is a heritable asset for the creditor. The testator may *constructively convert* moveables to heritage if he directs his executors to sell them, buy heritage, and give that to a beneficiary: but that is not foolproof because the beneficiary can reconvert by opting for the moveables instead.[6]

(4) One can ensure that the asset is not part of one's estate at all. Assets held in trust are an example. In particular take pension or life assurance proceeds: if payable to the testator or his executors they fall into the estate, but if to his widow or someone else they do not. Again this can benefit the widow at the children's expense, or *vice versa*.[7]

2. Approbate and reprobate

9.3 The identical English term "election" succinctly describes the purpose of approbate and reprobate. One cannot accept and reject the same legal document: one cannot take a benefit under it and at the same time insist on some independent benefit which clashes with its provisions. One must make a clear and free choice.

The idea has many applications. *Crum Ewing's Trustees* v. *Bayly's Trustees*[8] was not a case of legal rights. A testatrix had a power of appointment over funds under her father's will. Her children accepted sums which she gave them in exercising that power; they could not then challenge her appointment as executor under the father's will. Accepting one part of a deed was inconsistent with rejecting another part.

9.4 A valid election needs four conditions.

(1) It must be a free choice. If made in ignorance of alternative courses of action it can be set aside. That happened in *Walker* v. *Orr's Trustees*:[9] the electing children had insufficient knowledge of material facts: in particular they were not shown a copy of the will, not told the amount of the estate, and not urged to get independent advice; even 13 years later they could revoke the election.

The deceased's executor should thus ensure that potential claimants are aware of their legal rights and what options they have. The force and limits of this rule were stressed in *Donaldson* v. *Tainsh's Trustees*:[10]

---

[6] See Gloag & Henderson, para. 44.11.
[7] *Beveridge* v. *Beveridge's Exx.*, 1938 S.C. 160; see Clive, at p. 685.
[8] 1911 S.C. (H.L.) 18.
[9] 1958 S.L.T. 220.
[10] (1886) 13 R. 967 at p. 971 *per* Lord Justice-Clerk Moncrieff, approved in *Harvie's Exrs.* v. *Harvie's Trs.*, 1981 S.L.T. (Notes) 126 where an unadvised election was nonetheless valid.

"I do not say that independent legal advice is absolutely essential, but it is the duty of trustees to see and insist that a widow, before she makes up her mind to an election which will be injurious to her pecuniary interests, is acting not from a mere emotional feeling as to what she may suppose to have been her husband's wishes, but after full information and deliberation."

(2) The elector must have legal capacity to elect. A minor cannot make a binding election.[11] A *curator bonis* looking after an insane person's affairs should not exercise the power of election unless there are urgent reasons to do so, and he needs the court's approval.[12]

(3) The will which requires the election must itself be valid and enforceable.

(4) The legatee must be able, by election, to give effect to the legacy. Contrast *Brown's Trustees* v. *Gregson*[13] where the will made an invalid bequest of property situated in Argentina.

9.5 Election may be explicit: for the executor's protection it is best in writing. At the other extreme mere silence or delay scarcely ever constitutes election[14] (though after 20 years legal rights prescribe anyway). The test is conduct which shows a clear intention to accept or reject the legacy. Taking a pension shows nothing: it is consistent with either. Nor does becoming executor under the will: but to do so and then claim legal rights against it is a clear conflict of interest to be avoided.[15]

9.6 The effect of an election depends on the method used. An *express* discharge of legal rights covers the whole estate, testate or not, unless the elector reserves the right to claim from current or future assets which fall into intestacy.[16]

If discharge is implied from conduct it extends only so far as the will and legal rights conflict, so in principle legal rights are still claimable from the intestate estate. In practice the will often deals with election by a "forfeiture" or "full satisfaction" clause.

3. Forfeiture and equitable compensation

9.7 Election usually arises as a choice between legacies under a will and legal rights. At the very least one cannot take both if the two conflict. Two related problems complicate matters. What is the

---

[11] See para. 4.23.
[12] *Allan's Exrs.* v. *Allan's Trs.*, 1975 S.L.T. 227.
[13] 1920 S.C. (H.L.) 87.
[14] But *cf. Pringle's Exxs.* v. *Pringle* (1870) 8 M. 622.
[15] *Smart* v. *Smart*, 1926 S.C. 392.
[16] As in *Petrie's Trs.* v. *Mander's Trs.*, 1954 S.C. 430.

precise effect of a clause in the will that the legacies are in "full and final satisfaction of legal rights" or, conversely, an express forfeiture of the legacies if one claims legal rights? What then happens to the forfeited legacy? That is the question of equitable compensation.

(a) When is there forfeiture?

9.8 The answer depends on the terms of the will and the effect of section 13 of the 1964 Act. Several situations can be distinguished.

(1) Before 1964 if there were no "full satisfaction" clause the legatee need only elect to the extent that the will and legal rights were inconsistent. So, as in *White* v. *Finlay*,[17] if the will only dealt with part of the estate one could claim legal rights out of the rest.

(2) A "full satisfaction" clause was common. Its scope was always a question of the testator's intention as expressed in the will. In principle it meant (and still means) that by accepting a legacy one lost one's legal rights in the whole testate estate, and *vice versa* on claiming legal rights.[18]

(3) Suppose the will gave a liferent income, and the legatee elected for legal rights as a capital sum. Clearly the estate had to find extra cash in hand at once: other legatees suffered a *pro rata* reduction as a result. So *equitable compensation* occurred: the sum in the legacy went to them to compensate them. This might mean accumulating income over some time to pay them. That was the position in *Macfarlane's Trustees* v. *Oliver*;[19] the court held that once they had been compensated, the elector's rights revived: he could claim the liferent income again. Equitable compensation did not automatically mean permanent forfeiture of rights under the will.

(4) If the will expressly forfeited the legacy in the event of the legatee claiming legal rights, that was permanent. There was still equitable compensation, but the legacy did not then revive; *Macfarlane* did not apply. If there was a "full satisfaction" clause, that was taken to imply forfeiture[20] and had the same effect.

(5) Section 13 of the 1964 Act now implies "full satisfaction," and hence forfeiture, into almost every will made after 9 September, 1964. The old law still governs older wills. It provides:

> "Every testamentary disposition executed after [that date] by which provision is made in favour of the spouse or of any issue of the testator and which does not contain a declaration that the provision is made in full and final satisfaction of the right to any

---

[17] (1861) 24 D. 38.
[18] *Naismith* v. *Boyes* (1899) 1 F. (H.L.) 79.
[19] (1882) 9 R. 1138.
[20] *Rose's Trs.* v. *Rose*, 1916 S.C. 827.

share in the testator's estate to which the spouse or the issue, as the case may be, is entitled by virtue of *ius relicti, ius relictae* or legitim shall (unless the disposition contains an express provision to the contrary) have effect as if it contained such a declaration."

Unfortunately the Act does not abolish equitable compensation. It merely applies to all wills the old law on "full satisfaction" clauses, so stopping legal rights reviving *after* equitable compensation. This was made clear in *Munro's Trustees, Petitioners:*[21] a husband and two sons were left a liferent under a post-Act will; they claimed legal rights. That meant complete forfeiture of the liferent, and the income had to be accumulated for the benefit of a grandchild who took the fee under the will. This caused lawyers much consternation, since till then they thought they had seen the last of this horrendous doctrine.

(b) What is the effect of forfeiture?

9.9 Three related issues cause problems.

(1) *Whom does forfeiture affect?* Suppose there is a legacy to the elector and another related one to his children: such as liferent to one and fee to the other. The elector, taking legal rights, loses his legacy; do the children also lose theirs? That depends on the words of the will. If it says they forfeit, they do. If nothing is said expressly about them, the test is: are the two gifts interconnected or independent? If the latter, there is no forfeiture.[22] If the elector's own original forfeiture was not express but inferred (as under section 13) the children will certainly not be affected.[23]

(2) *What property is affected?* Despite the wide terms of forfeiture and full satisfaction clauses, the elector may not lose all legal rights. It may be that the will does not dispose of the whole estate. Or, as in *Naismith* v. *Boyes,*[24] some event after the testator's death makes it impossible to give effect to all the legacies. There a beneficiary entitled to the fee of the estate died and the fee fell into intestacy. In such cases the elector may claim legal rights out of the intestate estate. The rationale was explained in *Campbell's Trustees* v. *Campbell's Trustees,*[25] where there was an express forfeiture clause:

> "The forfeiture provisions were intended to protect the settlement as a whole and play no part when part of the estate falls into intestacy."

[21] 1971 S.C. 280. See Scot. Law Com. Memorandum No. 70, para. 4.31.
[22] *Ballantyne's Trs.* v. *Ballantyne*, 1952 S.C. 458.
[23] *Nicolson's Trs.* v. *Nicolson*, 1960 S.C. 186.
[24] (1899) 1 F. (H.L.) 79.
[25] 1950 S.C. 48.

(3) *What happens to the forfeited legacy?* We have seen that equitable compensation takes effect. But that only goes on till the other beneficiaries are compensated; moreover, the accumulation may become illegal under the Trusts (Scotland) Act 1961. What happens then depends on the will. The sum may be redirected to another person by a "destination-over" ("to X, failing whom to Y") or by accretion.[26] It may go to the residue or, failing that, fall into intestacy. If intestacy, the ironical result may be to send it back to the elector if he happens also to be the person entitled to succeed the deceased on intestacy.[27] But the courts understandably sometimes jib at such a result. In *Macnaughton* v. *Macnaughton's Trustees*[28] there was a forfeiture clause covering the elector and his children, and a destination-over: ultimately everyone chose legal rights so intestacy resulted. That should have given the elector the property; but the court ignored the strict rules and gave it to the children—"anyone but the elector" was the apparent rationale.

RESTRAINTS ON TIME: ACCUMULATIONS

1. Background

9.10 A testator may set up a testamentary trust to administer his estate after his death and carry out the instructions contained in the will. Among other things he may want property to be held in trust and the income accumulated in the fund for distribution to beneficiaries when, say, they reach adulthood. That is unobjectionable. At the other extreme one may try to have the income accumulated for ever and never paid out to beneficiaries. Or one may need to accumulate income for an indefinite period to permit equitable compensation. The law will not allow that: it limits the duration of accumulation.

English law frowns on perpetual trusts of any sort, except charitable trusts. In principle Scots law does not, and provided the purposes are sufficiently certain and are not contrary to public policy they are quite permissible. Trusts for hospitals, orphans, or dogs' homes would be valid. The only constraints are purely statutory.

The limits were originally laid down by the Accumulations Act 1800, known as the Thellusson Act after the testator whose ingenious trust inspired it. Thellusson was a wealthy English merchant who, in his will, directed that the residue of his estate was to be invested in land; the income was to be accumulated during the lifetime of his sons

---

[26] See paras. 10.13, 10.17, 11.13.
[27] *Tindall's Trs.* v. *Tindall*, 1933 S.C. 419.
[28] 1954 S.C. 312.

and grandsons; when the last one died the fund would be split among the family. Despite much litigation the trust was valid[29] and ultimately lasted some 60 years. What was striking was merely the sum involved (£600,000 at 1798 prices) and for that reason the Act ensued to prevent any repetition. Its direct successor is the Trusts (Scotland) Act 1961, section 5 and, extending the rules, the Law Reform (Miscellaneous Provisions) (Scotland) Act 1966, section 6.

2. The statutory rules

9.11 The two Acts lay down six possible maximum periods for accumulation, affecting both lifetime and testamentary trusts. The truster's intention is irrelevant: the rules apply whether he expressly directed accumulation or merely gave trustees discretion which had that result. The rules must be strictly observed. Accumulation must fall within one of the periods, which are alternatives, and one cannot add one period to another to extend it. Not surprisingly one cannot contract out of the rules:

> "No private arrangement or consent to defeat the provisions of the . . . Act, which . . . was dictated by public policy . . . can be given effect to by the Court. Were it otherwise . . . the Act might, without much difficulty, be so entirely defeated as to render it of no more effect than if it had been repealed."[30]

Note that, of periods (*a*) to (*f*), (*e*) and (*f*) affect only deeds which took effect after August 3, 1966. In principle (*a*) *ends* at the grantor's death; (*b*) and (*c*) *start* then; (*d*) to (*f*) can "straddle" it.

(a) The lifetime of the grantor (1961 Act, section 5(2)(a))

This applies to a direction in an *inter vivos* deed to accumulate during the grantor's lifetime. The accumulation may also relate to the joint lives of the grantor and someone else. Formerly such accumulations had to end at the grantor's death. Under the 1961 Act that is unnecessary provided the deed also "directs" accumulation under (*d*), (*e*) or (*f*): any of those periods can be used as an alternative, but (*b*) and (*c*) are not permissible (because they would here provide an *additional* period). *McIver's Trustees* v. *Inland Revenue* illustrates the operation of that rule: the deed directed accumulation till the grantor's son was 22; that did not come under (*d*) and so the accumulation lapsed when the grantor died.[31]

---

[29] *Thellusson* v. *Woodford* (1799) 4 Ves. 227; (1805) 11 Ves. 112.
[30] *Maxwell's Trs.* v. *Maxwell* (1877) 5 R. 248.
[31] 1974 S.L.T. 202.

(b) Twenty-one years after the grantor's death (section 5(2)(b))

This only applies where the date of death is the starting-point. If the period starts before or afterwards one of the other rules must be invoked. It is a maximum period, so that if for part of it the income is used for some other purpose and not accumulated, that does not extend the termination date.

(c) The minorities of persons living or in utero at the grantor's death (section 5(2)(c)).

This may be any person, not necessarily the grantor's family. While it refers to person(s), the maximum period will be about 21 years 9 months on the assumption of a posthumous child. "Minority" here means until age 21 rather than, as for most other purposes, 18.

(d) The minorities of persons who would, under the terms of the will or deed directing accumulation, be entitled if of full age to the accumulated income (section 5(2)(c))

This has no reference to the date of the testator's death: for instance, in *Re Cattell*[32] it applied to the minorities of persons born after his death. Furthermore it may permit accumulation during successive minorities as different beneficiaries are born and grow up. But it does require that they are actually entitled to the income at age 21 (and not later): they must be actual and not contingent—possible—beneficiaries, and so not dependent on trustees' discretion. As a result the income available for accumulation will steadily diminish as they successively reach majority.

(e) Twenty-one years from the making of the deed (1966 Act, section 6(1))

(f) The minorities of persons living or in utero at the date of the deed (1966 Act, section 6(1))

3. The effect of illegal accumulation

(a) The general principle

9.12 Illegal accumulation does not invalidate the trust itself. That continues after the end of the permitted period except for its accumulation provisions: "the deed is to be read as if it had expressly

[32] [1914] 1 Ch. 177.

declared that the accumulation directed should stop at the end of [the period]; and for the rest the deed is to be read and receive effect exactly as it stands."[33] Indeed the accumulation clauses may be referred to in order to interpret the rest of the deed, rather (on one view) like a revoked clause in a will.

(b) Disposal of income

9.13 The income which can no longer be accumulated must "go to and be received by the person[s] who would have been entitled thereto if such accumulation had not been directed."[34] What that means in practice depends on the terms of the will: the income may go to a beneficiary, go to residue, or fall into intestacy.

The test is whether the will makes a "present gift" to the beneficiary of the fund from which the income has been accumulated, rather than a right which takes effect at some future date.[35] If there is such a gift he gets the now unaccumulated income, but not otherwise. The Act does not operate to accelerate future rights. In that second case the income goes in the meantime to the residuary legatees if they are left a present gift of the residue. If they are not, it goes to the heirs on intestacy: the deed has made no provision for the event.

Contrast, then, *Landale's Trustees* v. *Oversea Missionary Fellowship*[36] and *Smith* v. *Glasgow Royal Infirmary*.[37] In *Landale* the residue was expressed to pass on the testator's death, and though the trustees could hold back enough to pay various annuities, they could make interim payments to the residuary beneficiaries, who therefore got the income. In *Smith* nothing was due to the legatees till the annuitants died; the income fell into intestacy. In neither case was the capital of the fund paid over, because it was still required for annuities; it was different in *Dowden's Trustees*[38] where there were no trust purposes which required the fund to be retained.

The beneficiaries on intestacy are ascertained as at the testator's death, despite the fact that the accumulated fund may emerge years later.

(c) Legal rights

9.14 It is disputed whether legal rights can be claimed out of accumulated income which falls into intestacy. The counter-

---

[33] *Elder's Trs.* v. *Treasurer of Free Church of Scotland* (1892) 20 R. 2, *per* Lord Kyllachy.
[34] Trusts (Scotland) Act 1961, s. 5(3).
[35] See Vesting, para. 11.4.
[36] 1982 S.L.T. 158.
[37] 1909 S.C. 1231.
[38] *Dowden's Trs., Petrs.*, 1965 S.L.T. 88; 1965 S.C. 56.

argument is based on the point that legal rights are fixed and valued at the testator's death whereas the accumulated funds emerged later; but the case law is inconsistent.[39]

4. Successive liferents

9.15 A right of fee in an asset allows the *fiar* to use it, draw income from it, and dispose of it in life or on death as outright owner. A liferent gives no right of disposal and lapses when the liferenter dies. The two commonly coexist through the mechanism of a testamentary trust: the fiar inherits a vested right immediately the testator dies but cannot use the property till after the liferenter's death.

A variety of liferent over land, the *entail* or *tailzie*, was for centuries an important means of ensuring that family estates were kept intact and not sold. Modern commercial society opposes such controls and restricts the maximum duration of liferents. Before 1968 the Entail Amendment Act 1848, section 48 applied to heritage, and the Trusts (Scotland) Act 1921, section 9 to moveables. They still govern deeds executed before November 25, 1968.

9.16 For later deeds the Law Reform (Miscellaneous Provisions) (Scotland) Act 1968 applies to both heritage and moveables. Under section 18 it is not possible to create a liferent in favour of someone who is not alive or *in utero* at the date of the creator's death. The section has the effect that the liferent property belongs absolutely to the liferenter at the date when he becomes entitled to the liferent or (if he is under 18 then) when he becomes 18. If the property is held by trustees they must make over the property to him at his expense. But none of this affects the rights of feudal superiors and holders of securities or other rights over the property.

RESTRAINTS ON PURPOSE: PUBLIC POLICY [40]

1. Illegality, immorality, and impossibility

9.17 If a legacy is immoral, illegal, or impossible, it is void. If on the other hand the legacy is subject to a condition which is illegal, immoral or impossible, the condition is treated as *pro non scripto* (as if unwritten) and ignored: the legacy is fully effective.

Impossibility is defined strictly; it is something more than mere improbability. If "if you marry X" is the condition, that is not

---

[39] *Moon's Trs.* v. *Moon* (1899) 2 F. 201; *cf. Lindsay's Trs.* v. *Lindsay*, 1931 S.C. 586.
[40] The purpose must also be certain, *i.e.* clear: para. 10.10.

impossible just because one is at the time married to Y. In *Barker* v. *Watson's Trustees*[41] the testator's daughter was undergoing addiction treatment in a hospital at the time he wrote his will; the condition attached to the legacy was that she and her husband were "reconciled" at the date of his death. That was valid: it was possible, though of course nothing could be done about it by the time the will was known. In any case it was not really a condition in the sense "if you do this you will get the legacy": "words descriptive of the place or mode of life of a person at the date of death of the testator do not, properly speaking, create a condition."

In *Barker* the court, rightly, dismissed the idea of an immoral condition. More such examples occur where the beneficiary is required not to live with someone related. In *Fraser* v. *Rose*[42] a father left his daughter a legacy which was conditional on her not living with her mother—moreover the executors were to throw her out of the house; the legacy was held to be payable unconditionally. By contrast, in *Balfour's Trustees* v. *Johnston*[43] the daughter had been taking an interest in an orphan; her father disapproved and made her legacy conditional on her not seeing the child—that was not contrary to public policy.

2. Public policy

9.18   The courts have evolved a concept of public policy as a ground on which to strike down provisions in a will. The basis of the doctrine is the testator's abuse of the power of testation; its scope is undefined and it rests on excessive self-glorification by the testator without any benefit resulting to anyone. "The testator's act may be regarded as going beyond the right of *testamenti factio* . . . [his] directions reach a certain pitch of grotesqueness, of extravagance, of wastefulness or of futility."[44]

It is recognised as a dangerous doctrine which risks arbitrariness, and for that reason will not be invoked except in particularly outrageous cases. The court will wish to be convinced that the defects of the testator's scheme greatly outweigh any public benefit.

9.19   The idea first came to the fore in the *McCaig* cases. McCaig, who built the famous Folly at Oban while alive, directed his testamentary trustees to use the revenue from his estate in perpetuity for the purpose of erecting artistic towers and statues of himself and his family on his estate. This would supposedly encourage young

[41] 1919 S.C. 109, *per* Lord Dundas at pp. 120–121.
[42] (1849) 11 D. 1466.
[43] 1936 S.C. 137.
[44] *Mackintosh's J.F.* v. *Lord Adv.*, 1935 S.C. 406, at p. 410 *per* Lord President Clyde.

Scots artists. The court struck the legacies down. Formally they did so on the ground that he could not disinherit the heirs on intestacy unless he created beneficial rights in favour of others. He did not: the artists would receive no prizes and the public got no benefit. Some *obiter* remarks show the judges' attitude:

"if it is not unlawful, it ought to be unlawful, to dedicate by testamentary disposition . . . the whole income of a large estate to objects of no utility, private or public, objects which benefit nobody, and which have no other purpose or use than that of perpetuating at great cost, and in an absurd manner, the idiosyncracies of an eccentric testator." [45]

In a subsequent case the court struck down provisions in McCaig's sister's will along rather similar lines. [46] Again no beneficial interest was conferred on anyone. The judges expressed the opinion that the directions were invalid as contrary to public policy: it was dangerous to permit a bequest which could only benefit the vanity of a testator who had no claim to be immortalised. One innocuous provision in the will was allowed to stand.

Later cases have been more clearly decided on the grounds of public policy as such. In *Aitken's Trustees* v. *Aitken* [47] the testator wanted part of Musselburgh High Street demolished and a massive bronze statue of himself erected. The object itself was reasonable: "interest in one's ancestors and . . . in their respectability if not their distinction, is a typical, and in some respects a not unlaudable, trait of the Scottish character." The manner of pursuing it was utterly fantastic. As a rule "the court is not to make itself the judge of what is for the public benefit. It is enough that the object is one, not immoral or contrary to public order, which a certain section of public opinion may regard as of public benefit." Here even that test was not met— quite the contrary; the provisions failed as "an irrational, futile and self-destructive scheme to carry out not unreasonable purposes."

Mackintosh's Judicial Factor v. *Lord Advocate* [48] concerned a testatrix's direction to spend her entire estate on erecting a mausoleum for her and to re-inter two close friends there. They were not relations; indeed she was illegitimate so (at that time) they could not be. [49] Now relations have a "right approaching in character to a right of custody" over graves, allowing them to apply for exhumation; she lacked that right. On that ground alone the court struck down the

---

[45] *McCaig* v. *University of Glasgow*, 1907 S.C. 231, at p. 242 *per* Lord Kyllachy.

[46] *McCaig's Trs.* v. *Lismore Kirk Session*, 1915 S.C. 426.

[47] 1927 S.C. 374, *per* Lord Sands at pp. 379–383.

[48] 1935 S.C. 406.

[49] Not the law now: the status of illegitimacy has virtually disappeared. Law Reform (Parent & Child) (Scotland) Act 1986, s. 2.

direction. That apart, it is clear that a reasonable provision for a tombstone or mausoleum is acceptable;[50] the court in *Mackintosh* were split as to whether the case was so unreasonable as to contravene public policy.

In a similar way a legacy to put flowers on a grave in perpetuity may be both too indefinite and unreasonable to be valid.[51]

Provided there is some public benefit public policy is satisfied. So a provision to establish a fund for an army regiment, though large, is acceptable.[52]

Further reading

Wilson & Duncan, *Trusts, Trustees and Executors*, Chaps. 7, 8.
M. C. Meston, "Accumulations" (1981) 26 J.L.S. (Workshop) 218.
M. C. Meston, "The Power of the Will," 1982 J.R. 172.

---

[50] See "Death and Debt", para. 3.5.
[51] *Lindsay's Exr.* v. *Forsyth*, 1940 S.C. 568.
[52] *Campbell Smith's Trs.* v. *Scott*, 1944 S.L.T. 198.

CHAPTER 10

INTERPRETATION OF WILLS

RULES OF EVIDENCE

1. General principles of interpretation

10.1 In interpreting the words of a will the fundamental principle is to give effect to the intention of the testator as expressed in the will. The testator's meaning must be deduced from the words he used. The court must read the will as a whole, along with any codicils— additional ancillary testamentary writings which alter it. Where provisions conflict it tries to reconcile them; if that fails the most recent receives effect. If at all possible the will is construed in a sense that avoids intestacy: it is assumed that the testator meant something by it. Words are presumed to have their ordinary, primary meaning; terms which have a recognised technical legal meaning, such as "heirs," will have their ordinary technical sense.[1]

Consequently one is normally not permitted to contradict the terms of the will by using *extrinsic* evidence to show that the testator actually meant something else. The reasons are obvious: there would be unlimited scope for inconclusive conjecture as to the testator's real intention; evidence might easily be concocted. That may be *direct* evidence of the testator's intention—oral and written statements made by him—or *indirect* evidence of surrounding facts and circumstances which he knew about at the time when he made the will: both are excluded. Revoked clauses in the will *may* perhaps be considered in order to show what the rest of the will means, but even that is doubtful.[2]

2. The use of extrinsic evidence[3]

10.2 Extrinsic evidence is however allowed if the will is unclear and the ordinary rules of interpretation provide no solution. In using it the court aims to put itself in the position of the testator at the time he made the will.[4] The aim is to explain the will, not to contradict it:

> "we must find the intention of the testatrix within the four corners of the deed which she has legally executed. We are,

---

[1] *Macdonald's Trs.* v. *Macdonald*, 1974 S.L.T. 87.
[2] *Devlin's Trs.* v. *Breen*, 1945 S.C. (H.L.) 27; *cf. Currie's Trs.* v. *Collier*, 1939 S.C. 247.
[3] See Walker and Walker, *Evidence*, pp. 282–298; Macphail, paras. 15.20 *et seq.*
[4] *Hay* v. *Duthie's Trs.*, 1956 S.C. 511, at p. 528 *per* Lord Carmont.

undoubtedly, to look at the whole deed; and . . . if there be any doubt in the terms, we are to take into consideration the circumstances under which the deed was executed . . . [But] it is only if the terms of the deed appear to be in themselves doubtful in their import or legal construction, that it is either necessary or legitimate to affect or explain them by extraneous circumstances."[5]

10.3 Extrinsic evidence is admitted for six overlapping purposes.

(1) To enable a will to be read. If it is in code it has to be deciphered; if it is in a foreign language it must be translated. The translation must be certified by an expert in the language.

(2) To establish whether a document is the testator's will. It may never have been meant as a will in the first place, the writer having lacked concluded testamentary intent; it may have been destroyed *animo revocandi*. In either event the writer's intention may not be plain from the document. So, for instance, in the case of a draft will one must consider the terms of any covering letter. Such evidence is essential where a will is said to have been revoked by the *conditio si testator*.

10.4 (3) To construe words in an unusual, secondary sense where their primary sense is ineffective. "A testator may give his own meaning to the words which he uses. His will becomes the dictionary from which the meaning of the terms used in it is to be ascertained."[6] In this way the provision can be implemented. Otherwise it would fail and intestacy would result.

Common examples at one time concerned the meaning of "child." Its primary sense was a legitimate, genetic child: adopted and illegitimate offspring were excluded. But external factors might point to the wider meaning: "a bequest by a testator, who is a bachelor . . . to his children may infer a gift to his illegitimate children surviving him, if he dies a bachelor, because the bequest would otherwise be inept."[7] That problem is now minimal: "children" now includes an adopted or illegitimate child unless the will says the opposite.[8]

10.5 (4) To prove what the testator knew about facts material to the construction of his will. For instance, in *Dunsmure* v. *Dunsmure*[9] the testator made a legacy of "any money I am entitled to under my

---

[5] *Blair* v. *Blair* (1849) 12 D. 97.
[6] *Borthwick's Trs.* v. *Borthwick*, 1955 S.C. 227, at p. 230 *per* Lord Justice-Clerk Thomson.
[7] *Scott's Trs.* v. *Smart*, 1954 S.C. 12. For adoption see *Hay* v. *Duthie's Trs.*, 1956 S.C. 511.
[8] But not for wills executed *before* September 10, 1964 (adoption) or November 25, 1968 (illegitimacy): 1964 Act, s. 23(2); Law Reform (Miscellaneous Provisions) (Scotland) Act 1968, s. 5.
[9] (1879) 7 R. 261.

late father's will." But he was also due money under his parents' marriage contract, and he knew it; in the circumstances the words covered both will and marriage contract. As this was a holograph will without professional advice the court felt particularly well-disposed to allow this extended meaning.

Similarly in *Livingstone* v. *Livingstone*[10] the testator referred in a codicil to "the sum of £6,000." The same sum occurred in the original will. Did the codicil give a fresh legacy or just repeat the old one? The value of the estate, insofar as the testator knew it, was a relevant factor suggesting the latter.

This rule applies particularly to a *legatum rei alienae*, a bequest of property the testator did not own. The law presumes that he made a mistake, and the legacy fails. If it is proved that he made the legacy deliberately, knowing the facts, the executors must try to implement his wishes and acquire the object for the legatee or, failing that, pay him the cash value instead.

(5) Two identical legacies in the same will are taken to be a mistake and only one is payable. Extrinsic evidence can rebut this presumption against double provisions.

10.6 (6) To identify the subject or the object of a legacy, if the will is ambiguous as to the property bequeathed or the beneficiary or purposes. Ambiguity can be *patent* (it is plain on a first reading) or *latent* (doubt arises only when the will is applied to the external facts).

It is sometimes said that only latent ambiguity permits extrinsic evidence. If a patent ambiguity cannot be solved by reading the will, the affected legacy is uncertain and lapses.[11] In fact the case law is not consistent and it is difficult to separate the categories. But (supposing latent ambiguity) only indirect evidence is normally allowed. The exception is where the will is meant to refer to one legatee but two or more people actually match the description: if the context gives no clues the testator's correspondence or oral statements are admissible evidence as to who was meant.[12]

If there is no ambiguity at all, the terms of the will stand or fall on their own. Extrinsic evidence cannot alter them. So in *Fortunato's Judicial Factor* v. *Fortunato*[13] a clearly worded legacy of a public house could not include an adjoining flat: in reaching this interpretation it was permissible to refer to other clauses in the will, but not to the circumstances in which it was made or the way in which the property was managed.

Despite applying the rules of interpretation and extrinsic evidence,

---

[10] (1864) 3 M. 20.
[11] See *Yule's Trs.*, 1981 S.L.T. 250 where "child" was read as a clear error for "grandchild."
[12] See Walkers, *Evidence*, pp. 285–288.
[13] 1981 S.L.T. 277.

a legacy may still be too uncertain to receive effect. It lapses and intestacy may result.

SUBJECTS AND OBJECTS OF LEGACIES

1. Types of subject and object

10.7 A legacy is a bequest of specified property to a specified recipient or for a specified purpose. The item is the subject, the recipient is the object.

The subject of the legacy is usually straightforward, though—as in *Dunsmure*—ambiguity may need to be resolved. Before 1868 it was not possible to leave heritage by will, but only by an immediate—*de praesenti*—conveyance taking effect on death and using the word "dispone"; there is now no restriction, and the only question is whether the testator intended a particular term to include heritage and, generally, what it meant.

10.8 The object is frequently a class of relation. Most of these terms have acquired a legal meaning which will apply unless the testator is proved to have used them in a different sense. "Child" we have seen. "Issue" refers to children, grandchildren, and other descendants— again the date of the will may determine whether it extends to illegitimate descendants. But a legacy to "dependants" will fail for uncertainty as the term has no precise meaning.[14]

"Next-of-kin" usually means the relations entitled to inherit if one dies intestate; in *Nelson's Trustees* v. *Nelson's Curator Bonis*[15] that was a daughter, but the term was taken to mean a nephew: this was decided in the light of the will having been altered in other respects to exclude the daughter from benefiting. The same point applies to "heirs."[16]

"Wife" or "husband" needs great care. Divorce does not revoke a will. Such a legacy is valid if "wife" was added simply to identify a named legatee, as in *Couper's Judicial Factor* v. *Valentine*.[17] If it is a family provision, for the recipient in the character of wife—as when the legatee is not named—the legacy either falls or goes to whoever is the wife when the legacy is payable. That happened in *Burns' Trustees*:[18] when the testator made his will and when he died, his nephew was married; when (32 years later) the legacy became payable to the nephew's wife, he was remarried; the new wife took the legacy.

---

[14] *Robertson's J.F.* v. *Robertson*, 1968 S.L.T. 32.
[15] 1979 S.L.T. 98; also *Borthwick's Trs.* v. *Borthwick*, 1955 S.C. 227.
[16] For date at which heirs identified see "Vesting", para. 11.30.
[17] 1976 S.L.T. 83.
[18] 1961 S.C. 17.

In the same way a legacy to a "fiancé(e)" is not conditional on marriage unless it says so.[19]

2. Uncertainty

(a) General rule

10.9 We have already seen that a will, or a legacy, may be ambiguous. That occurs whenever there is no item matching the subject or no person matching the object. The maxim is that *falsa demonstratio non nocet: dummodo constet de re* (or, as appropriate, *de persona*): mere misdescription does not invalidate the bequest if the ambiguity can be cured by extrinsic evidence. If it cannot the legacy fails; it is void for uncertainty.

A classic example concerning the object was *Cathcart's Trustees* v. *Bruce*.[20] The legacy was to "General Alexander Fairlie Bruce." There was in fact a General Alexander J., and a Mr Alexander F. From extrinsic evidence—letters—referring to the "General's" children as young men, it was clear that the real General was meant. There the description fitted neither possible beneficiary. It is a finer point if one is described accurately but not the other, as in *Nasmyth's Trustees* v. *N.S.P.C.C.*[21] where the legatee was the N.S.P.C.C. but the S.S.P.C.C. claimed it was meant. On the face of it there is no ambiguity: the court in *Nasmyth* said that "positive evidence" is needed to disregard the description and choose the inaccurately-named person, but it gave no guidance as to what exactly that meant.

The subject causes fewer problems. In *Magistrates of Dundee* v. *Morris*[22] trustees were directed to set up the Morgan Academy, but no cash legacy was itemised. That would not raise latent ambiguity. But it was not void for uncertainty: the will specified the size of the school, and thus allowed the legacy to be ascertained—as a sum sufficient to pay for the school.

(b) Class gifts; selection of objects by trustees

10.10 A legacy may be left to a defined class of people. If sufficiently certain, it is effective. But "if there can be a reasonable doubt as to who is comprehended within the so-called description, the courts will treat the bequest as void." So in *Salvesen's Trustees* v. *Wye* a bequest

---

[19] *Ormiston's Exr.* v. *Laws*, 1966 S.L.T. 110.
[20] 1923 S.L.T. 722; and *Keiller* v. *Thomson's Trs.* (1824) 3 S. 279.
[21] 1914 S.C. (H.L.) 76, *per* Lord Dunedin at p. 83.
[22] (1858) 3 Macq. 134 (H.L.).

to "any poor relations, friends, or acquaintances of mine" was invalid.[23]

One problem is whether to read such lists "disjunctively" (*i.e.* as separate provisions) or "conjunctively" (as one provision, with several criteria all of which must be met in each case). In *Salvesen's Trustees* the list was construed disjunctively, hence widely; "poor relations" would be acceptable but "friends" was not, so the whole list fell for uncertainty. Note that as a general tendency (though with exceptions) "and" is interpreted conjunctively and "or" disjunctively.

One may occasionally have to consider whether a gift is to individuals or a class, as in *Millar's Trustees* v. *Rattray*:[24] a legacy to "the children of [X], of whom there are ten" was taken to be a class which included three children born after the date of the will; the number simply identified the class without limiting it.

10.11 It is a fundamental principle that a testator cannot delegate to someone else the power to make a will—that, after all, is why a will cannot be made for an *incapax*. But he can by his own will appoint testamentary trustees and instruct them to choose beneficiaries from within a class defined by himself:

> "A party may, in the disposition of his property, select particular classes of individuals and objects, and then give to some particular individual a power, after his death, of appropriating the property, or applying any part of his property, to any particular individuals among that class whom that person may select and describe in his will."[25]

That class must itself be sufficiently certain: if trustees are given total discretion to distribute property as they think fit, with no guidance from the testator, that is void from uncertainty.[26] Subject to that constraint, instructions will be given effect.

10.12 Where the bequest is to "charities", the law is more generous. Admittedly the testator must create some mechanism for the charities to be selected: if, as in *Angus's Executrix* v. *Batchan's Trustees*,[27] he appoints no trustees or executors for that purpose, the bequest is ineffective. On the other hand the omission is not fatal if the legacy is sufficiently precise not to rely on trustees' discretion: as in *Ballingall's*

---

[23] *Salvesen's Trs.* v. *Wye*, 1954 S.C. 440. See Wilson and Duncan, pp. 194–199.
[24] (1891) 18 R. 989.
[25] *Crichton* v. *Grierson* (1828) 3 W.&S. 329, at p. 338 *per* Lord Lyndhurst L.C.
[26] *Sutherland's Trs.* v. *Sutherland's Trs.* (1893) 20 R. 925.
[27] 1949 S.C. 335. See Wilson and Duncan, pp. 175–179.

Judicial Factor v. *Hamilton*[28] where it was to "heart diseases and cancer research."

Subject to trustees or executors being appointed, the bequest to charities is effective. "Charitable purposes" are a class in their own right and need no further definition in the will. But note that they have different senses in England and Scotland. In England their meaning is precise: "trusts for the relief of poverty; trusts for the advancement of education; trusts for the advancement of religion; and trusts for other purposes beneficial to the community."[29] In Scotland that test only applies for tax purposes.[30] Otherwise the term has a loose commonsense meaning.

"Charity" is exceptional: other similar terms are ineffective. "Public purposes", for instance, is void for uncertainty:[31] it might include political donations. The problem occurs where the testator, unwilling to use one word, combines "charity" with a term which on its own would be uncertain. The test then is whether the two words are read disjunctively, referring to separate objects, or to take the other merely to explain and further define "charity." If the first, the whole clause is void; if the second, it is valid. So in *McPhee's Trustees* v. *McPhee*[32] "religious and charitable" was valid, while in *Rintoul's Trustees* v. *Rintoul*[33] "charitable or social institutions" was uncertain. But it depends how the court interprets the particular will: in *Wink's Executors* v. *Tallent*[34] "benevolent or charitable" was upheld. Word order, punctuation, and the general scheme of the will all influence the interpretation chosen.[35]

MULTIPLE LEGACIES AND LEGATEES

1. Destinations-over[36]

10.13 A destination-over is a provision in the will in the form "to A, failing B" or "to A or B." It names the original legatee or "institute" (A) and then a further legatee B to whom the property may pass in A's place.

B may be either a conditional institute or a substitute. A conditional institute is an alternative legatee; a substitute is a second

[28] 1973 S.L.T. 236.
[29] *Commissioners of Income Tax* v. *Pemsel* [1891] A.C. 531.
[30] *Inland Revenue* v. *Glasgow Police Athletic Association*, 1953 S.C. (H.L.) 13.
[31] *Blair* v. *Duncan* (1901) 4 F. (H.L.) 1.
[32] 1912 S.C. 75.
[33] 1949 S.C. 297.
[34] 1947 S.C. 470.
[35] See Wilson & Duncan, pp. 196–197.
[36] See Henderson, *Vesting*, pp. 49–55.

successive legatee. Now if A for some reason never inherits from the testator (perhaps he dies before him), in either case B inherits in his place. The difference arises if A does inherit. If there is conditional institution, B's right immediately lapses altogether. If there is substitution, B still takes the property after A dies—unless A defeats B's right by disposing of it either during his lifetime or by his own will.

The rule is clear; the problem is to decide if an ambiguously worded clause creates a substitute or a conditional institute. That depends on whether heritage or moveables are at issue. If heritage, substitution is presumed; if moveables (or a mixture of both), conditional institution. Each item of property is looked at separately, so that both presumptions may occur in the one will. But while the presumptions are strong, the terms of the will may rebut them.

In *Watson* v. *Giffen*[37] spouses jointly owned a house. The wife left her share "to and in favour of my said son . . . whom failing, to my own heirs and assignees and disponees whomsoever in fee." The son survived her but died intestate before her husband, who was her heir. The share went to the husband, despite the existence of the same words for moveables elsewhere in the will. By contrast, in *Crumpton's Judicial Factor* v. *Barnardo's Homes*[38] cash was left to charities "in case [X] dies without issue." He did, but not before outliving the testatrix: by his survivance the charities' right lapsed.

2. Cumulative and substitutional legacies

10.14   Testamentary writings may leave more than one legacy to the same person. The legacies may be cumulative or substitutional: if cumulative, both are payable; if substitutional, only one is.

The testator's intention may be clear upon reading the writings so as to reconcile their provisions and find out the testator's overall scheme. There may in fact not be two effective legacies: the later may have revoked the earlier. Failing that one must rely on legal presumptions.

(1) If one deed contains identical legacies, these are presumed to be substitutional. The testator is taken to have repeated one legacy through forgetfulness. Where the amounts differ, the legacies are cumulative. On the other hand, in *Gillies* v. *Glasgow Royal Infirmary*[39] there were two identical quarter-shares of residue: the court treated these as cumulative on the strained reasoning that these were not legacies as such.

(2) If the legacies are in different deeds, they are cumulative

[37] (1884) 11 R. 444.
[38] 1917 S.C. 713.
[39] 1960 S.C. 438.

whether identical or not. The principle was laid down in *Arres'
Trustees* v. *Mather*:[40]

> "When a testator by one or several instruments gives two or
> more legacies to the same individual, he presumably intends that
> they shall all have effect, and in the absence of any expression or
> other indication of intentions to the contrary [the law accepts
> this]. Nor will a mere speculative conjecture or plausible doubt
> be allowed to affect the legal presumption for cumulation, which
> is generally in accord with the real intention, and is the *prima
> facie* legal presumption precisely because it is so, for the
> aim . . . of the law is to ascertain and carry into effect the
> testator's intention. The presumption may . . . be overcome, not
> only by distinct expression that the later bequest was intended to
> be substitutional, but by anything which satisfies the court that it
> was so intended."

In reaching a conclusion the court may look not only at the scheme
of the deeds but also at extrinsic evidence. In *McLachlan* v. *Seton's
Trustees*[41] the history of the wills was crucial. The first was made
under duress, and consequently the testatrix later made a new will: in
it she deliberately repeated some (but not all) of her earlier legacies,
which were therefore not cumulative but substitutional.

3. Division *per capita* and *per stirpes*[42]

10.15 We have seen this distinction in intestate succession.[43] *Per
capita* division allows all the legatees to share equally. By contrast,
per stirpes division is initially made at the level of the *stirps*,[44] the
branch of the family tree indicated by the will as appropriate;
thereafter members of the *stirps* share equally *per capita*. Take a
legacy jointly to A's son B and C's sons D and E: if they take *per
capita* each gets one-third; if *per stirpes* (with the head of each *stirps*
being A and C respectively) B gets one-half while D and E each take
one-quarter.

When a bequest is left to a number of individuals, it is presumed
unless the will indicates otherwise that all who survive the testator
take equally *per capita*. If, however, the legatees are described as
members of a group or class (such as "the issue of X") *per stirpes*
division is a possibility. If they have the same degree of relationship to

---

[40] (1881) 9 R. 107. See also *Edinburgh Royal Infirmary* v. *Muir's Trs.* (1881) 9 R. 352.
[41] 1937 S.C. 206.
[42] See Henderson, *Vesting*, pp. 218–224.
[43] At para. 4.16.
[44] *Stirpes* is the plural of *stirps*.

the deceased (*e.g.* all are grandchildren) *per capita* division is preferred;[45] if different degrees (one is a child, the other are grandchildren), *per stirpes* at the degree nearer the deceased.

10.16 But general rules do not fully answer the problem, which is always one of interpreting the particular will. Even if it uses the term *per stirpes*, that just begs the underlying question: who is the head of the *stirps*? At what point in the family tree did the testator want the legacy to be divided? *Per stirpes* division occurs if "the children of X" does not merely identify *who* they are, but also *what* their share is: they inherit in place of X, X's share goes to them in aggregate, so division is *per stirpes* at the level of X.[46]

Per stirpes division is a two-stage process. First one identifies the various *stirpes* and divides the estate among them. Having ascertained what share each *stirps* gets, one divides that among its members. This second stage is in principle *per capita*.

Cobban's Executors v. *Cobban*[47] and *Laing's Trustees* v. *Samson*[48] illustrate the concept. In *Cobban* the estate was to be "divided equally between X and his children and my brother Y and his children:" this meant *per capita* division among all the beneficiaries. In *Laing's Trustees* division was among "my surviving brothers and sisters and the lawful issue of those who may be deceased": the issue got what their parent would have got, so division was *per stirpes* at the level of the brothers and sisters.

4. Accretion

10.17 A legacy may be to several legatees, such as "A, B and C." If all the legatees survive and acquire a vested right, the position is simple: each takes a proportionate share of the legacy, and if one of them later dies before receiving actual payment his right then passes to his heirs as part of his own estate. The problem arises if one dies before his right vests: does his share fall into intestacy[49] (or residue) or does it accrue to the other legatees? In the second case there is *accretion*.

The solution depends on whether the legacy is treated as "several" or "joint." If several, each share passes separately and there is no accretion. If joint, the legacy remains undivided and the share accresces to the survivors. The underlying issue is whether the

---

[45] *Campbell's Trs.* v. *Welsh*, 1952 S.C. 343.
[46] *Thomson* v. *Cumberland*, Nov. 16, 1814, F.C.
[47] 1915 S.C. 82.
[48] (1879) 7 R. 244. See *Boyd's Tr.* v. *Shaw*, 1958 S.C. 115.
[49] Including a destination-over will avoid intestacy.

testator intended one aggregate legacy to the beneficiaries *en bloc* or separate legacies merely payable out of one total fund.

10.18 In the simple case—"A and B" with nothing further said—the legacy is joint and there is accretion to the survivor. But if there are "words of severance" that points to the testator intending separate legacies: consequently accretion is excluded and intestacy results. *Paxton's Trustees* v. *Cowie*[50] explains what is meant:

"When a legacy is given to a plurality of persons named or sufficiently described for identification 'equally among them', or 'in equal shares', or 'share and share alike', or in any other language of the same import, each is entitled to his own share and no more, and there is no room for accretion in the event of the predecease of one or more of the legatees. The rule is applicable whether the gift is in liferent or in fee to the whole equally, and whether the subject of the bequest be residue or a sum of a fixed amount or corporeal moveables. The application of this rule may, of course, be controlled or avoided by the use of other expressions by the testator importing an intention that there shall be accretion in the event of the predecease of one or more of the legatees."

10.19 However, words of severance will not always bar accretion. They are simply strong evidence of the testator's intention, and that may still point to a collective legacy and thus accretion. Two common types of provision achieve this result:

(1) Words of survivorship: "equally among X, Y, and Z, and the survivor." If X fails to survive his share accresces to the others.

(2) A class gift: where beneficiaries are selected not essentially as individuals (out of the testator's regard for them personally) but as members of an identified group, normally relations.

Numerous cases discuss class gifts. "Equally among the children of [X]" is one instance.[51] Similarly a "one-third share," normally a clear sign of severance, would not prevent accretion where the will as a whole made clear that the legatee inherited merely as one of three sons.[52]

If the will names the beneficiaries individually, that makes a class gift unlikely. The fact that the legatees happen to form a class is not enough unless they explicitly inherit *as a class*. Adding their names suggests that their individual identity is more important than their membership of the class: for instance "A, B, C, and D, the children of

---

[50] (1886) 13 R. 1191, at p. 1197 *per* Lord President Inglis.

[51] *Muir's Trs.* v. *Muir* (1889) 16 R. 954.

[52] *Roberts' Trs.* v. *Roberts* (1903) 5 F. 541.

my late sister."[53] But names are not always fatal: the testator's apparent intention is always central. The names may be mere subsidiary identification—"my children (who are X and Y)" more important, there may be words of survivorship. Both features allowed accretion in *Menzies' Factor* v. *Menzies*.[54]

10.20   *Mitchell's Trustees* v. *Aspin*[55] indicates what care is necessary in drafting such clauses. Residue was to go in equal shares to children in liferent, and to their issue in fee; "failure" of any issue would divide that person's share equally *per stirpes* among the other children and issue. Perhaps the testator intended accretion: but he had not provided for the event of issue never existing at all, and (despite strong dissenting judgements) the Court of Session and House of Lords both ignored accretion and held that the share fell into intestacy.

Accretion is not limited to the death of a legatee; it can occur whenever a legacy fails for any reason. In *Fraser's Trustees* v. *Fraser*[56] a legacy was to A and B but the testator revoked B's share. Had there not been words of severance, it would have accresced to A; as it was, B's share fell into intestacy.

5. *Conditio si institutus sine liberis decesserit*

10.21   Normally if a legatee dies without acquiring a vested right his legacy lapses. Unless there is accretion or a destination-over, the bequest falls into residue or intestacy. The *conditio si institutus sine liberis decesserit* is an equitable exception to that rule: it implies into the will a conditional institution of the legatee's children to inherit in his place if he fails to survive. They inherit in preference to a substitute named in the will, a residuary legatee, an heir on intestacy, or anyone to whom the legacy would otherwise accresce. The theoretical rationale is that the testator overlooked the possible death of the institute and would have inserted a conditional institution to children if he had thought of it.[57]

The doctrine depends on the institute—the original legatee—being closely related to the testator. The courts have arbitrarily limited the relationships to which it applies. It covers the testator's children, grandchildren, and other descendants (but not stepchildren). It does not apply to brothers or other collaterals, with one exception: nephews and nieces are included if the testator was *in loco parentis* to

---

[53] *White's Trs., Petrs.*, 1957 S.C. 322.
[54] (1898) 1 F. 128; similarly *Young's Trs.* v. *Young*, 1927 S.C. (H.L.) 6.
[55] 1971 S.L.T. 133; 1971 S.L.T. 166 (H.L.).
[56] 1980 S.L.T. 211.
[57] English law has a similar rule: Wills Act 1837, s. 33 (1).

them.[58] But in practice the *loco parentis* test is meaningless. How the testator viewed the nephew during his lifetime is unimportant; what matters is simply that he "has placed himself in a position like that of a parent towards the legatees—that is to say he has made a settlement in their favour similar to what a parent might have been presumed to make."[59]

10.22 In effect the *conditio* is presumed automatically from the relationship. The presumption may be displaced, but the onus of proof is on those who oppose its application and not those who assert it. Three factors will assist rebuttal:

(1) Express exclusion of the *conditio*. Even so, a simple survivorship clause—"to my children surviving at my death"—will not by itself defeat it. The *conditio* overrides accretion: if a child predeceased, *his* descendants get his share; only if he had none does it go to the surviving children.

(2) A bequest made from personal regard for the legatee rather than in view simply of his relationship. It is not essential for the *conditio* that the beneficiaries form a class, all of whom are instituted, but it makes it easier to displace it if the beneficiaries are selected members named individually.[60]

(3) The testator did not overlook the existence of the institute's children. An example is *McNab* v. *Brown's Trustees*:[61] the testatrix left property in liferent, and then in fee to her two sons equally and the survivor of them and "the issue of either of them who predeceases me." One son died after the testatrix but before the liferent expired: he had not predeceased her, so his children could not invoke the *conditio*.

10.23 The original potential legatee must have been validly instituted in the first place. Conditional institution under a destination-over will suffice. So the *conditio* is excluded if he had died before the date of the will,[62] or before any codicil which affected his legacy.[63] Probably the *conditio* applies if he survives the testator but dies before acquiring a vested right.[64] Indeed, in *Reid's Trustees* v. *Reid*[65] the court went further. The testator's nephew died after drawing an income benefit under the will: on the nephew's death his interest

---

[58] *Hall* v. *Hall* (1891) 18 R. 690.
[59] *Bogie's Trs.* v. *Christie* (1882) 9 R. 453, *per* Lord President Inglis.
[60] *Knox's Exr.* v. *Knox*, 1941 S.C. 532.
[61] 1926 S.C. 389.
[62] *Travers's Trs.* v. *Macintyre*, 1934 S.C. 520.
[63] *Miller's Trs.* v. *Miller*, 1958 S.C. 125.
[64] *McGregor's Trs.* v. *Gray*, 1969 S.L.T. 355; *cf. Mitchell's Exx.* v. *Gordon's Factor*, 1953 S.L.T. 134.
[65] 1969 S.L.T. (Notes) 4.

passed to his children under the *conditio* rather than to the testator's heir-at-law under intestacy.

10.24 Suppose the institute would have inherited a further legacy by accretion. In principle the *conditio* does not apply to the additional accresced provision: only to the institute's original share. In practice the will often introduces complications:

(1) It may give the institute's children the benefit of accretion, stating that they are to take "such share, original and accrued, as their parent would have taken if he had survived."

(2) It may *also* contain words of survivorship. These override (1): the accrescing share goes to the survivors. Take a legacy to "A, B, and C, and the survivors": A dies leaving children; B dies with none; C survives. A's original (one-third) share goes to his children; B's accresces to C, and A's children get none of it.[66]

(3) Suppose that in (2) C had also not survived. Applying (2) would cause intestacy in respect of B's and C's shares. In that case, reversing the normal rule, *if*(1) is also present it is given full effect: A's children get everything.[67]

LEGACIES: CLASSIFICATION AND PAYMENT

1. Classification

10.25 How a legacy is classified is important for two reasons. First, it determines exactly what rights the legatee has in respect of the property bequeathed. Second, it dictates the order of priority in which legacies are paid, and thus in which they lapse or are reduced if the estate is too small to pay them all: that raises the issues of ademption and abatement.

(1) *Specific (or special) legacies.* These are legacies of a specified item, like a house or the right to receive a debt, or an identified investment: "my 1,000 shares in X Company Ltd." The legacy is confined to that item, and lapses if the testator no longer owns it when he dies: it is "adeemed." The item is regarded as assigned on death to the legatee, who can bring an action for its delivery not just from the executor but from anyone in possession of it.[68]

(2) *Demonstrative legacies.* These, like special legacies, refer to a particular item, but state the source or funds from which the testator wishes it to be provided or paid. The question is then what happens if the source is insufficient for the legacy. A special legacy would lapse

---

[66] *Miller's Trs.* v. *Brown*, 1933 S.C. 669. See Murray, pp. 168–173; Henderson, pp. 102–109.
[67] *Beveridge's Trs.* v. *Beveridge*, 1930 S.C. 578.
[68] In that case the executor is also nominally a defender.

to the extent that the fund is insufficient. A demonstrative legacy, by contrast, gives the legatee a claim against the residue for the excess.

(3) *General legacies.* These are generic, "bequeathed indefinitely without any character distinguishing [them] from others of the same kind belonging to the deceased;"[69] "a legacy not of a special article or debt, but of a certain quantity or value which may be measured in money (as is usual) or in goods of a specified description."[70] The legatee has a right to sue the executor to enforce its payment or delivery.

(4) *Residue.* This covers the whole of the testator's estate (heritable and moveable) which remains after paying the testator's debts and carrying out the antecedent purposes—such as legacies—of his will or wills. It includes property not disposed of by the will and legacies which fail initially or (perhaps because they are conditional on some event) lapse after the testator's death. Residuary legatees have no right to insist on particular assets from the estate, unless they all agree on a division. The executors have discretion whether to transfer the assets *in specie, i.e.* physically, or to sell and distribute the proceeds.

A will should dispose of residue: otherwise that property devolves under the rules of intestacy. In that case the heirs on intestacy are those as at the testator's death, not those at the later date when a legacy lapses and the intestacy becomes known.[71]

2. Ademption of specific legacies

10.26 A specific legacy is adeemed if it no longer belongs to the testator when he dies. It lapses entirely: the legatee gets nothing. The test is twofold: was the legacy specific, and was the item part of the estate at death? That is purely factual: in modern law the testator's intention in disposing of the asset (was it deliberate?) is irrelevant.

The problem is usually whether the legacy still survived at the date of death. *Ogilvie-Forbes' Trustees* v. *Ogilvie-Forbes*[72] summarised it: "the question is whether a testator has at the time of death the same thing existing, it may be in a different shape—yet substantially the same thing." There a legacy of a house was adeemed by its transfer to a limited company, albeit a company controlled by the testator. By contrast, in *Ballantyne's Trustees* v. *Ballantyne's Trustees*[73] there was ademption where the bequeathed sums, identified as being in a bank

---

[69] Erskine, *Inst.*, III.ix.11.
[70] McLaren, Vol. I, p. 575.
[71] *Lord* v. *Colvin* (1865) 3 M. 1083.
[72] 1955 S.C. 405, at p. 411 *per* Lord President Clyde.
[73] 1941 S.C. 35.

account at Glasgow, were uplifted and re-deposited by the testator in a new account at Hawick.

There is no ademption if the item was not yet finally disposed of. In *McArthur's Executors* v. *Guild*[74] a hotel sale was conditional on the licence being transferred to the buyer; that happened after the testator died; ademption had not occurred. Much the same happened in *Tennants' Trustees* v. *Tennants*[75] where shares had been transferred but not yet registered with the company. (Note that, even if ademption is absent, the legatee might hold those shares subject to a constructive trust in the buyer's favour, requiring him to complete the transfer and to forward any dividends received in the meantime.[76])

The risk of ademption can be minimised by wording legacies to refer to assets owned at death. "Any car I may own at the date of my death" is an example.

3. Abatement of legacies

10.27   The testator's debts, including executry expenses and IHT, must be paid or provided for before any legacies. So must legal rights, if claimed. The estate may then not be large enough to pay all the legacies. They must abate—be reduced. The will may itself state how, but failing that the order is as follows:

(1)   Residuary legacies abate first.

(2)   General legacies next abate *pari passu* (equally).

(3)   Demonstrative legacies do not abate until the specified fund is exhausted, but then abate like general legacies.

(4)   Specific legacies are payable though no assets remain for general legacies.

Legacies' order of priority does not depend on their mere numbering in the will unless the will says so. Other factors may point to a different order.[77]

4. *Legatum rei alienae*

10.28   This is a legacy of an item which did not belong to the testator. The law presumes that he made the legacy by mistake (and it lapses) unless it is proved to have been deliberate. In that second case the executor must try to purchase the item to give to the legatee; if he cannot the legatee receives the cash value instead. But, as was pointed out in *Meeres* v. *Dowell's Executor*,[78] it is not enough to show that the

---

[74] 1908 S.C. 743.
[75] 1946 S.C. 420.
[76] See R. Burgess, "The Unconstructive Trust?", 1977 J.R. 200.
[77] *McConnel* v. *McConnel's Trs.*, 1931 S.N. 31 (H.L.).
[78] 1923 S.L.T. 184.

testator ought to have known the facts; he must actually have done so.

5. Precatory bequests

10.29 Instead of the testator instructing his executors what legacies to pay, he may use words like "I would prefer that . . . ." Normally this is taken as a polite form of instruction which the executors must follow.[79] Sometimes the request is outwith the executors' power to fulfil. In *Milne* v. *Smith*[80] the testator left a legacy to his son and hoped that his partnership would be carried on. This was a precatory condition attached to the legacy; it could not be enforced (neither the son nor the other partner might be willing), so the legacy was payable unconditionally.

Alternatively the testator may request a legatee to dispose of the legacy in some way. To the extent that this attempts to restrict the legatee's right of ownership, it is unenforceable under the doctrine of *repugnancy*.[81] The most it can do is to create a destination over the property, which the legatee can evacuate by disposing of it as he wishes while alive.

6. Interest on legacies

10.30 In principle legacies are payable with interest from the testator's death to the date of payment. There is no fixed "legal rate": the rate is what the estate earned or should have earned if properly administered.[82] But circumstances may waive interest: for instance, the estate may have been insolvent for part of the period.[83] In any event the will often makes legacies payable interest-free.

CONDITIONAL LEGACIES

10.31 A legacy may be payable subject to conditions. These may be suspensive (payment is postponed till the condition is fulfilled) or resolutive (the legacy lapses if a specified event occurs, such as remarriage).

The condition may be ineffective for several reasons, and it is then disregarded and the legacy takes effect unconditionally. It may be

---

[79] *Reid's Trs.* v. *Dawson*, 1915 S.C. (H.L.) 47.
[80] 1982 S.L.T. 129.
[81] See Murray, pp. 39–44.
[82] *Kearon* v. *Thomson's Trs.*, 1949 S.C. 287.
[83] *Waddell's Trs.* v. *Crawford*, 1926 S.C. 654.

impossible. It may be *contra bonos mores*, contravening public policy: the normal example is a restraint on cohabitation or marriage. It may be uncertain: in this respect England requires a tougher test for resolutive than suspensive conditions (because they defeat a right already given to the legatee) but Scots law does not, "it [being] only necessary in order to allow of the condition being enforced that it be expressed in terms sufficiently determinate to advertise the beneficiary and the Court of the general course of conduct which has been enjoined."[84]

A condition may be potestative: it requires for its final fulfilment the act of someone other than the legatee. The condition may then be taken as fulfilled when the legatee has done all he or she can to fulfil it. So in *Miller & Another, Petitioners*[85] she was willing to look after the testatrix as required in the will; only the testatrix's confinement to hospital prevented her doing so. She was entitled to the legacy.

The conditions may be inconsistent with the bequest: if so they are disregarded. This is another example of the doctrine of "repugnancy" which resolves conflicts between mutually-contradictory provisions. The classic instance occurs where property is left in fee—outright ownership—and conditions are attached which are appropriate to a lesser right such as a liferent. In particular, the beneficiary's right of fee may be subject to the trustees not making payment till a specified age such as 25. Then, as in the leading case of *Miller's Trustees* v. *Miller*,[86] the beneficiary can insist on payment unless he is legally *incapax* (*e.g.* as under 18) or payment is being withheld in order to safeguard some other purpose of the trust. Withholding property purely to manage it for the owner is not consistent with full ownership.

Powers of Appointment

10.32   In principle a testator cannot delegate his power of testation. However, when making a legacy he may create a power of appointment in respect of the property in question: a power to select to whom the property will subsequently pass. He either reserves the power to himself or grants it to the legatee or some third party; the recipient of the power cannot himself delegate it to someone else.

Powers of appointment are *special* or *general*. Under a special power beneficiaries are chosen from a defined class. A general power gives an unlimited choice. That is in effect as wide a power of disposal as any owner can have: so if the testator purports to give a legatee a

---

[84] *Balfour's Trs.* v. *Johnston*, 1936 S.C. 137 *per* Lord Moncrieff.
[85] 1977 S.L.T. (Sh. Ct.) 67. See Wilson & Duncan, p. 85.
[86] (1890) 18 R. 301.

liferent *plus* a general power, he in fact makes the legatee unrestricted owner. The power is incompatible with the liferent, which on its own would allow assets to be used but not disposed of. The one exception, where the liferent remains in force, is an alimentary liferent.
A power must be exercised according to its terms. Any unauthorised exercise is *ultra vires* and a "fraud on the power" which can be challenged by anyone who is rightfully entitled to benefit under the power.[87]

Further reading

Murray, *Law of Wills*.
Henderson, *Vesting*, Chaps. 7, 15, 17.
"Fraud on a Power", 1976 S.L.T. (News) 157.
M. C. Meston, "Bequests to Heirs," 1974 S. L. T. (News) 109.
M. C. Meston, "*Per capita* and *per stirpes* division; The *conditio si institutus*; Accretion" (1981) 26 J.L.S. (Workshop) 195, 203, 212.
G. Robertson, "*Per Stirpes* Division," 1979 S.L.T. (News) 133.
J. R. Scott, "The *Conditio si Institutus*," 1958 S.L.T. (News) 229.
W. H. D. Winder, "Ademption of Legacies," 1957 S.L.T. (News) 185.

---

[87] *Callander* v. *Callander's Exr.*, 1976 S.L.T. 10. See Gloag & Henderson, para. 43.29; Murray, chap. 17.

CHAPTER 11

VESTING

GENERAL RULES

1. The concept of vesting

11.1 Property is said to "vest" in someone when he acquires an indefeasible right to it. In the context of succession that has two practically important aspects.

(a) Vesting in the executor

Under the old law a deceased person's heritable property passed directly to his heir on his death. By contrast the moveables vested in the executor for the purpose of administration when he obtained confirmation of his title: he was then empowered to ingather it and distribute it to the beneficiaries under intestacy or the deceased's will. Any dealings by the executor with the property before confirmation constituted unauthorised "vitious intromission" which laid him open to liability for all the deceased's debts.

Under the Succession (Scotland) Act 1964[1] all the deceased's property—heritable and moveable—now vests in the executor upon confirmation. There is one important exception. Heritable property subject to a special destination vests purely to allow the executor to convey it to the next-entitled person, *if* that is necessary. So in a destination of form "A, then B," on A's death his executor's role is to transfer ownership to B. In the more usual survivorship destination, "A and B and survivor," B is already joint owner, automatically becomes full owner, and the property does not need to vest in the executor at all.[2]

(b) Vesting in beneficiaries

11.2 While a testator still lives, his legatees have a mere *spes successionis*, the chance to inherit on his death. He can normally revoke his will at any time, so they cannot have an indefeasible vested right. That arises on his death at the earliest; the will may itself postpone vesting till some later date. Legal rights and rights on

---

[1] s. 14(1).
[2] s. 18(2). See Meston, pp. 82–83; (1965) 10 J.L.S. 73.

intestacy vest on the death of the spouse, parent or intestate respectively.

Precisely what right does vesting give the beneficiary? It has been called a "right of property."[3] But it is not outright ownership of the items involved. He may be unable to recover them from a third party who acquires them from the executor for value and in good faith;[4] if they include a house, he cannot mortgage that (because he has as yet no recorded title to it); and he cannot necessarily demand possession of them, because the will may postpone payment or transfer till a later time.

What the beneficiary has, rather, is a personal right against the executor to compel him to pay over or deliver the vested estate in terms of the will or intestacy. Legal ownership at this stage rests with the executor: it passes to the beneficiary only when transferred by delivery (in the case of moveables) or recorded written disposition or notice of title (for heritage).

11.3 The beneficiary can dispose of his vested right by *inter vivos* assignation: outright, or in security for a loan. It forms part of his estate on his death, so may be subject to IHT. Most important, it does not lapse in that event but passes to his heirs in their turn under his own will or intestacy.

2. Vesting and payment

(a) General principles

11.4 Vesting is quite distinct from receiving possession or payment under a legacy or intestacy. Possession is immaterial to vesting. The two may coincide, but need not. For debts must be paid before any legacy: that alone can delay payment for up to 12 months after death.[5] Moreover, a will may provide that a legacy vests on the testator's death but is not payable until some specified future event: usually the end of a liferent[6] or the legatee reaching 18 or some other age.

In that case, if the beneficiary survives the date of vesting but dies before receiving payment, his legacy goes to his heirs. If he had no vested right, it passes instead by destination-over or with residue under the testator's will, or by the *conditio si institutus*[7] or the rules of intestacy.

---

[3] *Haldane's Trs.* v. *Murphy* (1881) 9 R. 269, at p. 295 *per* Lord Young. *Cf.* (1986) 31 J.L.S. 148, 396; (1987) 32 J.L.S. 218. See paras. 10.25, *supra*, and 13.34.

[4] Succession (Scotland) Act 1964, s. 17.

[5] McLaren, Vol. II, p. 1164.

[6] See Gloag & Henderson, *Introduction*, Chap. 40.

[7] See para. 10.21.

(b) Vesting, minority and taxation

11.5 Questions of vesting may thus involve disputes between claimants for the legacy. But they also have important tax ramifications. In particular, in a testamentary trust it is crucial for IHT whether a beneficiary has an "interest in possession" in trust assets: a "present right of present enjoyment."[8] If he does, he is treated as owning the assets (so they are part of his estate for IHT), and the trust is denied the advantageous status of an accumulation and maintenance settlement.[9] *Stenhouse's Trustees* v. *Lord Advocate*[10] illustrates the concept: a will gave trustees power to allocate funds to the testator's daughters once aged 22; they did so; the daughters took a vested right and, being adult, could insist on immediate payment. Combining those factors, they had an interest in possession in the funds.

11.6 The problem often concerns bequests to minors. The testator wishes to delay payment till they are adult, with trustees administering the funds and the income arising from them until then. He has several choices:

(1) The bequest may vest on his death, the trustees having power to accumulate the income rather than pay it out. That has three effects. The income cannot be accumulated beyond age 21.[11] If this is a "bare trust", with no other purposes to fulfil (such as a liferent), under the doctrine of repugnancy *all* the funds must be paid over at age 18.[12] For purposes of IHT the legatee owns the funds, and has an interest in possession despite the mere fact of accumulation; similarly he pays income tax on the income.

(2) Vesting may be postponed to a specified age, say 21 or 25. This allows the funds to be withheld beyond age 18, though the will may also give the trustees discretion to pay them over at an earlier age. Again the child *must* get the income from age 21. He *may* be given a liferent (and so a right to the income) prior to that age: if so, IHT and income tax are treated as in (1). If not, they fall not on him but on the trust as a separate entity.

(3) The trust may be an accumulation and maintenance settlement. Tax law restricts the duration (25 years) and beneficiaries (the testator's grandchildren and other defined relations); all the unaccumulated income must be used for the beneficiary's maintenance, education or benefit; and the beneficiary must initially have no

---

[8] *Pearson* v. *I.R.C.* [1980] 2 W.L.R. 872; IHTA 1984, ss. 5(1), 49(1), 59. For IHT see para. 12.10.
[9] IHTA 1984, s. 71.
[10] 1986 S.L.T. 73.
[11] See para. 9.11.
[12] See para. 10.31.

interest in possession but will get one before (at latest) age 25. In practice the child usually gets the income from age 21, with the funds vesting at age 25. In that case income tax and IHT fall on the trust, not the child, till those ages respectively.

3. Rules of interpretation

11.7 The date of vesting may range from the testator's death to the date of payment; earlier and later times are not possible. The date chosen depends on "the intentions of the testator, in so far as they can be discovered or reasonably inferred from the deed taken as a whole, and from the circumstances, legitimately collected, under which the deed was made . . . It is a *quaestio voluntatis*. That is the cardinal rule and guide."[13]

That dictum stresses a salient aspect of the law of vesting. The words of the will are crucial. No two wills are identical; each case must be decided on its own facts. The courts have developed numerous rules to ascertain when vesting occurs (some of them arbitrary rather than logical), but ultimately these are merely guidelines, presumptions which must yield to the clearly expressed words of the will. Unfortunately the will is often unclear. The court may have a gut feeling what the testator really meant, but if he did not say so clearly, they have little choice but to apply those rules even if that gives a different outcome. As is often said, "the court will not make a testator's will for him."

All the usual rules for interpreting wills apply. In particular, the scheme of the will and any codicils is read as a whole, while the family circumstances in which the testator made the will are relevant. There is a presumption against putting a construction on the will which results in partial or total intestacy, as the testator is taken not to have intended that: if he had, would he have made the will in the first place?

The will may expressly declare when vesting is to take place. That is some help, but is not decisive; the declaration has to be read in the light of the rules of interpretation. The courts will accept it (perhaps reluctantly) if it makes the testator's intentions clear; but if it conflicts with the scheme of the will it simply obscures matters and may be disregarded.[14]

11.8 One presumption is especially important in the absence of some contrary indication of the testator's intention: that in favour of vesting at the earliest possible date. This means vesting *a morte testatoris*, on the testator's death. Given two reasonably possible

---

[13] *Carleton* v. *Thomson* (1867) 5 M. (H.L.) 151, at p. 153 *per* Lord Colonsay.
[14] *Carruthers' Trs.* v. *Carruthers' Trs.*, 1949 S.C. 530.

interpretations of the will, the courts prefer the one which allows that. But if that is impossible, they go to the other extreme:

> "If the term of vesting is not the date of the death of the testator, it is difficult to find any other period of vesting except the period of distribution . . . except some special cases where the testator has either expressly or by implication assigned a term of vesting other than the period of distribution . . . Where no other period is suggested the term of vesting is either (1) the death of the testator, or (2) the period of distribution."[15]

CONDITIONAL LEGACIES

1. Types of condition

(a) Payment

11.9 A legacy may be made payable on condition of a specified event occurring. This only postpones vesting if the condition is attached to the legacy itself. If the legacy is unqualified, and the condition relates merely to payment, vesting occurs in principle on the testator's death.[16]

(b) Certain and uncertain events

11.10 Some types of event are, by the nature of things, inevitable; some are not. The first is a *dies certus*: it must occur, though the exact date may be unpredictable; the legacy is taken as unconditional. The second is a *dies incertus*:[17] it may or may not occur, and there is a true condition. The first does not suspend vesting, the second may.

Suppose, then, property goes to X in liferent and Y in fee. The liferenter's death is *dies certus*. Though payment to Y is postponed until then, his right vests in him on the testator's death: so if he dies during the liferent his heirs get his legacy. To delay vesting would require an additional factor, such as words in the will or a destination-over whereby another legatee took in Y's place as conditional institute on his death.

Conversely, marriage or survival to a specified age are both *dies incertus*. So in *Mackintosh* v. *Wood*[18] a testatrix left her son one legacy due on her daughter's marriage, and another due on the

---

[15] Lord President Inglis in *Marshall* v. *King* (1888) 16 R. 40, at p. 43.
[16] *Alves' Trs.* v. *Grant* (1874) 1 R. 969.
[17] Certain and uncertain day, respectively.
[18] (1872) 10 M. 933.

daughter's death; on the son dying earlier the first legacy lapsed, but the second did not because, depending on a *dies certus*, it had already vested.

(c) Suspensive and resolutive conditions

11.11 Even if the condition relates to a *dies incertus*, it will not necessarily postpone vesting. That depends on whether the condition is suspensive or resolutive. The first suspends vesting until the condition is fulfilled and the legatee's right thus completed. The second allows vesting subject to defeasance:[19] the legacy vests immediately but falls if the relevant event occurs.

The type of event determines the type of condition. A suspensive condition involves a factor personal to the legatee, such as his survival or marriage. The legacy only vests on the event. A resolutive condition is extraneous to him: say, the birth of children to someone else. The birth, and only that, defeats his already-vested legacy.

2. Survivorship clauses and destinations-over

11.12 These are two common clauses by which a testator recognises the possibility of a legatee dying before the date of payment and regulates what then happens to the legacy. Both are taken to fix vesting at the date of payment (be that at the testator's death or postponed till later) unless the will selects some other date.

(a) Survivorship clauses

A survivorship clause is usually in the form "to X, Y and Z and the survivors or survivor," or words to similar effect. The survivors are identified at the date of payment; predeceasing legatees have no vested right and their shares pass to the survivors by accretion[20] or (if words of severance exclude that) fall into intestacy.

The classic exposition of the rule came in *Young* v. *Robertson*[21] where a clause in this form instructed a gift of fee to be paid at the expiry of a liferent. The House of Lords held that the fee vested in those alive at that date. Lord Westbury's dictum has since been taken to apply, not just to cases involving liferents, but all words referring to survivorship:

> "I apprehend it to be a settled rule of construction, that words of survivorship occurring in a . . . will . . . should be referred to

---

[19] See para. 11.15.
[20] Or to their children, if the *conditio si institutus* applies: para. 10.21.
[21] (1862) 4 Macq. 314.

the period appointed by [it] for the payment or distribution of the subject-matter of the gift . . . The application of that rule would lead to this determination in two cases. [i] If a testator gives a sum of money or the residue of his estate to be paid or distributed among a number of persons, and refers to the contingency of any one or more of them dying, and then gives the estate or the money to the survivor, in that simple form of gift which is to take effect immediately on the death of the testator, the period of distribution is the period of death, and accordingly the contingency of death is to be referred to the interval of time between the date of the will and the death of the testator. In such a case, the words are construed to provide for the event of the death of any one of the legatees during the lifetime of the testator. [ii] . . . if a testator gives a life estate in [his property], and at the expiration of that life estate directs [it] to be divided among a number of objects, and then refers to the possibility of some one or more of those persons dying, without specifying the time, and directs in that event the . . . distribution to be made among the survivors, it is understood by the law that he means the contingency to extend over the whole period of time that must elapse before the . . . distribution takes place. [Therefore] the survivors are to be ascertained in like manner by a reference to the period of distribution, namely, the expiration of the life estate."

Young v. *Robertson* thus allows for two alternatives, failing indication to the contrary in the will: vesting *a morte testatoris* or, if later, at the date of payment.

(b) Destinations-over

11.13 A destination-over states who is to inherit in the event of a beneficiary's failure to live till the date of vesting. It provides an alternative beneficiary. The basic form is "*to A, whom failing to B.*"[22] A is the institute, the first potential beneficiary; B is the conditional institute, his right arising only in the event of A's death prior to the date of vesting. The legacy vests at the date of payment (following *Young*) and the destination-over takes effect then unless the will says otherwise.

Contrast conditional institution and substitution. The conditional institute inherits only if the institute fails; so vesting has to be postponed to find out if the institute survives the date of payment. A

[22] Since "failing" is judged at the date of vesting, contrast its sense where immediate defeasible vesting occurs. See paras. 11.14, 11.32.

substitute beneficiary inherits *after*, rather than instead of, the institute: "to A, then B" is the sense. B can inherit as substitute whether or not A survives the date of payment. Consequently there is no need to postpone vesting, and *Young* v. *Robertson* does not apply. The legacy vests in the institute A on the testator's death, and then in B on A's death *unless* A has evacuated—revoked—the destination by will or in his lifetime.[23]

So care is needed in wording a destination-over. Is substitution or conditional institution wanted? The drafter can ask two questions: (1) What sort of property is at issue? Substitution is strongly presumed with heritage, conditional institution with moveables or— as is usual—a mixed estate of heritage and moveables. (2) Do the words themselves override the presumption and point to one or the other? "Whom failing" is neutral on its own. Stating (expressly or by implication) that the destination depends on the institute dying before vesting suggests conditional institution.[24]

The moral is to specify the date to which the institute and conditional institute must respectively survive to obtain a vested right. This is essential if vesting and payment are not to be simultaneous. "To A if in life at the date of distribution, whom failing to B if then in life" illustrates one solution.[25]

Note, too, that the form "*to A and B*" is unwise for any destination-over. It can in rare cases imply that A and B have successive rights, as with "A and his heirs" (his heirs' rights would not arise before his death unless the will clearly said so). But in general it suggests concurrent rights.[26]

(c) Destinations-over to relations

11.14 A destination-over to named beneficiaries causes no problem. But it may instead refer to a class of relations: "*to A failing whom his heirs*," "*issue*," or "*children*." There the destination is "derivative": the conditional institute is not named as such but described only in terms of his relationship to the institute.

The law treats a destination-over to "*heirs*" in the same way as one to a named legatee. It suspends vesting until the date of payment. The problem here is simply who the heirs are. In this case one identifies them at the date of vesting unless the will selects a different time.[27]

A destination-over to "*A failing whom A's issue*" or "*children*" is

---

[23] See para. 10.13.
[24] See Henderson, *Vesting* at pp. 49 *et seq.*
[25] Elder, *Forms of Wills*, no. 142, p. 116.
[26] *Cobban's Exrs.* v. *Cobban*, 1915 S.C. 82; *Black's Trs.* v. *Nixon*, 1931 S.C. 590.
[27] *Wylie's Trs.* v. *Bruce*, 1919 S.C. 211. For destinations in title deeds *cf. Baillie's Trs.* v. *Whiting*, 1910 S.C. 891, *Macdonald's Trs.* v. *Macdonald*, 1974 S.C. 23. See para. 11.30.

treated differently. It does not, *by itself*, suspend vesting.[28] There is immediate "vesting subject to defeasance" in A: his right vests *a morte testatoris* but, if he predeceases the date of payment leaving issue or children, it lapses and they inherit instead.[29]

3. Vesting subject to defeasance

(a) The scope of the doctrine

11.15 Unlike a suspensive condition, a resolutive condition allows a legacy to vest unless and until a specified event occurs. Vesting is defeasible by the event. If the event must occur before a set date (normally that of payment), and it does not, vesting at that point becomes absolute and indefeasible.

The classic case of defeasible vesting requires the birth of children or issue (to the legatee or someone else) before the legacy becomes payable at the end of a liferent. The scope and rationale of the doctrine have been explained thus:

> "When a gift is made in such terms that it would take effect absolutely at the death of the testator but for the single contingency of the possible birth of issue to a particular person, that is a possibility which interferes so little for practical purposes with the primary legatee treating the legacy as his own, subject to his being divested by the single event, that it must be presumed that the testator intended that he should so treat it. . . . it is for the benefit of the [legatee] that he should be able to deal with his expectant interests as if they were vested in him . . . rather than that he should be prevented from dealing with them at all on the ground that they are kept in suspense."[30]

In this form the concept is relatively new,[31] and the courts have never been over-fond of it. Logic would apply it to other resolutive conditions, but that rarely happens. It occurs with simple legacies to a class—"the children of X" and the like.[32] Other isolated examples are a legacy made conditional on a named person remaining unmarried[33] or insane.[34] The problem there is: how to ensure the legacy is repaid if the event occurs? That practically limits the rule to "prepayment" defeasance during liferents. The courts are very reluctant to extend

---

[28] The will may contain other words which do suspend vesting: *e.g.* a survivorship clause.
[29] *Wylie's Trs., supra; Allan's Trs.* v. *Allan*, 1918 S.C. 164.
[30] *Johnston's Trs.* v. *Dewar*, 1911 S.C. 722, *per* Lord Kinnear.
[31] Emerging in *Taylor* v. *Gilbert's Trs.* (1878) 5 R. (H.L.) 217.
[32] But only partially: see para. 11.31.
[33] *Smith's Trs.* v. *Smith* (1883) 10 R. 1144.
[34] *Yule's Trs.* v. *Deans*, 1919 S.C. 570.

the doctrine beyond three well-defined situations, all involving the birth of issue.

(b) Types of defeasible vesting

11.16 (1) A bequest *to A in liferent and A's issue in fee, whom failing to B in fee.* If any issue are alive when the testator dies the fee vests in them at once. If there are none the fee vests in B, but as soon as any issue are born during the liferent B's right lapses and the fee vests in them.[35] (The fee will not later revert to B if they die before the liferenter.) If no issue are born by the end of the liferent—the date of payment—B's right then becomes indefeasible.[36]

With the style just cited, the *birth* of issue is the defeating event. That is the effect of *"failing issue,"* which only requires issue to exist at some point after the testator's death, however briefly.[37] The will may specify a different event. It may require the issue to outlive the liferenter (*"leaving issue"*); or, as in *Taylor,*[36] to reach the age of majority. In either case B's right is not defeated if they die earlier.

11.17 (2) A bequest *to A,* followed by a direction to trustees *to hold for A in liferent and his issue in fee.* The initial bequest must give A the fee outright, and not merely a liferent. The effect of the direction is to impose an additional trust purpose; if it lapses A's legacy becomes absolute.[38] So the fee vests immediately in A: if he dies leaving issue, it transfers to them; if not, it remains part of A's own estate on death. Under this formula the issue must actually outlive A; there is no defeasance if they predecease him.[39]

11.18 (3) A bequest *to A in liferent and B in fee, whom failing to B's issue.* A destination-over usually suspends vesting till the date of payment. Destinations to "issue" or to "children" are the exception: the legacy vests *a morte testatoris* in B, subject to defeasance if he dies before payment *and* leaves issue who survive him.[40]

(c) Suspensive conditions and double contingencies

11.19 There is no defeasible vesting unless the possible birth of issue (or other such event) is the *only* thing to stop the legatee taking an

---

[35] Also defeasibly, to allow issue born later in the liferent to share in the legacy: see para. 11.31.

[36] *Taylor* v. *Gilbert's Trs., supra,* 31.

[37] *Carleton* v. *Thomson* (1867) 5 M. (H.L.) 151. Henderson, *Vesting* discusses styles of wording at pp. 138 *et seq.,* 207 *et seq.*

[38] *Tweeddale's Trs.* v. *Tweeddale* (1905) 8 F. 264; *Scott's Trs.* v. *De Moyse-Bucknall's Trs.,* 1978 S.C. 62.

[39] *Lindsay's Trs.* v. *Lindsay* (1880) 8 R. 281.

[40] *Allan's Trs.* v. *Allan,* 1918 S.C. 164.

immediate absolute vested right at the testator's death. It is excluded if the will in some other way suspends vesting.

For instance, a legacy cannot vest until the legatee (whether an individual or class) exists and is identified. "The fee will not vest until the occurrence of the event which will determine who are the persons called, or the individuals composing the class are ascertained."[41]

There may also be suspensive conditions. The legatee may have to reach adulthood: if that happens during the liferent, his right then vests but is still defeated if issue are born before payment.[42] With a survivorship clause there is simply vesting outright at date of payment, and thus no place for defeasible vesting before then.

11.20 Again there may be more than one destination-over: a "double contingency." Take *"To A in liferent and his issue in fee, whom failing to B, whom failing to C"* or *"whom failing to B or his issue."* The last-named legatee (C in one case, B in the second) may find his right defeated in two quite different ways. Vesting is suspended to the date of payment.[43]

The "double contingency" rule has two rather arbitrary limits which allow defeasible vesting. Firstly, the contingencies may not be successive but alternatives. Thus in *Coulson's Trustees* v. *Coulson's Trustees*[44] they were the legatee leaving issue *or* leaving a widow. Secondly, they may both simply involve the birth of issue to previously-named liferenters: *"to A in liferent and his issue in fee, whom failing to B in liferent and his issue in fee, whom failing to C."* The courts treat that as one contingency in duplicate; there is defeasible vesting in C.[45]

INTERMEDIATE AND ACCELERATED VESTING

11.21 As we have seen the date of vesting is as a rule *either* the date of the testator's death *or*, if later, the date of payment. *Young* v. *Robertson* illustrates that. There is no half-way house. No-one, neither institute nor conditional institute, obtains a vested right before then.

However, there are exceptions. The testator's intention, seen in the will, is paramount. He may select some other intermediate date and displace the rule in *Young*. If an unforeseen event occurs, such as a

---

[41] *Steel's Trs.* v. *Steel* (1888) 16 R. 204 *per* Lord President Inglis at p. 208. But the class may be enlarged after that as new members are born: see para.11.31.
[42] As in *Taylor, supra.*
[43] *Lees' Trs.* v. *Lees,* 1927 S.C. 886.
[44] 1911 S.C. 881.
[45] *Moss's Tr.* v. *Moss's Trs.,* 1958 S.C. 501.

legatee's early death, another legatee cannot obtain accelerated vesting or payment if that would frustrate the intention and defeat the purpose of the will. There are four distinct problems.

1. Double events [46]

11.22 A legacy may depend on the legatee surviving two events: a certain age (typically 18) and the expiry of a liferent. It cannot be *paid* till both have occurred; but it may *vest* at that age even if the liferent has not expired.

Reaching majority is a *dies incertus*: if it is a condition of the legacy (and not merely identifying the time of its payment) it suspends vesting till then. The end of the liferent is *dies certus*, and does not suspend vesting. So in principle the legacy vests at age 18, whether that be before or after the liferent expires.

However, there may in addition be a destination-over. Its wording is crucial. Normally it can be read as referring to failure to survive the date of payment: so vesting occurs then or at majority, whichever is later. But if it expressly applies to the date of majority, that (whenever it is) is the vesting date. [47]

2. Survivorship clauses [48]

11.23 If a legacy is payable to "*A, B, C and the survivor*," in principle it vests at the date of payment. If A fails to survive that date, it vests then in B and C. But suppose A and B both die earlier, C thus becoming the last survivor. There are two possible interpretations at that point. One is that the will is concerned simply with survivorship as among A, B and C, "*inter se*": if so C at once takes a vested right, which will not lapse if he then himself dies before the date of payment. The other is that survivorship refers to the date of payment, and the legacy only vests if C survives till then.

The second interpretation is normal. But as always one must look to the precise words of the clause and the whole scheme of the will. They may displace the *Young* rule by pointing clearly to survivorship *inter se* as the test. There is no rigid form of words for this, but it should be made clear that the whole legacy goes to the one survivor (or "longest liver") when the other legatees die. [49] A reference to "survivors"—plural—will almost certainly rule this construction out. [50]

[46] See Henderson, *Vesting*, pp. 263–267; Elder, *Forms*, p. 131.
[47] *McAlpine* v. *Studholme* (1883) 10 R. 837; Henderson, *Vesting*, pp. 56, 266.
[48] See Henderson, *Vesting*, pp. 84 *et seq.*; Elder, *Forms*, p. 128.
[49] *Laing's Trs.* v. *Horsburgh*, 1965 S.L.T. 215; Henderson, *Vesting*, pp. 84 *et seq.*
[50] *Playfair's Trs.* v. *Stewart's Trs.*, 1960 S.L.T. 351.

3. Destinations-over [51]

11.24 In a destination-over, the institute A's right depends on his surviving to a set age or date. Does the condition "carry over" and apply to the conditional institute B as well? If it does, the legacy vests in B at the date originally envisaged for A; but if not, it may vest as soon as A dies. The answer depends on what the condition is and who B is.

Take the simplest case: A is to survive to (say) age 18. There is nothing else to delay payment and thus vesting. The condition is purely personal to A: it does not affect B. If A dies earlier, the legacy vests in B at once. [52]

11.25 More commonly A is to survive until a liferenter dies. The destination-over usually suspends vesting until that date. If A dies earlier, B must still wait till then for vesting. That applies whether B is a named individual or merely A's "heir." For that reason the heir's identity is ascertained, *not* at A's death, but at the date of vesting, on the fiction that A actually died then. [53]

11.26 Complications start if B inherits as A's "issue" or "child." One must distinguish two situations.

(1) *By itself* this allows A's right to vest on the testator's death, subject to defeasance: it falls when A dies during the liferent leaving issue B. Is there then vesting in B at once, or only when the liferenter dies? Logic and precedent favour the first, but the law is unsettled. [54]

(2) Additional words may suspend vesting. Take a survivorship clause: "*to A and B, or (if either dies before the date of payment leaving issue) to his issue,*" or "*(if he leaves no issue) to the survivor of A and B.*" There is no vesting in A or B until the date of payment—the ordinary *Young* rule. But suppose A dies first: can the legacy vest in his issue at once, or must they also live till payment? Here the law contrasts "substitutional" and "original" bequests. In the first (and normal) type A's issue get the same share A would have had had he lived: they must therefore fulfil the same condition, *i.e.* survive till payment. [55] In an original bequest (which is very rare) the shares are not thus linked; there is vesting in the issue at once. [56]

---

[51] See Henderson, *Vesting*, pp. 92 *et seq.*, 109 *et seq.*, 154; Elder, *Forms*, pp. 128, 130.

[52] *Cattanach's Trs.* v. *Cattanach* (1901) 4 F. 205.

[53] *Thompson's Trs.* v. *Jamieson* (1900) 2 F. 470; *Wylie's Trs.* v. *Bruce*, 1919 S.C. 211.

[54] *Davidson's Trs.* v. *Davidson*, 1909 2 S.L.T. 20; *Wardlaw's Trs.* v. *Wardlaw's Exrs.*, 1940 S.C. 286.

[55] *Addie's Trs.* v. *Jackson*, 1913 S.C. 681.

[56] *Campbell's Trs.* v. *Dick*, 1915 S.C. 100; criticised in *Robertson's Trs.* v. *Mitchell*, 1930 S.C. 970.

4. Accelerated vesting and payment[57]

11.27   There are two main reasons to postpone vesting or payment of a legacy: to allow accumulation of income arising from it, or to give someone a liferent of it. Both may occur in one will; in each case the property is usually administered by means of a trust. But the period may be cut short: the accumulation becomes illegal; the liferenter renounces the liferent, or forfeits it by claiming legal rights instead. What happens to (firstly) the income which was to be accumulated or taken by the liferenter, and (secondly) the capital sum itself? As a general rule the event does not hasten vesting or payment: that must still await the date envisaged in the will.

11.28   With accumulations two issues arise.

(1) How is the no-longer accumulated income from the fund disposed of? The words of the will are crucial. It may give a legatee a "present gift" of the fund so that, in the absence of accumulation, he is entitled to the income. If it does not the income falls into intestacy. This is a question of payment rather than vesting, as *Wilson's Trustees* v. *Glasgow Royal Infirmary* makes clear:[58]

> "Absolute vesting is indeed a condition of success on the part of the legatee, but something more is required. A legatee . . . whose legacy falls to be paid or delivered at a postponed date is not necessarily . . . entitled to receive the intermediate income even although his right to the *corpus* is absolutely vested in him. It is always a question of intention, depending upon the express or implied directions of the testator."

So in *Wilson's Trustees* the legacy was payable on the death of the testator's widow: all income till then went to his heir on intestacy. By contrast, in *Landale's Trustees* v. *Overseas Missionary Fellowship*[59] the legacy was immediate, subject only to accumulation and to payment of an annuity to another beneficiary: when accumulation ended the legatee got all the surplus income left over after deducting the annuity. Alternatively, as in *Stewart's Trustees* v. *Whitelaw*,[60] a liferenter may have a vested immediate right to the income.

(2) The legatee *may* be entitled to immediate payment, not just of income arising from the legacy, but of the legacy itself. This applies only if he has an indefeasible vested right *and* is an adult *and* no trust purposes remain to be fulfilled. This reflects the general principle in

---

[57] See Henderson, *Vesting*, pp. 297 *et seq.*; Wilson & Duncan, *Trusts*, pp. 112 *et seq.*, 138 *et seq.*
[58] 1917 S.C. 527 *per* Lord Skerrington at p. 532.
[59] 1982 S.L.T. 158.
[60] 1926 S.C. 701.

Miller's Trustees v. *Miller*[61] that someone with a complete vested proprietary right cannot be denied possession of the item except to protect his own interests (as under age and so *incapax*) or someone else's (as beneficiary under the trust). *Landale's Trustees* illustrates the point in reverse: there the trustees had still to retain sufficient funds to allow them to pay the annuitant.

11.29 Analogous points apply where a liferent is renounced. The legatee may be able to claim payment under *Miller's Trustees* if he already has a vested right. But "where vesting and not mere payment is dependent upon the death of the liferenter, nothing that the liferenter does in the way of abandoning his or her right can accelerate the period of vesting, because the testator has fixed it finally, and it is not for anybody else to make a new will for him."[61a] Otherwise one might defeat his scheme and prejudice other beneficiaries. The same applies if someone forfeits a liferent by claiming legal rights instead.[62]

On the other hand the will itself may expressly or implicitly link vesting to renunciation.[63] Many cases hinge on what exactly its words mean; their context is decisive. So "lapse" has been held to refer to renunciation, unlike "expiry,"[64] while "termination" has gone both ways.[65] Clear precise wording avoids such semantics.

If vesting is not accelerated, what happens to the income which would have gone to the liferenter? If the will allows, it may be accumulated or may fall into residue. If the will fails to cover the point (as in *Buyer's Trustees* v. *Nunan*[66] where the liferent was itself of residue) the income must go as it arises to the heirs on intestacy.

Class Gifts

11.30 A legacy to a class—"children," issue," or other relations—is inevitably more imprecise than one to a named individual. The membership of the class may change through time. So it is important to know at what point they are identified, and when the legacy vests.

Often the answer is clear. The facts of life and death may dictate one date when (unless the will says otherwise) the legacy vests and the class must be identified. So "my children" points to the testator's

[61] (1890) 18 R. 301.
[61a] *Jacks's Trs.* v. *Jacks*, 1913 S.C. 815, *per* Lord Kinnear at p. 826.
[62] *Munro's Trs.*, 1971 S.C. 280.
[63] *Muirhead* v. *Muirhead* (1890) 17 R. (H.L.) 45.
[64] *Whitelaw's Trs.* v. *Whitelaw's Trs.*, 1981 S.L.T. 94; *cf. Middleton's Trs.* v. *Middleton*, 1955 S.C. 51.
[65] *Chrystal's Trs.* v. *Haldane*, 1960 S.C. 127; *Hurll's Trs.* v. *Hurll*, 1964 S.C. 12.
[66] 1981 S.C. 313, *sub nom. Collie & Buyers*, 1981 S.L.T. 191.

death; some may die later, but the class cannot enlarge.[67] The "heirs" of the testator or of a legatee, being the people entitled to inherit from him, are normally ascertained at the date of vesting.[68]

11.31 However, take a legacy to "*the children* [or *issue*] *of X*." X may outlive the testator. The class is open-ended: it may grow or wither after the testator dies. The law takes a pragmatic approach. The class is finally fixed at the date of payment: later-born children are excluded.[69] (Otherwise one could not know how much to pay each child.) Four main results are possible:

(1) If payment is at the testator's death, the legacy vests then in the children then alive.

(2) If it is later (say, the end of a liferent) the legacy initially vests in children alive at the testator's death (or, if none, the first born afterwards), subject to *partial* defeasance in favour of any others born before the date of payment.[70] So all children alive at any time between the testator's death and payment are in the class (they need not survive the whole period), though their exact number and shares are not known till payment.

(3) Suppose the legacy is conditional on children reaching (say) age 18. If so it vests in the first who does, subject to partial defeasance in favour of those who later reach 18. The class is finally ascertained at the point when the eldest child's share is payable: later-born children are again excluded.[71]

(4) The legacy may depend on X "*leaving issue*." Some issue must outlive X for the class to exist. But, provided that happens, the effect of *Hickling's Trustees* v. *Garland's Trustees*[72] is that the legacy vests in *all* the issue, including (retrospectively) any who had survived the testator but died before X. The decision is bizarre; plainly the testator wanted only the surviving issue to inherit, and where possible that is the interpretation the courts prefer.

11.32 There may also be a destination-over: "*to the issue of X, or failing issue* [or *if X dies without leaving issue*] *to Y*." Y's initial right is defeated when the legacy vests in the issue. The form of wording determines when they are identified.

(1) With "*failing issue*" the legacy vests in the issue as soon as any

---

[67] Except for posthumous children, who are treated as already born when the testator died: see para. 1.12.

[68] *Wylie's Trs.* v. *Bruce*, 1919 S.C. 211; *Barr's Trs.* v. *Inland Revenue*, 1943 S.C. 157; Henderson, *Vesting*, pp. 92 *et seq.*, 225 *et seq.*

[69] *Wood* v. *Wood* (1861) 23 D. 338; Henderson, *Vesting*, pp. 188–215.

[70] *Carleton* v. *Thomson* (1867) 5 M. (H.L.) 151.

[71] *Scott's Trs.* v. *Scott*, 1909 S.C. 773.

[72] (1898) 1 F. (H.L.) 7.

exist. Again there is partial defeasance in favour of other issue born before payment. After vesting, they need not live till payment.

(2) With "*leaving issue*" only issue who outlive X get a vested right. The destination-over rules out "retrospective" vesting and allows the courts to distinguish *Hickling's Trustees*, which did not contain one.

As always, these rules yield to a contrary direction in the will. It may, for instance, suspend vesting until the date of payment: explicitly, or by a survivorship clause, or by a destination-over to heirs or a named legatee.

Further reading

R. Candlish Henderson, *Vesting*.
C. de B. Murray, *Laws of Wills*, Chap. XV.
Stair Memorial Encyclopaedia, Vol. 25, paras. 900–956.
G. L. Gretton, "Vesting, Equitable Compensation and the Mystery of the Shadow Liferent," 1988 S.L.T. (News) 149.
G. L. F. Henry, "Vesting Subject to Defeasance" (1959) Conv. Rev. 173.

CHAPTER 12

TAXATION

INHERITANCE TAX[1]

(a) BACKGROUND AND PURPOSE

12.1 At least since the 1600s taxes have been levied on people's property at their death. Death is inevitable: it is an ideal occasion for governments to raise revenue. Death taxes were gradually extended to include property transferred within a limited period before death. This reflected the need to make their avoidance more difficult, and (during this century) the avowed aim of using taxation to redistribute wealth within society.

From 1894 to 1975 the main tax was estate duty. This was "progressive," like income tax: the larger the estate, the higher the duty. It applied to transfers on death and within the previous seven years, to property the deceased owned or had a liferent of. Certain transfers were exempt; transfers between spouses were not, *but* if the surviving spouse was only given a liferent and duty was payable on the property, it was exempt when that spouse subsequently died.

Capital transfer tax replaced estate duty in 1975. This was cumulative throughout life and on death, so that each successive transfer attracted tax at a higher rate. A special ten-yearly charge applied to trusts where no beneficiary had an "interest in possession" in the trust funds: discretionary trusts, except for (among others), accumulation and maintenance trusts.[2] Gifts between spouses were now exempt.[3]

Capital transfer tax was severely modified in 1986 and renamed inheritance tax (IHT). Lifetime transfers are now cumulated for only seven years, and the tax has a flat rate.[4] It applies to transfers made by individuals domiciled[5] in the UK (wherever the item is located) and of property situated in the UK (wherever the owner is domiciled).

---

[1] Some aspects were covered earlier: common calamities and survivorship, deeds of arrangement, and legitim (paras. 1.11, 5.23 and 4.23). This book only briefly touches on trusts.

[2] See para. 11.4.

[3] But the estate duty liferent exemption is preserved where the liferent began before November 13, 1974: IHTA 1984, Sched. 6, para. 2.

[4] Currently (1989–90) 20 per cent on lifetime transfers in excess of £118,000 in cumulative total; 40 per cent on death.

[5] "Domicile" has a special wide meaning for IHT: IHTA 1984, s. 267.

(b) Basic Concepts

1. Chargeable transfers

12.2 IHT is charged on the *value transferred* by a *chargeable transfer*. A chargeable transfer is any *transfer of value* made by an individual except for an *exempt transfer*. A transfer of value is a disposition made by a person as a result of which the value of his estate immediately afterwards is less than it would be but for the disposition; the value transferred is the amount by which it is less.[6] On death a person is treated as if he made a transfer of value of his whole estate.[7]

A person's *estate* is the aggregate of all the property to which he is *beneficially entitled*. That is wider than ownership: it includes property over which he has a power of disposal, and trust property in which he has an interest in possession as a beneficiary, such as a liferent. Conversely certain *excluded property* is disregarded and debts are deducted.[8]

12.3 Thus IHT is charged on the loss to the transferor's estate. This has three implications.

(a) Omissions

Where the value of his estate is diminished by his omission to exercise a right, he is treated as making a disposition at the latest time when he could have exercised the right, unless he shows the omission was not deliberate. Two omissions are ignored: waiving remuneration which would be taxable under Schedule E income tax, or waiving a dividend within 12 months before the right to it arose.[9]

(b) Commercial transactions

A disposition is not a transfer of value if it is shown that it was not intended to give anyone a gratuitous benefit *and* (1) it was an arm's length transaction between two people who were not *connected persons*, *or* (2) it was what one would expect in such a transaction. Relatives, trustees and settlor, partners (and their relatives), and companies controlled by one person are instances of connected persons.[10]

---

[6] IHTA 1984, ss. 1–3.
[7] IHTA 1984, s. 4(1).
[8] IHTA 1984, ss. 5, 6, 49(1).
[9] IHTA 1984, ss. 3(3), 14, 15. For legal rights renunciations see paras. 4.23, 5.24 *supra*.
[10] CGTA 1979, s. 63.

IHT might be minimised by artificially splitting one transfer into several which, taken individually, are worth less than the undivided transfer. For instance, one gift of 60 per cent of a company's shares is worth more than two separate transfers each of 30 per cent. To prevent this, "transaction" has a wide sense, including a series of transactions or *associated operations*: essentially operations which are interdependent or relate to the same property.[11]

(c) Gross and net transfers

12.4 IHT is levied on the gross—total—loss to the donor's estate. Now suppose X gives Y £100,000. If Y agrees to pay the IHT, that is the relevant figure; it is a *gross chargeable transfer*; the IHT comes out of it. If X is to pay, his total loss is £100,000 *plus* IHT; the £100,000 is a *net chargeable transfer* which must be *grossed up* to obtain a total figure on which the IHT is levied. The gross figure is therefore that which, after IHT is deducted from it, will leave the net cash sum.[12]

The difference can be large. Take the above case, with IHT at 20 per cent.[13] A gross chargeable transfer produces IHT of £20,000. A net one gives a bill of £25,000 (20 per cent of a £125,000 total, in effect 25 per cent of the cash sum). Grossing up is complex, and is usually done by using published tables of figures.

In principle the estate is not grossed up on death, because plainly the IHT must come out of the estate. However, a specific (non-residuary) legacy may be left "free of tax": it gives rise to IHT, but that is paid out of the residue. The legacy must therefore be grossed up to determine what the IHT attributable to it amounts to.[14]

2. Cumulation

12.5 Once any applicable exemptions have been deducted from transfers for value,[15] the resulting chargeable transfers are cumulated for seven years. It is a rolling period: new transfers are added on while old ones drop out of the cumulative total seven years after they were made. The tax due on each new transfer thus depends critically on the total gross value of any transfers in that prior period. But, once the

---

[11] IHTA 1984, s. 268; two exceptions concern (a) operations straddling March 27, 1974, and (b) leases.

[12] A dividend displays the same idea. The shareholder receives it net of basic rate tax, but the gross figure (including the "tax credit") must go in his income tax return.

[13] For simplicity this ignores annual exemptions and assumes that the £118,000 threshold has already been exceeded.

[14] See "Calculation of tax", para. 12.22.

[15] *e.g.* annual exemption: see para. 12.18.

IHT is paid, only the donor's death can usually reopen it; later fluctuations in the gross total will not affect it retrospectively.

12.6 Some transfers are chargeable (and cumulated) at once. The main type is a gift to a simple discretionary trust. If the donor dies within seven years IHT is recalculated at the death rate applying at date of death.

12.7 But many gifts are *potentially exempt transfers* (PETs): gifts by one individual to another, to a trust in which someone has an interest in possession, an accumulation and maintenance trust, or a trust for a disabled person. They are neither charged nor cumulated at once. If the donor dies within seven years they are then retrospectively cumulated as at their original date: as a result they not only bear IHT themselves,[16] but (by raising the total) may cause more IHT to be payable on later gifts.

In each case (1) IHT is calculated on the lifetime gross value: the gift is not grossed-up afresh on death; (2) "taper relief" reduces the extra tax if the interval till death exceeds three years.

3. Gifts subject to reservation

12.8 A gift is *subject to reservation* if, during the seven years before the death, the recipient did not at all times have possession and enjoyment of the item to the entire or virtually entire exclusion of the donor.[17] For instance, the donor gifts shares to a discretionary trust but is a potential beneficiary; or he receives the dividend from shares or occupies a house rent-free. "Virtually" disregards minimal benefits to the donor such as staying in the house on short visits, but otherwise the rule applies if the donor retains *any* benefit from the gifted item.[18]

There is no "reservation" if the donor pays a commercial rent for his occupation, nor if he is later unexpectedly compelled by old age or infirmity to move in with the recipient because he cannot cope for himself. Conversely it is probably reservation to occupy as a guest without an enforceable contract.[19]

12.9 Reservation has two IHT consequences. The initial gift is treated in the normal way, *e.g.* as a chargeable transfer if it is to a discretionary trust. However a second charge could arise on the donor's death: if he waived the reservation while alive he made a PET,

---

[16] At the rate in force at the date of death.

[17] Finance Act 1986, s. 102, affecting gifts made after March 17, 1986.

[18] Finance Act 1986, s. 104.

[19] *Chick* v. *Stamp Duties Commissioner* [1958] A.C. 435; but the case law, which concerns analogous estate duty rules, is not consistent.

and if it lasted until his death the item is charged as part of his estate. IHT is not payable twice, but only on whichever of the two transfers produces the higher IHT bill.

(c) VALUING THE ESTATE

1. Assets included in the estate

12.10 The executor must submit a valuation of the deceased's estate when he obtains confirmation to it. The IHT return also includes within it the inventory for confirmation. But the estate to be itemised for IHT differs from that which requires confirmation or which the deceased owned:

(1) Items passing under a survivorship destination do not need confirmation, but IHT is due on the deceased's share (usually half the value).

(2) The estate for IHT consists of all the property to which he was beneficially entitled immediately *before* he died. That includes property of which he merely had an interest in possession (such as a liferent) or which he had a power to dispose of (such as a tenancy, if assignable).[20] But it omits items to which he had legal title as trustee, though these may need confirmation if he was the sole trustee.[21]

(3) A gift under reservation divests the donor of ownership, but the item is deemed to remain part of his estate for IHT.

12.11 Conversely some assets are *excluded property*. For IHT purposes they do not form part of the estate on death:[22]

(1) Property situated abroad, *if* the deceased was domiciled there.

(2) A *reversionary interest*, such as that of a fiar in liferented property. With some exceptions[23] his interest is free from IHT if he dies during the liferent.

(3) A liferenter's interest in possession, if it reverts on his death to the settlor or his spouse.[24]

(4) The executor may elect to exclude woodlands.[25]

(5) Pension benefits are included if they *must* be paid to the executors. More usually the pension fund trustees are to pay a widow or dependant but may have discretion to pay the executor; such benefits are not part of the estate.[26] A similar point applies to life assurance policy proceeds.

---

[20] IHTA 1984, ss. 5(1), (2), 49(1).

[21] See para. 13.25.

[22] They also attract no IHT if gifted *inter vivos*. Only the main types are listed here.

[23] *E.g.* if he had paid for it: IHTA 1984, ss. 47, 48.

[24] Unless they paid for it: IHTA 1984, s. 54.

[25] IHTA 1984, ss. 125–129.

[26] If the scheme was approved by the Inland Revenue for income tax or personal pensions: IHTA 1984, ss. 58, 151; Finance (No. 2) Act 1987, s. 98.

2. Debts and liabilities

12.12   The deceased's legally enforceable liabilities are deducted in valuing his estate. Not every liability may be deductible:

(1) It must have been incurred for some consideration—not gratuitously—or imposed by law (*e.g.* taxes or rates).[27]

(2) All or a proportion of the consideration may be property which had itself come from the deceased. If so the same proportion of the debt may be disallowed.[28]

(3) One deducts only so much of a guarantee as is unlikely to be reimbursed. An existing IHT liability is deducted but any reimbursement will be added to the estate.

(4) Reasonable funeral expenses are allowable, including the cost of a gravestone.[29]

(5) Other executry expenses are not deductible, with one exception: extra costs relating to foreign property, to 5 per cent of its value at most.[30]

12.13   So far as possible a secured debt reduces the value of the item it is secured over. In the case of heritage it may be deducted from the original inventory value or the IHT account: either produces the same IHT but the first reduces the confirmation dues payable.

3. Basis of valuation

12.14   Property is valued at the price which it might reasonably be expected to fetch if sold in the open market. Sale may in fact be impossible: private companies only permit restricted transfer of their shares. A hypothetical sale is nevertheless assumed.[31]

Though the estate is defined as that immediately before the death, valuation takes account of changes resulting from it. Thus it includes life assurance policy proceeds payable to the executors.[32] Nevertheless it also includes interests which lapse on death (such as liferents) or pass by survivorship.

12.15   *Related property* must be taken into account in valuing items. The main example is property in the estate of the deceased's spouse. Aggregating the two may give a higher value than taking them separately: *e.g.* 60 per cent of a company's shares as opposed to two

---

[27] IHTA 1984, s. 5(3), (5).
[28] The rules are complex: Finance Act 1986, s. 103.
[29] IHTA 1984, s. 172; Inland Revenue Statement of Practice 7/87.
[30] They may be deductible for income tax: see para. 12.33.
[31] IHTA 1984, s. 160; *I.R.C.* v. *Crossman* [1937] A.C. 26.
[32] If payable to someone else, *e.g.* the widow, they fall outwith the estate.

holdings of 30 per cent. If so the deceased's value is his proportion of the aggregate.

Publicly-quoted shares are valued at the lower of (a) one quarter of the difference up from the lower to the higher of the two quoted prices, or (b) halfway between the highest and lowest recorded prices. If the stock market was closed on the date of death one may use the previous or next trading day. Unquoted shares must be valued on the "open market" basis.[33]

The executor must enter the most precise valuation he can, relying on an expert where necessary: a stockbroker (for quoted shares), the company (unquoted shares), an accountant (a partnership), and the like. For a house one can consult local house prices, a surveyor, or (if the Capital Taxes Office raises queries) the district valuer. If an estimate is necessary (with items like income tax repayments) the inventory should say so; the executors must undertake to give the exact figure when possible. A "nil" value may occur (*e.g.* for shares of a company in liquidation): the item must still be included in order to get confirmation.

12.16 Post-death changes in value usually do not affect the IHT valuation. But if assets fall in value and the executors[34] sell at a loss they can in three cases use the sale price for IHT. This may make it wiser to sell assets rather than transfer them to residuary legatees *in specie* (in kind) and lose this relief.

(1) Sale of quoted shares or unit trusts within 12 months after death. There must be a loss on the aggregate total of all the investments.[35]

(2) Sale of land within three years after death.[36]

(3) Sale within three years of property valued on death under the "related property" rules.[37]

(d) Exemptions and Reliefs

12.17 Certain transfers are disregarded entirely for IHT and do not enter into the cumulative total.[38] Others receive partial relief and only a proportion is deducted. Their careful use in a will and in lifetime transactions can minimise IHT.

---

[33] These are the rules for CGT: CGTA 1979, s. 150 (3).
[34] Usually, strictly, the person liable to pay the IHT.
[35] IHTA 1984, ss. 178–189.
[36] IHTA 1984, ss. 190–198.
[37] IHTA 1984, s. 176.
[38] IHTA 1984, ss. 18–42.

1. Exemptions: lifetime only

12.18 (1) *Annual exemption* of gifts to a total of £3,000. Where several gifts are made in a year, the earlier ones benefit first. If a PET is retrospectively "added in" on death, it is treated for this purpose as made later in the year than all transfers which are not PETs: this avoids reallocating the exemption.

(2) *Small gifts* of up to £250 to one person. This cannot be used to partly exempt a larger gift.

(3) *Normal expenditure out of income* which does not harm the spender's standard of living. This usually exempts premiums he pays on a life assurance policy in another person's favour (which the law treats as gifts).[39] Indeed the policy can be designed to pay off the IHT on the estate.

(4) *Dispositions for the maintenance of relatives*: to a spouse or ex-spouse, for the education of either spouse's child, or to care for a dependent relative.

(5) *Gifts in consideration of the recipient's marriage*. The maximum exemption is £5,000, depending on how and whether the donor is related.

(6) *Dispositions allowable for income tax or conferring retirement benefits*.

2. Exemptions: lifetime and death

12.19 (1) *Transfers between spouses* by gift, intestacy, legal rights, or will. This does not apply if the transfer only takes effect after a specified period or a liferent, or depends on a condition which is not met within 12 months. It is limited to £50,000 if the recipient is not domiciled in the UK.

To minimise tax one should also consider the IHT position on the second spouse's death. Using the exemption may sometimes make that worse. If one's spouse is already well off it may be better in the long run to transfer directly to children or grandchildren.[40]

(2) *Gifts to charities* or political parties, or to trusts for the benefit of employees.

(3) *Gifts for national purposes* (to specified bodies like universities and museums). Certain nationally important property—land, pictures, and the like—may be exempted if given to non-profit making bodies which will hold it for the public benefit. An analogous exemption covers gifts to individuals and trusts: it is conditional on

---

[39] Except for "back to back" schemes where the spender draws an associated annuity: IHTA 1984, s. 263.
[40] Post-death rearrangement can achieve this result.

making undertakings about upkeep and public access, and IHT falls due if there is a later non-exempt transfer or a breach of the undertakings.

(4) *Death on active service* gives rise to no IHT charge.

3. Reliefs

12.20 (1) *Business property* and *agricultural property* both attract reliefs of between 30 per cent and 50 per cent. There are stringent conditions such as using or occupying the property for two years before death. If property is eligible for both reliefs, agricultural property relief is the one given.[41]

With woodlands which are not part of "agricultural property" the executor can elect within two years after the death to treat them as excluded property.

(2) *Mutual transfers* occur when a donor receives an asset back from the donee and later dies. Without relief he could pay IHT twice, on the initial gift and on death. To avoid this IHT is charged on whichever one event creates the larger tax bill.[42]

(3) If the donor dies between three and seven years after making a PET, *taper relief* reduces the resulting IHT by up to 80 per cent. Similarly if the transfer had originally borne IHT at lifetime rates: but the relief cannot exceed the extra death-rate tax.[43]

(4) If the deceased had received property less than five years previously through a chargeable transfer or PET, *quick succession relief* applies on his death. This is up to 100 per cent of the IHT on *the proportion* of the first transfer which actually increased his estate. To illustrate: A inherited property worth £100,000; after IHT on that sum he only received £80,000. On A's death the relief is based on eight-tenths of £20,000. It does not matter if the deceased disposed of the property in the interval between receipt and death.[44]

(e) CALCULATION OF TAX

1. Ordinary procedure

12.21 This is relatively simple. The order is:
(1) Calculate estate for confirmation (in inventory).
(2) Deduct the deceased's debts.

[41] IHTA 1984, ss. 105–124. The reliefs are effectively wasted unless used for non-exempt transfers. Especial complexities occur with partly-exempt transfers: IHTA 1984, s. 39A.
[42] Finance Act 1986, s. 104.
[43] IHTA 1984, s. 7, for transfers after March 17, 1986.
[44] IHTA 1984, s. 141.

(3) Add other chargeable assets (*e.g.* liferent).
(4) Add chargeable transfers made in previous seven years.
(5) Deduct exemptions and reliefs.
(6) Compute IHT on resulting total at death rates.
(7) Compute IHT on lifetime transfers at death rates.
(8) IHT chargeable on estate is (6) *minus* (7). Quick succession relief can now be deducted from (8).
(9) To compute extra tax due on lifetime gifts, from (7) deduct taper relief and then IHT already paid on them while the deceased was alive. The gifts' recipients pay the extra tax.

The main complication is the effect of death on lifetime transfers. An illustration may help. Suppose X died in June 1989 leaving an estate of £60,000. He had made certain gifts while alive:

(1) a PET of £206,000 in May 1988—no IHT was due at the time.

(2) a gift of £16,000 into a discretionary trust in May 1989. This attracted *two* years' annual exemptions (£6,000): if an annual exemption is not used in any particular year it can be carried forward into the next (but no further). The sum of £10,000 therefore went into the cumulative total. As X had made no previous chargeable gifts, no IHT would then arise.

When X dies:

(1) the PET becomes chargeable. It gets two years' annual exemption. IHT is due at 40 per cent on the chargeable amount in excess of £118,000 (the rate at date of death), *i.e.* £82,000.

(2) the gift to the trust now bears extra tax for three reasons: (a) the PET has entered the cumulative total; (b) the PET has taken over the 1988 exemption, so only the 1989 exemption of £3,000 is available; (c) the PET has used up the nil rate band, so tax is now due at 40 per cent on the whole chargeable sum (£13,000).

(3) the estate of £60,000 of course bears IHT at 40 per cent.

The extra tax under (1) and (2) is borne by the donee and the trust respectively.

2. Incidence of tax

12.22 On which assets (and therefore which beneficiaries) does the resulting IHT fall? That is a distinct issue from *liability*: whom can the authorities compel to pay the tax? The person liable can, after paying, insist on reimbursement from the person on whom incidence falls.

IHT is a testamentary expense and falls primarily on the residue of the estate. Thus "specific" (in this sense, non-residuary) legacies do not bear their own tax: that falls on the residue. They are "free of tax." Settled property bears its own tax. That said, a testator may vary these rules by instructing that a legacy bears its own tax. He may leave a *share* of residue free of tax (thus casting its IHT on the rest of the residue) but not *all* the residue, because some part of it must ultimately bear the IHT. "Free of tax" does not mean exempt from IHT. It merely reallocates the IHT due. The specific legacy must be grossed-up, thus increasing the overall value of the estate and the IHT. The procedure varies depending on the composition of the estate.

(1) Exempt specific legacy and chargeable residue: the legacy is simply deducted and IHT is due on the residue.

(2) Tax-free specific legacy and exempt residue: the legacy is the only chargeable item. No IHT is due on the residue itself but it bears the IHT due on the grossed-up legacy. If the IHT exceeds the residue the legacy abates to pay the excess.

(3) Tax-free specific legacy and chargeable residue (or another gift which bears its own tax): the legacy is not the only chargeable item. One must (a) gross-up as in (2) and total up the estate; (b) find out the IHT rate for the estate; and (c) gross-up again at that rate to arrive at the actual tax payable.

Legal rights are (for the purpose of this calculation) treated as a gift bearing its own tax. Now only at age 18 can a minor child elect whether to claim legitim; but the executor must make a provisional election for IHT purposes within two years after the death. The IHT can be recalculated if the minor subsequently reverses the executor's choice.[45]

(f) LIABILITY AND PAYMENT

1. Liability to pay tax

12.23 If extra tax is payable on lifetime transfers the order of liability is:

(1) the person who received the item, had an interest in possession or vested right in it, or took the benefit of it under a trust.

(2) the executor, but only if (1) does not pay within 12 months after the death or need not pay because his liability is limited.

12.24 Those liable for IHT on transfers on death are:

(1) The executor, in respect of (a) property which was not part of a settlement immediately before the death and (b) settled land within the UK which vests in the executors.

(2) The trustee, in respect of property which was part of a settlement before the death. So the executor need not pay IHT on the

---

[45] IHTA 1984, ss. 42, 147; *Capital Taxes Encyclopaedia*, D.6.41–6.43.

deceased's liferent assets, though he will often agree with the trustee to do so and be reimbursed.

(3) Anyone in whom the property vests after the death, or who takes an interest in possession—except a purchaser.

(4) If property was held in trust before the death, anyone who gets the benefit or income from it after the death.

Executors' and trustees' liability is limited to the value of the assets they receive in that capacity, or would have received but for their neglect or default. Others' liability is limited to the value of the property in question.

2. The tax return

12.25 If tax is payable the executor sends the IHT account/ inventory [46] to the Capital Taxes Office (CTO); they return it and he lodges it with the commissary department of the local sheriff court. If no tax is payable he just does the latter. He must do this within 12 months after the end of the month in which death occurred, whether IHT is due or not; if he fails to, the CTO can demand an account from anyone in whom any of the estate vests. He must lodge a corrective inventory if the valuation is later amended. After confirmation the CTO may challenge the valuation, and will formally assess the tax payable.

For smaller estates the executor simply lodges an inventory with the sheriff court.[47] This is done in two cases:

(1) *Excepted estates*: estates where (i) the total gross value does not exceed £100,000, no more than £15,000 being situated outwith the UK; (ii) all the property passed under the deceased's will, intestacy, nomination, or survivorship; *and* (iii) the deceased died domiciled in the UK and had made no lifetime gifts chargeable to IHT or capital transfer tax. So there must be no settled property, or PETs on which IHT is due. The CTO may ask for the inventory within 60 days after confirmation.

(2) *Small estates*: where the "small estates" confirmation procedure is used and the gross estate for IHT purposes is no more than £17,000.

3. Payment

12.26 The executor must pay the IHT when he lodges the account, and at any rate within six months after the end of the month when the

---

[46] Form A-3, with Warrant Form A2 and payment of the tax as provisionally calculated.
[47] Using Forms B-4 and B-3 respectively.

death occurred. But for certain assets he may instead opt to pay by 10 equal annual instalments:[48] land; controlling shareholdings; some unquoted minority holdings; and a business or interest in one. He will be wise to opt: it avoids borrowing to pay before confirmation, and once estate funds are available he can then pay in a lump sum if he chooses.

12.27 When the executry is finished the executor can ask the CTO for a "clearance certificate" covering any or all of the estate assets.[49] This certifies that the due IHT has been paid and (in the absence of fraud, non-disclosure of material facts, or subsequent changes in the valuation or distribution of the estate) discharges any possible liability. With "excepted estates" discharge is automatic 60 days after confirmation.

CAPITAL GAINS TAX

1. Capital gains before death

12.28 If any CGT remains unpaid in respect of disposals made by the deceased, it is payable by the executors as a debt of the estate. The annual exemption applies.[50] There may be a net gain or loss in the year of death. If a gain, it can be set against the deceased's previous losses; if a loss, conversely, it is "carried back" for up to three tax years and set against gains.

2. Capital gains during executry administration [51]

12.29 Death is not a chargeable disposal: no CGT arises on any unrealised gains, and no reliefs can be claimed on unrealised losses. The executors are treated as acquiring the deceased's assets at their market value at the date of death. This is the IHT value; if the executors subsequently opt for a later lower value for IHT,[52] it applies for CGT as well. In lowering IHT they can thus raise the CGT on a subsequent disposal, and they should weigh the overall effect with care.

The date of death value is the base point for computing later gains and losses. If the executors dispose of assets (except to legatees) they are chargeable as a single self-contained body, distinct from them-

---

[48] Starting at the six month point.
[49] Using Form C-e.
[50] Currently (1989–90) £5,000.
[51] CGTA 1979, ss. 47–49.
[52] *E.g.* they sell shares at a loss in the next 12 months.

selves as individuals. They cannot set their gains (or losses) against losses (or gains) made by the deceased or by beneficiaries. They have the annual exemption for three years only, and other exemptions where appropriate; indexation relief deducts inflation from the gain. As well as ordinary expenses, they may deduct an appropriate proportion of the costs of obtaining confirmation and of administration.[53]

12.30 It is not a disposal for CGT if the executors in course of administration transfer assets to a legatee. "Legatee" means anyone who acquires (for himself or as trustee) under a testamentary disposition or intestacy: including a post-death deed of arrangement, *mortis causa* donation, or (it seems) legal rights. The legatee acquires as at the date of death and the value then; he, not the executry, takes all gains and losses on a subsequent disposal.[54] The same goes for disposals under intestacy or (it seems) legal rights.[55]

So the executors must consider whether to hand over assets to a beneficiary or to sell them and give the proceeds. Their choice—if they have one[56]—may involve several factors. Would the executry suffer heavy CGT? Beyond that, who can best minimise CGT: executors or beneficiaries? Which can best set gains against losses? Which has most exemptions? The executry has only one aggregate annual exemption; each beneficiary has his own.[56a]

INCOME TAX

1. The deceased's income

12.31 The executor must inform the Inland Revenue of the death and submit an income tax return for the period from April 6 last to the date of death. They can make an assessment within three years after the end of that tax year, which may relate to any tax year ending less than six years before the death.

If tax is due, that is a deductible debt of the estate. Conversely there may be a tax repayment: among other reasons the deceased gets a full year's personal reliefs on death, but only a *pro rata* amount will have been set against tax under PAYE while alive. This is an asset of the

[53] *I.R.C.* v. *Richard's Exrs.*, 1971 S.C. (H.L.) 60. They may use the true cost or a standard scale of costs: In. Rev. Statement of Practice 7/81.

[54] And can deduct the cost of transferring the asset to him.

[55] See Scobbie (1988) 33 J.L.S. 341.

[56] *E.g.* with residue or legal rights; *cf.* a specific legacy which is transferred *in specie*, physically.

[56a] Note that the Finance Act 1989, s. 124 abolished the *general* CGT "hold-over" relief on gifts. That on business assets survives.

estate and should be confirmed to. In both cases an estimate may be needed, with a corrective inventory later if necessary.

Any business which the deceased ran as a sole trader or in partnership is treated for tax purposes as terminating on his death. (Whether it in fact ends is another matter. That depends on the will, the partnership deed, and the beneficiaries' own wishes.) Accounts must be prepared: the period from April 6 last will be reassessed on an "actual year" as opposed to "preceding year" basis; likewise the previous two tax years if, in their case, that results in more tax.

Two exceptions apply:

(1) if the spouse inherits and carries on the business (unless she claims the termination basis).

(2) if the executor and all the surviving partners elect within two years to treat the business as continuing. The executor will only elect if the partners give an indemnity for any resulting higher tax bill.[57]

12.32 Investment income received after death is usually executry income (even though it may be in the deceased's estate for IHT purposes). One exception, treated as the deceased's income, is interest accrued before death on securities[58] whose nominal value totalled over £5,000 (such as government stocks, "Gilts").[59] Dividends and most bank and building society interest are (subject to a proposed change from 1991) received net of basic rate tax, but higher rate tax may be due on the grossed-up amount.

12.33 Some executry expenses are tax deductible. They are (1) interest on a loan raised to pay IHT before confirmation (for moveable property and for one year only) *and* (2) mortgage interest on the deceased's only or main residence, if it is also the surviving spouse's (or will be when she leaves job-related accommodation).[60]

2. Executry income

12.34 The executry is taxable as a separate entity from the deceased and from the executor as an individual. It pays the basic rate on income arising during administration and receives no personal reliefs.[61]

Income bears income tax, but capital receipts are chargeable to CGT. Classification is difficult where the deceased had a business. Income tax is due if the executors actively continue trading; CGT if they merely realise the assets. Each case is decided on its facts.[62]

---

[57] ICTA 1988, s. 113 (1).
[58] ICTA 1988, ss. 713–715. Accrual is on a daily basis.
[59] ICTA 1988, ss. 713–715.
[60] ICTA 1988, ss. 358, 364.
[61] The appropriate form is R59.
[62] *I.R.C.* v. *Donaldson's Trs.*, 1955 S.C. 320.

12.35 Liferenters will be entitled to the free income[63] of the estate from the date of death. Residuary legatees will also get income which the residue produces (with the complication that they also receive capital, and the executors must distinguish the two for tax purposes). The executors pay the income net after deduction of basic rate tax;[64] the beneficiary includes the gross amount in his tax return so, after crediting the deduction, he may be liable for higher rate tax. But where the income had already been subject to IHT (as having accrued before death) the IHT is credited against this extra income tax.[65]

12.36 If complex the executry administration may take two or three years. At its end the residue is paid out or the executry converts into a continuing trust. Only then is the beneficiaries' income finally known, and their earlier tax assessments may need adjustment accordingly. Liferenters and residuary legatees use different procedures.[66]

12.37 If an executor receives any income after the close of the administration he passes it on to an entitled beneficiary or the trust (as appropriate), in whose hands it is taxed. For this purpose—and for CGT—the administration is complete at the point when debts and prior legacies have been paid or provided for and the residue has been ascertained.[67]

Further reading

Stair Memorial Encyclopaedia, Vol. 25, paras. 959–1032.
Foster, *Capital Taxes Encyclopaedia*, *esp.* sections B, D and E.
A. R. Mellows, *Taxation for Trustees and Executors.*
B. McCutcheon, *Inheritance Tax.*
E. Scobbie, "Tax-efficient Executry Administration" (1988) 33 J.L.S. 341.

Numerous books cover tax law in detail. Most relevant Law Society P.Q.L.E. publications contain useful detailed surveys of the practical problems.

---

[63] *i.e.* after paying debts and legacies, and apportioning executry expenses between income and capital.
[64] Along with a certificate stating the income and tax (Form R185E).
[65] ICTA 1988, s. 699.
[66] ICTA 1988, ss. 695–701; see *Stair Memorial Encyclopaedia*, Vol. 25, paras. 983–987.
[67] ICTA 1988, s. 702(*a*).

CHAPTER 13

EXECUTRY ADMINISTRATION

STRUCTURE AND BACKGROUND

13.1 When a person dies his property must be gathered in and then distributed to his beneficiaries. The executor is responsible for this. He is appointed either by will (an *executor-nominate*) or by the sheriff (an *executor-dative*). A second step is essential to allow him to administer the estate: he must obtain from the sheriff *confirmation* of his title. Administration without confirmation is an unauthorised "vitious intromission" which may make him liable for all the deceased's debts.

13.2 Before 1964 only moveables passed *via* the executor; heritage went directly to the heir by *service*. The Succession (Scotland) Act abolished the separate rules for heritage.[1] They remain relevant for two purposes: administering estates of those who died before the Act was in force, and reviving a "lapsed trust" through the heir of the last surviving trustee.[2]

In the case of moveables, the rules evolved over centuries. Before the Reformation in 1560, church officials—"commissaries"—dealt with succession under canon law. They were then replaced by commissary courts under royal control; by the 1800s these had jurisdiction over executries within their area or *commissariot*. Ultimately the sheriff took over their functions, with the sheriff clerk responsible for the administrative aspects.

13.3 The deceased's domicile determines which sheriff has jurisdiction to grant confirmation or appoint an executor-dative. That is the sheriff in whose commissariot he was domiciled[3] when he died. The Edinburgh commissary office deals with those who had a Scots domicile but no known local domicile within Scotland, or who left property within Scotland but were domiciled elsewhere.

Commissary jurisdiction is primarily administrative and non-contentious. The sheriff himself is only involved in appointing executors-dative or, where legal difficulties occur, issuing a special warrant for confirmation. Confirmation says who is entitled to be executor. It makes a holograph will probative,[4] but otherwise does

---

[1] Succession (Scotland) Act 1964, s. 14 (1).

[2] 1964 Act, s. 37(1) (*d*); Law Reform (Miscellaneous Provisions) (Scotland) Act 1980, s. 6.

[3] On domicile see para. 14.2, *infra*.

[4] Succession (Scotland) Act 1964, s. 32.

not determine the validity of a will or of a beneficiary's right to inherit: that may require separate litigation.

THE OFFICE OF EXECUTOR

1. Executors and trustees

13.4 A will may appoint the same people both as executors and as testamentary trustees. In practice the two functions tend to overlap. Legally, and for tax, they are distinct. The executor's duty is to collect the estate and distribute it to beneficiaries; the trustee's is to hold it and administer it according to the trust purposes, (say) during a liferent. The executry administration is complete once debts and legacies are paid; at that point the trust takes over.

Furthermore an executor, unlike a trustee, represents the deceased: *eadem persona cum defuncto*, he stands in his shoes; if he pursues a debt he can be met by the same defences as the deceased. As such his personal liability for his actions is normally limited to the value of the estate confirmed to.

That said, trustees and executors have much in common. Being an executor is an administrative duty, not a benefit: he is not entitled to payment unless the will allows.[5] Executors have the same powers and, conversely, restrictions, as the law imposes on trustees. So— executors-dative apart—they can assume new executors or resign.[6] Conversely, if the will only appoints a trustee, he is entitled to be confirmed as executor.[7]

2. Entitlement to be appointed executor

(a) Executors-nominate

13.5 A testator may expressly appoint someone to be executor. Usually he names him, but it is enough if he can be identified: such as "the same executor as X has".[8] The will may ask someone else to make the choice. Alternatively appointment is implicit if the person is given powers which an executor would have: "to collect and divide my estate" or "to give effect to this will".

13.6 Suppose the testator appointed no executor, or his choice has failed by his proposed executor either refusing office, being incapaci-

[5] See para. 13.47.
[6] Executors (Scotland) Act 1900, s. 2; 1964 Act, s. 20.
[7] Executors (Scotland) Act 1900, s. 3.
[8] See *Martin* v. *Ferguson's Trs.* (1892) 19 R. 492.

tated or dying (whether before or after him). Under the Executors (Scotland) Act 1900 the deemed executors-nominate are his testamentary trustees or (if none exist) any general disponee, universal legatee or residuary legatee.[9] If there are several such legatees they must all either accept or expressly decline office. If any are untraceable, or have died causing partial intestacy, this last option is barred.[10]

(b) Executors-dative

13.7 Perhaps the deceased left no will; or he did, but an executor-nominate was not appointed. In either case an executor-dative is required. If several people compete for appointment they are selected in order of preference; those falling within the same category are entitled to be appointed jointly. An applicant need not notify other potential competitors. If they want to be informed they should lodge a "*caveat*" with the sheriff court: renewable monthly, it simply asks the court to give notification of any applications.

13.8 The order of preference is:

(1) General disponees (and the like) when the 1900 Act cannot be used. Any of them may be appointed executor-dative without the others' consent.

(2) The deceased's spouse is exclusively entitled if he or she inherits the whole intestate estate under prior rights.[11] If the estate exceeds prior rights the spouse is entitled concurrently along with (3).

(3) Those who inherit the "free estate" from the deceased under section 2 of the 1964 Act. The equivalent before 1964 was the "next-of-kin", which differed in many ways: it excluded the spouse and maternal relatives. It seems that next-of-kin can still be appointed executor-dative even if not entitled to inherit under section 2: this is an anachronism and the Scottish Law Commission favours its abolition.[12]

Those who inherit directly have, if they apply, preference over those who inherit by representation. So a surviving child has priority over a predeceasing child's offspring.[13]

(4) The deceased's creditors.

(5) Legatees who receive a specific legacy or a liferent.

(6) The beneficiary's property may already be under the adminis-

---

[9] Executors (Scotland) Act 1900, s.3. "Universal legatee" denotes the estate is all moveable; "general disponee" that it includes heritage.

[10] See Currie, p. 71.

[11] Succession (Scotland) Act 1964, s. 9(4).

[12] Memorandum No. 71 (1986), paras. 5.16–5.21.

[13] Succession (Scotland) Act 1964, s. 5(2).

tration of a court-appointed *judicial factor*. Three types are relevant: a factor *loco tutoris* for a pupil child, a *curator bonis* for a minor, and a *curator bonis* for a person of unsound mind. Any may apply to be appointed executor-dative to the person from whom the beneficiary inherits. If a child has no factor, the sheriff may specially appoint a commissary factor in order to be executor and obtain confirmation.[14]

(7) The procurator fiscal, if asked to by someone with a claim on the estate. This is very rare.

(8) The funerator: the undertaker or whoever has paid his bill. This only occurs if next-of-kin are unknown or cannot or will not be executor.[15]

13.9 If the entitled person declines to be executor, the next-entitled can take his or her place. For instance, a widow may be exclusively entitled under (2) but prefer her son to be executor. She should formally decline office and his application will explain the facts. If the estate exceeds prior rights he is independently entitled under (3) and no declinature is needed.

(c) The executor-creditor

13.10 Confirmation as executor-creditor is unusual and differs from other confirmations. It is a type of diligence: a way for a creditor to enforce his debt. So, uniquely, it need cover only that amount and not the whole estate. But it is impossible once another executor has been appointed, and ineffective if the estate is sequestrated within twelve months after the death. In practice the creditor simply sues for his debt.[16]

(d) Disqualification

13.11 Age is no disqualification: a pupil or minor child can be an executor. But it is very unwise: his tutor or curator will have to act on his behalf or along with him, and—especially with estate abroad—the child's signature may not be accepted to allow him to uplift property. There are better alternatives. If the guardian is the surviving spouse she can be appointed executor-dative in her own right. Failing that the court can appoint a relative to be *curator bonis* or commissary factor, and then, in that capacity, to be executor-dative.[17]

---

[14] Currie, pp. 117–122; Walker, *Judicial Factors*, pp. 88–90.
[15] Currie, p. 132.
[16] Currie, pp. 143 *et seq.*; Wilson & Duncan, *Trusts*, pp. 463 *et seq.*
[17] Currie, pp. 90–91, 120–123, and 479–484 (styles).

Insanity is a bar. Section 3 of the Executors (Scotland) Act can supply an alternative executor-nominate. Otherwise the executor's *curator bonis* can be appointed executor-dative in his place.

Bankruptcy is no bar. The only guarantee against financial mishaps or fraud is the bond of caution which executors-dative must lodge before confirmation.

Executors need not be resident in the UK. For convenience they should be.

3. Appointing executors-dative—procedure

(a) The petition

13.12 The applicant lodges a petition in the appropriate sheriff court.[18] This "initial writ" must state:

(1) the date and place of death. Sometimes these are not exactly known. It is sufficient to follow the words of the death certificate and to describe the location: *e.g.* "on the road between X and Y near Z." If death was presumed by virtue of disappearance the court decree specifies a date.[19]

(2) if the deceased died intestate. If he died testate it must mention the will and any declinature of office by executors-nominate.

(3) where the deceased was domiciled, to prove jurisdiction. If it was abroad, the applicant must lodge an expert opinion that he is entitled to be executor under the law of that place.

(4) the applicant's relationship to the deceased, to show his entitlement. It must eliminate potential preferable claimants, in particular any who died before the deceased. If a spouse survives, it must explain why she is not the applicant *or* state that the estate exceeds her prior rights. But the relationship—even if illegitimate—needs no proof by supporting evidence like birth certificates.[20]

13.13 Any documents referred to in the petition are lodged along with it. It is displayed in the court or the sheriff clerk's office (the sheriff clerk certifying that this has been done) but other possible claimants are not directly notified unless they lodged a *caveat*. If the petition is unopposed no hearing is needed and the sheriff grants decree nine clear days after certification.[21]

---

[18] With copies—the number varies—and a fee.
[19] Presumption of Death (Scotland) Act 1977, s. 10; see para. 1.4.
[20] *McLaughlin, Petr.*, 1987 S.L.T. (Sh. Ct.) 87, disapproving Currie, p. 113.
[21] The exact interval varies between sheriffdoms.

(b) The bond of caution

13.14 This is a guarantee that the executor-dative will perform his duties and not embezzle the estate. It is not required from a surviving spouse who inherits the whole estate by prior rights,[22] nor (except very rarely) from executors-nominate.

The cautioner must be subject to the jurisdiction of the Scottish courts, have been approved by the Court of Session, and not be a beneficiary. Almost invariably it is an insurance company. The bond is a standard form and the company makes a charge based on the value of the estate.

Caution is required for the gross estate in the inventory. The only debts deductible are those (like mortgages) which are secured over items of heritage and appear as deductions within the inventory rather than the IHT account. In theory the executor can apply by initial writ to reduce the amount of caution, but this is not worthwhile.

All the executors sign the bond and send it to the company for completion. It is probative and must be entirely executed, with due authentication, *after* the sheriff's decree. The relevant details (names and addresses and capacity of executor's appointment) must match the initial writ and the inventory precisely.

After being appointed and taking out caution the executor-dative can apply for confirmation.

CONFIRMATION

13.15 The grant of confirmation is the executor's title to administer the estate. It reproduces the inventory[23] of the estate (but not the associated IHT account) and the associated oath sworn by the executor that it is valid.

For convenience one usually also obtains certificates of confirmation for individual items in the inventory. The executor then sends the confirmation or certificate to whoever possesses or registers the item—banks, company registrars, and the like. He can then have it endorsed in his name, encashed, sold, or in due course transferred to a beneficiary.

---

[22] Law Reform (Miscellaneous Provisions) (Scotland) Act 1980, s. 5. See S.L.C. Memorandum No. 71 (1986), paras. 5.27–5.36.

[23] The IHT form comprises the inventory and IHT account, but is often all called the "inventory". I distinguish the two parts here for clarity.

1. The inventory estate: classification

13.16 The concept of confirmation dates back to the Middle Ages. Executors were always required to state on oath an inventory of the deceased's estate as far as they knew it. In practice it was common to obtain partial confirmation to save expense, omitting items or minimising their value. The inventory had no tax function.

Those halcyon days ended with the Probate and Legacy Duties Act of 1808 which introduced an inventory duty and, with it, the modern distinction between estate subject to confirmation and that to be declared for tax purposes. By its terms:

> "before [anyone] shall be confirmed executor he shall exhibit upon oath or solemn affirmation, in the proper commissary court in Scotland, a full and true inventory . . . of all the personal or moveable estate and effects of the deceased . . . distinguishing what shall be in Scotland and what elsewhere."[24]

13.17 At that time confirmation affected only moveable property located within Scotland. For items elsewhere the executor had to obtain the local equivalent—in England, probate or letters of administration; *vice versa* for an English executor in Scotland. Though Scots law determined who *inherited* a domiciled Scot's moveable estate, wherever located, each country's executry procedure was quite separate.

Modern law considerably extends the scope of confirmation.

(1) It includes heritage.[25]

(2) It is recognised throughout the UK and may include property outwith Scotland *if* the deceased had Scots domicile; otherwise it includes only estate in Scotland. Conversely grants of probate or administration carry Scottish estate: no separate confirmation is needed.[26]

(3) Confirmation does not in principle affect property outwith the UK. However the courts in Commonwealth countries have discretion to accept and "reseal" it, giving it the same effect as a local grant of administration. Conversely Edinburgh sheriff court may, on certain conditions, reseal a Commonwealth grant for use here.[27] Estate outwith the Commonwealth normally requires a fresh local grant.

For (2) and (3) to apply there must be some confirmable estate in

---

[24] s. 38.

[25] Succession (Scotland) Act 1964, ss. 14, 15.

[26] Administration of Estates Act 1971, ss. 1–6: if domiciled in the place where the grant was issued.

[27] Colonial Probates Act 1892; Currie, pp. 258 *et seq.*

Scotland. If not the executor must get a grant of administration in the country where the property is. The Scottish Law Commission favours allowing a Scots confirmation in such cases.[28]

13.18   The inventory should therefore list and value the confirmable estate, item by item, in order under these headings:

Heritable estate in Scotland

Moveable estate in Scotland

Real and personal estate in England and Wales

Real and personal estate in Northern Ireland

A summary for confirmation then gives the total values for each head (lumping Scottish estate together) and the aggregate total. Finally foreign property is itemised and valued.

Itemised confirmable values are extended into the column of values on the form. Values in the summary and foreign values are not extended.

2. The inventory: particular items

13.19   The treatment of certain items can raise difficulties.

(1) *Heritage* and (outwith Scotland) *real property*. The description must be sufficient to identify the property as a separate item in the estate. A full conveyancing description is not necessary, but can have advantages: it ensures accurate identification if the property is later conveyed to a beneficiary, not by a full conveyance, but by a docket on the confirmation.[29]

Suppose the deceased had contracted to buy or sell a house but died before money was paid and the property conveyed. In either case the house must be confirmed to in order to complete the executor's title and allow subsequent conveyance. In the first case it is entered at full value and the price is a deductible debt for IHT; in the second it is given a nil value and the unpaid sale proceeds go in as an asset.

13.20   (2) The deceased's aggregate share of *partnership assets* appears as one moveable item. It may include heritage registered in the deceased's name as an individual: that needs an extra separate entry at a nil value in order to complete title. If the deceased had a one-man business its assets appear individually in the inventory and its liabilities are deducted in the IHT account.

13.21   (3) The IHT form asks for separate details of *joint property*: heritage, shares, bank accounts, and the like. Their treatment in the inventory varies.

[28] Memorandum No. 71 (1986), paras. 5.22–5.23.
[29] Currie, p. 157; Succession (Scotland) Act 1964, s. 15 (2).

(a) *Heritage, company shares,* and *unit trusts*: one confirms in the inventory to the proportionate share registered in the deceased's name—usually one-half. The exception is a survivorship destination of heritage: the share is omitted from the inventory but listed in the IHT account. (One must check that the deceased had not validly revoked the destination.)

(b) With bank accounts, by contrast, joint names do not imply joint ownership. They merely allow each person to operate the account. He owns only the money he paid in, which may be all or none. The inventory therefore states the proportion contributed by the deceased, and that is confirmed to.

Take an account in name of "X and Y and the survivor." The survivor can uplift the money without confirmation: that conveniently covers immediate expenses. But—except for the survivor's own contribution—the executor can reclaim the money for distribution to the appropriate beneficiary.

There are two exceptions. If the funds derived from either spouse's housekeeping allowance the spouses own them in equal shares; similarly items bought with those funds.[30] Or the deceased may have gifted his share to his co-holder: but that needs very clear proof.[31]

(c) Until recently household goods belonged to whoever bought them. But spouses are now presumed to own "matrimonial property" in equal shares, unless proved otherwise (and contributing unequally to the cost is not proof enough).[32] This covers most items bought for use in the matrimonial home except cars, money and shares. Thus only the deceased's half-share is confirmed to.

13.22 (4) *Life assurance* policy proceeds need confirmation only if payable to the executors; otherwise they are not part of the estate and can be paid on production of the death certificate.

The deceased may have assigned the policy in security for a loan which was not repaid before he died. Two complications arise.

(a) The policy proceeds go to the lender to pay off the loan; the estate is entitled to any surplus remaining. The inventory shows the gross proceeds *minus* loan, and thus the executor confirms to the net surplus. The entry is headed in the lender's name because the estate's claim is against the lender rather than the insurance company. It is also acceptable to confirm to the gross sum and deduct the debt separately in the IHT account: but the drawback is that the higher inventory total leads to higher caution and confirmation dues.

(b) There is usually a second security: a standard security over a

---

[30] Family Law (Scotland) Act 1985, s. 26.
[31] *Forrest-Hamilton's Tr.* v. *Forrest-Hamilton,* 1970 S.L.T. 338.
[32] Family Law (Scotland) Act 1985, s. 25.

house. When calculating prior or legal rights the loan must be allocated to the two securities in proportion to their values.[33] One may, but need not, use the same method in the inventory; or one can deduct the whole amount from the policy. The latter simplifies the inventory and maximises the heritage on which IHT can be paid by instalments; but in that case one must remember to reallocate at the prior/legal rights stage.[34]

13.23 (5) A *lease* is confirmed to (as heritage) unless it ends on the death. Even if the deceased could not assign his interest while alive, the executor can do so.[35]

13.24 (6) *Stocks and shares* are listed as Scottish or English depending on where the company is registered; government stock is English. One must also include (a) dividends declared before the date of death, though paid later, and (b) interest accrued till then (calculated on a daily basis; special rules apply to government stock).[36]

13.25 (7) Property held by the deceased as *trustee* passes automatically by accretion to the remaining trustees, without confirmation. But if he was the sole surviving trustee the property is now in limbo. It can be put as a note at the very end of the inventory: this allows his executor to transfer it to a beneficiary or to someone the beneficiary selects.[37]

The same applies if the deceased held as a confirmed *executor* on another person's estate. If he was not merely executor but *beneficiary* two entries are needed: that whole executry estate (as a note) and his own beneficial interest (as a confirmable item in the body of the inventory). Other procedures are sometimes possible.[38]

3. The oath[39]

(a) Who swears the oath, and before whom?

13.26 The executor must personally swear an oath that the inventory and associated details are true. He may instead solemnly affirm on grounds of religious belief or non-belief. If there are several

[33] *Graham* v. *Graham* (1898) 5 S.L.T. 319; see para. 4.13.

[34] If *two* borrowers have a joint policy in respect of a joint loan the debt must be divided between them; this affects how the policy proceeds are treated. See Gretton (1988) 33 J.L.S. 141.

[35] Succession (Scotland) Act 1964, s. 16(2); Meston, pp. 86–89.

[36] A beneficiary may suffer income tax on these (because they are paid after death). If so he has a credit for the IHT. See para. 12.35.

[37] Executors (Scotland) Act 1900, s. 6.

[38] For procedure when an executor dies see in more detail para. 13.56.

[39] See Currie, pp. 187 *et seq.*

executors only one need swear. If the inventory is compiled purely for IHT and no confirmation is required,[39a] a relation or beneficiary or anyone with an interest may swear.

The person before whom the oath is sworn must be completely impartial and independent. He should not be the executor's partner, co-executor, or a beneficiary. Subject to that he can be any of the following:

(1) *In Scotland*: a sheriff principal, sheriff, commissioner appointed by either, sheriff clerk or his depute, notary public, magistrate, or justice of the peace.[40]

(2) *In England or Northern Ireland*: anyone in (1), a commissioner for oaths appointed by the English or Northern Irish courts (respectively), or (in England) a solicitor entitled to administer oaths.

(3) *Abroad*: a local magistrate, British consul, notary public practising in that country or admitted and practising in Great Britain or Ireland, someone locally authorised to administer oaths, or certain senior officers in the Forces.

(b) Contents

13.27 The details must be accurate, consistent, and connect up with any will, initial writ, or related documents such as minutes of declinature. Certain preliminaries precede the oath:

(1) The deceased's full name and address. Previous names, addresses and aliases are included if needed to tie in with the will. Date of birth, date and place of death, and occupation or designation follow.

(2) The names and addresses of all executors being confirmed.

(3) Date and place of the oath. The oath is only valid for six months and must be re-sworn if the inventory is not lodged within that time.

(4) The name and address of the person administering the oath (stating his capacity), and those of the executor swearing it—the *deponent*. The names should link up with their surnames and initials as signed after the oath, while previous names and addresses may tie in with the will or initial writ.

13.28 The oath itself states the following:

(1) The deceased's name and domicile, to show jurisdiction: "domiciled in the Sheriffdom of X in Scotland" or as appropriate if of foreign or unknown domicile.

(2) The deponent's right to act as executor-nominate or dative,

[39a] *e.g.* under para. 13.36.
[40] Executors (Scotland) Act 1900, s. 8.

along with co-executors (using the order in the will). At this point the oath must, as appropriate:

    (a) identify the will, when it was recorded, or the decree appointing as executor-dative.

    (b) state any special capacity, such as "attorney under power of attorney dated . . . "

    (c) explain if any executors-nominate have died or declined appointment.

    (d) state the executor-dative's capacity as *per* the initial writ. For small estates there is no separate initial writ and the oath must also eliminate anyone with a preferable right to be appointed.[41]

    (e) reiterate if the deponent's or deceased's name or address were different in the will.

(3) Who the other executors are.

(4) Where the estate is and whether confirmation is required.

The deponent and the person administering the oath sign it.

4. Associated documents and procedure

13.29 Except for an executor-dative's decree of appointment, all documents referred to in the oath must be lodged along with the inventory. They must be docketed to identify them. The docket is a note written on the document (*not* on a separate sheet):

> "[Place, date] Referred to in my deposition of this date to the inventory of the estate of the late [X]."

It is signed by the deponent and the person administering the oath. The date must of course match that of the oath.

13.30 Unless the will is in English, attested, and clearly names the executor, additional procedure is needed to establish the executor's right to appointment.

    (1) An *attested will* may have been defectively executed, or its testing clause left uncompleted. The defect can be curable by a petition under section 39 of the Conveyancing (Scotland) Act 1874.[42] While a separate Court of Session or sheriff court action is possible, the point usually arises when seeking confirmation.

    The executor applies by initial writ for (a) proof that the will was duly executed *and* (b) special authority for appointment as executor-nominate or (if the will named no executor) as executor-dative. The

---

[41] Using Form B-3 with no initial writ; see para. 13.33. For larger estates these details go in the initial writ.

[42] See para. 6.10. Section 38 may also cure the testing clause.

initial writ must state how the will is defective (itemising any missing details), that the will is subscribed by the testator and bears to be[43] attested by two witnesses, and that the subscriptions are genuine. Proof is by affidavits. They are sworn, before a notary public or justice of the peace or anyone else locally authorised, by the two witnesses, anyone else present when the will was executed, and (if the will has several pages) whoever found it or had custody of it. Those swearing docket the will appropriately to link with their affidavits. The initial writ, will (or extract),[44] affidavits, and inventory are lodged with the sheriff clerk's office. The sheriff rarely requires a full hearing before granting decree and confirmation.

(2) The will may omit to name the executor and merely identify him as, say, "my son." Confirmation should be sought by initial writ, with affidavits that the executor is in fact the person referred to.

13.31 (3) A will which is *holograph* or adopted as holograph always requires to be validated by affidavits from two people who knew the testator and can swear that the handwriting and signature are genuinely his. They should see the original will before it is sent for registration and extract. Furthermore the initial writ procedure is used if there is some question whether the writing or signature is genuine and valid.

An informal writing does not need to be "set up" if it was adopted by another formally valid will which is itself lodged.

13.32 (4) A will executed *abroad* but not meeting Scots formalities is effective if executed validly under the law of the place of execution or of the testator's domicile, habitual residence, or nationality.[45] The inventory should refer to and be accompanied by an opinion by someone qualified in that local law that it is valid and that the named executor is entitled to administer the estate. An initial writ is not necessary.

Similarly a will in a foreign language must be lodged along with a translation certified by an expert as accurate.

A foreign will may be unavailable because it is deposited permanently with a local notary. It is acceptable to lodge a copy certified by him, if accompanied by an opinion by *another* expert as to local validity. A British consul or a notary public should also authenticate the copy.[46]

---

[43] *i.e.* is on the face of it attested.
[44] See para. 13.37.
[45] Wills Act 1963, ss. 1 and 2; see para. 14.17.
[46] See Currie, pp. 267–272.

5. Small estates

13.33 A "small estate" is one whose gross value, without deducting debts and funeral expenses, does not exceed £17,000.[47] An optional simplified confirmation procedure is available.[48] The sheriff clerk administers the oath and completes the inventory; there is no separate initial writ for executors-dative, but a bond of caution is still needed. The sheriff clerk must be satisfied of several points:

(1) There must be no competition for the post of executor.

(2) The value is no more than £17,000. The executor should give him a list which itemises and values the estate.

(3) The executor is entitled to appointment, either under the will or by relationship to the deceased. The details go in the oath. In intestate cases he can be asked for proof of identity and relationship: two witnesses attend the sheriff clerk's office with him and swear affidavits (not all clerks require this). If there is a will the clerk checks its validity.

6. Additional confirmations

13.34 It may emerge that property was omitted or wrongly valued in the original inventory. The executor must lodge an additional or corrective inventory (or "eik") if IHT is payable and confirmation is required.

If confirmation is not needed the matter is usually simply resolved by correspondence with the Capital Taxes Office.

For confirmation purposes the inventory or eik states the new or revalued items. These are confirmed to. The executor also needs an eik where, though the estate is no larger, items were wrongly described originally so that he cannot obtain title to them without correction. In that case the eik adds on the item as corrected and deducts the value of the original entry from the estate.

Only the original executor can use an eik. If he has died or become incapable a new executor must apply afresh for confirmation *ad omissa*.[49] Nor is it available if the "small estates" procedure was originally used: the executor must repeat that procedure or (if the new items take the estate above £17,000) get confirmation *ad omissa*.

7. Payment without confirmation

13.35 Not until the executor has been confirmed can he insist that the executry assets be paid or handed over to him. Whoever holds the

[47] Confirmation to Small Estates (Scotland) Act 1979, s. 1(3); Confirmation to Small Estates (Scotland) Order 1989 S.I. 1989 No. 289.
[48] Using Form B-3.
[49] See para. 13.56.

assets can require to see the confirmation. If the holder chooses not to and pays earlier he takes the risk of paying the wrong person; the true confirmed executor will be entitled to demand payment again.

Confirmation is however dispensed with in several (largely statutory) situations. The claimant must instead produce proof of the death.

(1) Property subject to a *survivorship destination* belongs automatically to the survivor without confirmation. But the destination must be in a title deed. Contrast a destination in a bank account. There the survivor can operate the account and so demand payment without confirmation; but he does not necessarily *own* the funds and may have to hand them over to the executor.[50]

(2) The deceased may have *nominated* someone to receive funds on his death. The method and maximum amount differ between funds under various statutes. The nominee can insist on payment: usually he is also beneficially entitled to the money and can keep it, but in rare cases the nomination is (like the bank account) for mere administrative convenience and he must pass it on to the executor.[51]

(3) In other cases payment is a privilege, not a right. Building societies, pensions, and company shares are examples. The holder has discretion whether to pay, but it must treat all claimants on the estate alike. It will usually require evidence of the claimant's entitlement to inherit. It may ask the claimant to grant an indemnity in case a confirmed executor later appears, and may also require evidence that no IHT is payable on the item.[52] For numerous public bodies a blanket statutory maximum of £5,000 is laid down.[53] Others, such as banks and companies, set their own limits on both the individual item and the total estate.

(4) If the Crown takes as *ultimus haeres* it requires no confirmation.

13.36 Though assets pass without confirmation they must still be included in an appropriate inventory for IHT purposes. If no confirmation is required and no tax is payable, then (by concession) one may instead lodge a simpler Form 20 to have the estate certified free of IHT.

8. Recording documents[54]

13.37 It is common to *register* the will at the start of the executry *for*

---

[50] See para. 5.2.
[51] See Currie, pp. 285 *et seq.*
[52] The C.T.O. can certify this using a Form 20.
[53] Administration of Estates (Small Payments) Act 1965; S.I. 1984 No. 539.
[54] See Currie, pp. 296–301; Halliday, *Conveyancing*, Vol. I, paras. 4–53 *et seq.*; Walker and Walker, *Evidence*, pp. 229, 240.

preservation in the Books of Council and Session.[55] While not essential it avoids the risk of losing the will, and is particularly wise if the estate is large or there is to be an ongoing trust. The original document is kept in the register and an *extract* is issued—an official authenticated copy which is probative evidence of its terms. A special certified extract can be obtained for use abroad. If the will has to be validated with affidavits, these should be obtained *before* sending for registration.

13.38 When seeking confirmation, the inventory and associated documents (including the will or extract but not the IHT accounts) are recorded in the Commissariot Books of the sheriff court. The inventory and IHT account are forwarded to the Capital Taxes Office; the documents are returned to whoever lodged them. The executor can then obtain the following:

(1) confirmation (in respect of the whole inventory);
(2) certificates of confirmation (one for each separate item);
(3) a certified copy of the confirmation, to use for foreign estate;
(4) an ordinary copy, for private records: this lacks the force of an extract.

Both types of register are open to public inspection.

THE EXECUTOR'S DUTIES

1. To gather in the estate

13.39 The executor must uplift the deceased's assets to allow him to pay his debts and distribute the remaining assets to his beneficiaries. Confirmation is his title to do so. Though any dealing with the assets before confirmation is vitious intromission, he "purges" it by being confirmed within a year and a day. In any case he can take preliminary steps beforehand. He can sue for a debt owed to the deceased; but he needs confirmation to be able to extract the court decree, discharge the debt, or enforce it.

The executor is in breach of duty if he negligently fails to pursue debts or other assets. A beneficiary has several remedies. He can sue the executor to make him account for the assets. He can sue a debtor in the executor's name, provided he gives the executor an indemnity against possible court expenses. If he is due a specific legacy, he can bring an action against whoever has the item, to have it delivered.

---

[55] In the registers at Meadowbank House, Edinburgh. Registration of a living person's will is also to be made possible: Administration of Justice Act 1982, ss. 23–25.

2. To pay the deceased's debts

13.40 The executor must pay debts in order of preference: privileged debts; preferential debts; lastly, ordinary debts.[56] He should not pay ordinary debts till six months after the death unless he is sure there are assets enough to pay the others: if he gets it wrong he must compensate the others personally. If necessary he will advertise inviting creditors to notify claims. He must check the incidence of the debts: on what assets do they fall? IHT and secured debts raise the point. Whoever inherits an asset burdened by a security (say, a house) takes *cum onere*—subject to the security—unless the will says otherwise, and must pay the estate the value of the debt secured on it.

The executor need not pay debts exceeding the value of the confirmed estate. If the estate is absolutely insolvent, and likely to remain so, he should take steps to have it sequestrated or a judicial factor appointed.[57]

3. To distribute the estate

13.41 Creditors must be paid before beneficiaries. But the executor need not wait indefinitely. If the estate is solvent he can start distribution after 12 months (at most); earlier if, after due inquiry, he is satisfied outstanding debts have been met. Any creditor who chooses to delay till later cannot sue an executor who has in the meantime distributed the estate with due care.

Potential legal rights claimants should be notified and asked to elect to claim or not. A child cannot validly elect; if his tutor or curator elects, the child can have the election set aside within four years after reaching age 18. The executor should retain funds to meet a possible claim at that age.

13.42 The beneficiaries can then be paid. If they are short of money the executor will often make a payment to account as soon as he is certain that funds permit. If legacies exceed the value of the estate they must be abated in order of preference, residue first and specific legacies last.[58]

13.43 A specific legacy is transferred *in specie*—physically. Moveables are delivered. For heritage a docket[59] can be noted on the confirmation or certificate of confirmation which is given to the

---

[56] See chap. 3.
[57] Bankruptcy (Scotland) Act 1985, s. 8(3). See Walker, *Judicial Factors*, pp. 42–46; McBryde, *Bankruptcy*, pp. 32–33, 41, and 236–238.
[58] See para. 10.25.
[59] Succession (Scotland) Act 1964, s. 15 (2). Notice of title is also an option.

beneficiary. Alternatively it can be formally conveyed. If so the disposition links up with the deceased's title: title is *deduced* through the confirmation. The will may instead be an acceptable link, but that may soon end, and it is best avoided.[60] General legacies are paid in kind or in cash according to their terms. Residuary legatees can take their legacies in kind if they agree collectively, but otherwise they cannot insist on particular items. Their primary right is to cash, and the executor can sell the items and distribute the proceeds; he will have to weigh up the CGT consequences. Complex rules govern the transfer of leases, including agricultural leases and crofting tenancies.[61]

13.44 Due care must be taken to ascertain and pay the correct beneficiaries. If the wrong person is paid three distinct issues arise:

(1) The beneficiary can sue the executor in an action of accounting to enforce his legacy. (This is also his remedy if the executor is simply unduly slow to pay.) But the executor has no liability to illegitimate or adoptive relations of whom he had no notice when he distributed the estate; he need not check first if they exist.[62]

(2) Can the executor recover the asset from the payee? That depends on general principles of restitution, which are themselves unclear. The correct criteria are probably that the error was excusable and that the payee has not disposed of or spent the asset in good faith: failing them, restitution is barred. But some decisions go further and state that liferent and annuity payments are irrecoverable.[63]

13.45 (3) Can the beneficiary sue the payee? It seems he can if he brings in the executor as a defender.[64] But a purchaser in good faith *cannot* be challenged. In the case of heritage he is protected by section 2 of the Trusts (Scotland) Act 1961 or section 17 of the 1964 Act, depending on whether he bought directly from the executor or from another beneficiary. Section 17 only applies if his title rests on the executor's confirmation: not if it derives from a will or special destination. Section 2 extends to moveables as well.[65]

4. Fiduciary duties

13.46 The executor is a trustee and has the same powers and duties.

---

[60] Opinion of the Professors of Conveyancing (1965) 10 J.L.S. 153; (1966) 11 J.L.S. 84; Scot. Law Com. Memorandum No. 71 (1986), para. 5.1.

[61] Succession (Scotland) Act 1964, s. 16; Meston, pp. 86–89.

[62] Succession (Scotland) Act 1964, s. 4(3); Law Reform (Miscellaneous Provisions) (Scotland) Act 1968, s. 7. The Scottish Law Commission favours a wider rule: Memorandum No. 71 (1986), paras. 5.2–5.9.

[63] *Rowan's Trs.* v. *Rowan*, 1940 S.C. 30; *cf. Darling's Trs.* v. *Darling's Trs.*, 1909 S.C. 445; see D. R. Macdonald, 1989 J.R. 49.

[64] *Armour* v. *Glasgow Royal Infirmary*, 1909 S.C. 916.

[65] For the S.L.C. view see Memorandum No. 71 (1986), para. 5.10.

As a fundamental principle he must not be *auctor in rem suam*: he must not allow his own personal interests to prevail over the interests of the executry estate. So he must derive no personal advantage at the expense of the estate.

It is quite acceptable in law for the executor to be a legatee (though for a solicitor it breaches professional ethics). But there must be no transactions between himself (as an individual) and the executry: he may not purchase assets of the estate. It matters not that the price was fair: the conflict of interest is plain, and a beneficiary can have the sale set aside.[66] Such transactions are allowed only if clearly authorised by the testator or, subsequently, by all the affected beneficiaries.

In *Inglis* v. *Inglis*[67] the executor had a farm tenancy assigned to himself without the other beneficiaries' consent. Fair price or not, he had to account for any profit he made from the transaction. The *auctor* principle overrode section 16 of the 1964 Act which governs transfer of the deceased's interest in a lease. The Scottish Law Commission proposes that it should no longer do so provided the interest in the lease is impartially valued.[68]

13.47 The executor can recoup his out-of-pocket expenses from the estate. Beyond that he must act gratuitously: unless the will allows he cannot charge a fee, nor (since he benefits indirectly) can his partners if he is in a firm. He can however appoint an outsider to act as factor or solicitor.[69] The typical will, avoiding the problem, authorises executors to "appoint one of their number to act as solicitor, with his usual professional remuneration."

13.48 Executors make decisions by majority. Each is liable only for his own acts and omissions, not his co-executors'—though blatant and continued neglect of executry affairs may itself be a breach of duty. If they wish to appoint agents, such as solicitors, they must choose them with care and should (however slightly) supervise their activities. But provided they do that they need not answer to beneficiaries for their agents' mistakes.

13.49 Beneficiaries are entitled to see accounts up to the end of the executry detailing the executor's dealings with the estate. At that stage he can also ask the beneficiaries to give him a discharge for his actions. It is not necessary, and they can still sue if a breach of duty is discovered, but by it they will acknowledge having duly received their entitlement from the estate.

---

[66] *Johnston* v. *Macfarlane*, 1987 S.L.T. 593; *Clark* v. *Clark's Exrs.*, 1989 S.L.T. 665.
[67] 1983 S.L.T. 437; 1983 S.C. 8.
[68] Memorandum No. 71, paras. 7.1–7.10.
[69] Trusts (Scotland) Act 1921, s. 4(*f*).

13.50 All these rules are primarily to protect the beneficiaries. A breach of duty cannot be challenged if they *all* authorise it in full knowledge of the facts. But, that aside, the obligation to account and to hand over legacies never lapses by prescription.

CESSATION OR LAPSE OF OFFICE

1. Declinature

13.51 An executor can decline appointment. A written minute is needed: either written on the will, in a separate document, or excerpted from minutes of a meeting where he attended and recorded his declinature. A sole executor should if possible first appoint an alternative and then resign, recording this in a combined minute of assumption and resignation.

In principle executors-nominate are all entitled to be confirmed jointly. So if only some apply, the others' declinature *must* be produced along with the inventory, referred to in it and docketed to link the two. The initial writ for an executor-dative must likewise be accompanied by declinatures from anyone with a preferable exclusive right to appointment, (say) an executor-nominate or a widow who takes the whole estate under prior rights.

If the potential executor is mentally incapable his *curator bonis* can decline on his behalf. Otherwise a medical certificate stating his incapacity is needed. If he is abroad or untraceable the sheriff may still grant confirmation: but delays will result, a special warrant will be required, and possibly caution as well.

2. Resignation

13.52 An executor-nominate can resign. If acting alone he should first appoint a new executor. An executor-dative can neither resign nor assume new executors.[70]

3. Removal

13.53 An executor is regarded as a trustee and can be removed by the courts for the same reasons:

(1) If an executor is insane or physically or mentally disabled, or disappears or leaves the UK for a continuous period of at least six

---

[70] Succession (Scotland) Act 1964, s. 20.

months, beneficiaries or co-executors can ask the Court of Session or the sheriff court where confirmation was granted to remove him.[71]
(2) An executor cannot be removed merely because of a potential conflict of interest with the estate: so he can be a beneficiary. But he can if he actively pursues his own interests against the estate (say by claiming legal rights) or if he causes deadlock by obstructing his co-executors. Beneficiaries or co-executors should petition the Court of Session. In many cases the other executors will continue the administration. But that will be inappropriate if there are none, or if financial problems are suspected: the court can then appoint a judicial factor to complete the executry.[72]

13.54 Confirmation makes a will probative but says nothing as to its essential validity; the will can be reduced in the Court of Session if invalid. So can the confirmation itself, if it emerges that the wrong person was confirmed. In either case the original executor's appointment lapses.[73] However, the law protects those to whom the executor had sold heritage or securities over heritage: if they acquired in good faith and for value their title cannot be challenged on grounds of the reduction.[74]

13.55 An executor-dative's appointment can be recalled at any time before confirmation. If a new executor seeks appointment (either to remove the existing one or after his death) he applies by initial writ. In cases of simple recall the applicant seeks the sheriff's consent by writing a minute on the original initial writ: *e.g.* if the initial writ was incorrect, one of several executors-dative has died or wishes to withdraw, or no executor-dative is required because a will has turned up.[75]

4. Death

13.56 If one of several executors dies, the others continue in office unless (rarely) they were expressly appointed to act jointly.[76] But if a sole executor dies the executry lapses. There are several ways to revive it and dispose of the estate: the choice depends on when the lapse occurs. One must envisage four people: an original deceased A, his executor B (who has died), B's own executor C, and an executor D who concludes A's executry.

[71] Trusts (Scotland) Act 1921, s. 23.
[72] See Walker, *Judicial Factors*, pp. 33–37; Wilson & Duncan, *Trusts*, pp. 293–297, 416.
[73] Currie, pp. 306–308.
[74] Succession (Scotland) Act 1964, s. 17.
[75] See Currie, pp. 130–131, 494–495.
[76] Executors (Scotland) Act 1900, s. 4; McLaren, *Wills*, Vol. II, p. 898.

(1) Suppose B had confirmed to A's property. *His* executor C, by noting it in B's inventory, can recover it and transfer it to a beneficiary, anyone chosen by the beneficiary, or someone entitled to carry on the executry administration.[77] This covers most cases, but not all. If A's estate requires further administration, it needs a new executor D; mere noting does not allow C to do it. Moreover a beneficiary cannot compel C to note and transfer. ((2) answers each problem.)

(2) Alternatively a new executor D is confirmed directly to A's estate: confirmation *ad non executa*.[78] He may undertake the administration. He can be anyone who has a beneficial interest in the estate: a legatee, heir on intestacy, or their executor representing their claim. (So he *may* coincidentally be the same person as C.) This procedure is also available if B did not die but was merely incapacitated.

(3) If B omitted some of A's assets from his confirmation, a new executor obtains confirmation *ad omissa* to them. He is chosen as in (2), but procedure differs: there will be fresh confirmation dues and IHT because B did not report the items.

(4) If B was appointed but died before confirmation, a new executor must confirm to A's estate. The rules are similar to (3).

(5) A beneficiary can petition the Court of Session to transfer assets directly to him if the executor through death or incapacity failed to do so.[79] Being relatively costly this is a last resort.

There is the complication that where A died before the 1964 Act the old law governs how his estate is wound up.[80] In that event the above procedures will not apply to heritage: the heir may have to make up title by "service."

13.57 It is worth noting how the rules for *lapsed testamentary trusts* differ. (1) and (5) both apply to trustees. (2) applies only if the last trustee had also been confirmed executor. Otherwise there are two options if further trust administration is needed:

(1) to ask the Court of Session to appoint a new trustee.[81]

(2) the last trustee's heir inherits the office if the trust deed says so. He is then entitled to be "served heir of provision in trust"—a quaint relic of pre-1964 procedure.[82]

---

[77] Executors (Scotland) Act 1900, s. 6.

[78] Executors (Scotland) Act 1900, s. 7. Form X-1 is used.

[79] Trusts (Scotland) Act 1921, s. 24.

[80] Succession (Scotland) Act 1964, s. 37(1) (*d*). See McDonald, *Manual*, para. 7.3; Meston, pp. 84–85.

[81] Trusts (Scotland) Act 1921, s. 22; Wilson & Duncan, *Trusts*, pp. 270 *et seq.*, 281–285.

[82] Revived by Law Reform (Miscellaneous Provisions) (Scotland) Act 1980, s. 6. But the "heir" is identified under the 1964 Act as the law in force when the trustee dies: *MacMillan, Petr.*, 1987 S.L.T. (Sh.Ct.) 50.

Further reading

Currie, *Confirmation of Executors*, especially Chaps. 1, 4, 8–14, and Forms at pp. 445 *et seq.*

Halliday, *Conveyancing Law & Practice*, Vol. IV.

McDonald, *Conveyancing Manual*, Section 7.3.

Meston, *The Succession (Scotland) Act 1964*, Chap. 8.

Morley, *Accounting*, Chaps. 1, 2.

Wilson & Duncan, *Trusts, Trustees and Executors*, Chaps. 28–32.

G. L. Gretton, "Trust and Executry Conveyancing" (1987) 32 J.L.S. 111.

Law Society of Scotland Post-Qualifying Legal Education papers regularly touch on substantive law and taxation as well as executry practice. They included detailed case studies. Among recent articles on executries:

N. R. Allan: "Conveyancing" (1981), pp. 34–43.

A. M. C. Dalgleish: "Insurance Policies" (1988), pp. 83–100.

C. Glasse: "Commissary Considerations" (1986), pp. 72–211.

W. Jones: "Commissary Considerations" (1988), pp. 65–82.

C. B. Miller: "Executry Conveyancing" (1988), pp. 5–29.

"Registration of Death; Procedure on Sudden Death" (1981), pp. 7–13.

CHAPTER 14

PRIVATE INTERNATIONAL LAW

INTRODUCTION

14.1 Problems of private international law or "conflict of laws" arise commonly in practice. If a person, whether a Scot or a foreigner, dies leaving property in Scotland, the Scottish courts may in various circumstances have to decide to what extent foreign law governs succession to his estate. Foreign law may be relevant in the administration of the estate and in ascertaining to whom it passes under rules of intestate succession. If a will was made, questions may arise of the deceased's capacity to test; the formal validity of its execution or its revocation; the essential validity of its provisions, for instance as regards rules of public policy; and the construction to be placed on those provisions. Certain fundamental rules should be borne in mind in this context.

GENERAL ASPECTS

1. Domicile

14.2 The concept of domicile is fundamental to questions of choice of law. In essence it denotes the "territory subject to a single system of law in which a man [or woman] has established his permanent home".[1] Every person must have a domicile; he may only have one at any one time. This may be acquired by birth—a domicile of origin— or by choice; acquisition of a domicile of choice requires actual residence but also a settled intention to change one's permanent home. In most questions of succession the domicile at date of death is relevant.

A child derives its domicile from its father or (in some cases where the child is illegitimate, the father dead, or the parents separated) its mother: a domicile of dependence. A minor child can acquire its own domicile. Before 1974 a woman automatically took her husband's domicile on marriage, but no longer.[2]

Note that domicile has a wider meaning for inheritance tax

---

[1] Anton, p. 155. See generally at pp. 155–183.
[2] Domicile and Matrimonial Proceedings Act 1973, ss. 1, 3, 4. In England (but not Scotland) the minor must be married or aged at least 16.

purposes, including residence in the UK in 17 out of the previous 20 years of assessment.[3]

2. Characterisation

14.3 Characterisation of a legal question is the process of determining the juridical category into which it falls.[4] This will decide the appropriate class of conflict of law rule to apply. For instance, are presumptions of death substantive or procedural for purposes of private international law? Is property moveable or immoveable? The problem arises because different legal systems' conflict of law rules themselves conflict: they classify such questions differently.

The general principle is to characterise from the standpoint of the *lex fori*, the place where the question is being litigated; but in doing so account is taken of any potentially relevant rules of foreign law in the context of their own legal system. So Scots law will decide whether a question in a Scottish executry is a matter of executry administration or of rights of succession.

14.4 However, this must be qualified in three respects.

(1) Legislation may dictate how a rule is to be characterised. So, section 3 of the Wills Act 1963 provides that where a law in force outside the United Kingdom falls to be applied in relation to a will, any requirement of that law whereby special formalities are to be observed by testators answering a particular description, or witnesses to the execution of a will are to possess certain qualifications, shall be treated as a formal requirement whatever that law says to the contrary.

14.5 (2) The *lex situs*—the law of the place where the property is located—determines whether property is moveable or immoveable.[5] Thus in *Macdonald* v. *Macdonald*,[6] where a domiciled Scotsman died leaving land in various Canadian provinces, it was held that because land was immoveable according to their law, it was not subject to Scottish legal rights over moveable estate.

Classification as moveable or immoveable is based, broadly speaking, on the physical nature of the property; it is distinct from the internal rules of classification as heritable and moveable (in Scots law) or real and personal (in English law) which a legal system applies in disputes where no foreign element arises. So, in English law, leases are personalty for domestic purposes but immoveable in inter-

---

[3] IHTA 1984, s. 267.
[4] See generally Anton, pp. 43–72; Morris, pp. 481–488.
[5] See Anton, pp. 385–390.
[6] 1932 S.C. (H.L.) 79. See also *Lashley* v. *Hog* (1804) 4 Pat. App. 581.

national law; debts secured on land, in Scots law, are moveable for most purposes but probably immoveable in international law.

Similarly the doctrine of conversion, whereby heritable property devolves *as if* moveable where the deceased intended its conversion (*e.g.* by selling it and giving the beneficiaries the cash proceeds), does not alter its immoveable status in international law. Take *Re Berchtold*:[7] a domiciled Hungarian owned a house in England; it was immoveable under English choice of law rules; English internal law applied; by its rule of conversion the house then devolved as if personalty.

14.6 When the Crown or a foreign government takes as *ultimus haeres* in the absence of other beneficiaries, is that (a) a true right of succession or (b) an instance of its right to all ownerless property— *bona vacantia*—situated within the state?[8] If the former, only immoveables may fall to the Crown, moveables going to the state where the deceased was domiciled; if the latter, the Crown takes both. Some states favour (a), others (b). For UK purposes both Scotland and England follow (b) (despite the term *ultimus haeres*): the Crown's claim is caduciary (i.e. by way of lapse), arising from the royal prerogative by failure of the normal succession.

In international law the position is less clear. The problem arises when a domiciled foreigner leaves moveables in Britain which his own government claims. In England, *Re Maldonado*[9] allowed the claim to be characterised under the foreign law: as that law applied (a), the foreign government inherited; had (b) applied, the British Crown would have got the items. In Scotland the point has not arisen, though in *Goold Stuart's Trustees* v. *McPhail*[10] it was implied that *Maldonado* might be followed if it did. If so this would overturn current Scots practice, which favours approach (b). In view of the confusion the Scottish Law Commission proposes that Scots law adopt (a) for all purposes.[11]

14.7 Numerous cases show how important characterisation is.

(1) Does the claim concern executry administration or rights of succession? If the former, the *lex fori*—as the law of the place where administration is taking place—applies; if the latter, the *lex situs* or *lex domicilii* depending whether the rights involve immoveables or moveable property. The *lex fori* decides the initial question of

---

[7] [1923] 1 Ch. 192.
[8] Anton, pp. 516–519; McMillan, pp. 10–13.
[9] [1954] P. 233.
[10] 1947 S.L.T. 221.
[11] Memorandum No. 71, paras. 6.8–6.13.

characterisation (*Scottish National Orchestra Society Ltd.* v. *Thomson's Executor*[12]).

(2) Is the question one of succession or matrimonial property? If the latter, the spouses' *lex domicilii* as at marriage—not death—will apply. This problem has arisen in two contexts: legal rights and revocation of wills. Since *Lashley* v. *Hog*[13] Scots law has treated legal rights arising on the death of a spouse or parent as a right of succession. By contrast, if proprietary rights arise on marriage—by an express marriage contract or under a regime of community of spouses' property—English and South African law[14] characterise the matter as one of matrimonial property; so, probably, will Scots law.[15] Where it is argued that a will has been revoked by marriage (*e.g.* under English law) Scots and English courts[16] both refer the question to the domiciliary law at date of marriage: unlike South Africa[17] we do not explicitly characterise the issue as concerning matrimonial property, but the result is the same.

(3) Are rules of evidence or substantive rights of succession at issue? If the former, the *lex fori* applies exclusively and foreign rules are ignored. In *Re Cohn*[18] two domiciled Germans were killed in a bomb blast in London: their moveable property devolved under German law. English law presumed that the elder died first; the German Civil Code, that they died simultaneously. Uthwatt J., considering the German rule in the context of the Code, held that it was substantive rather than merely procedural, and thus must be given effect by the English courts.

3. Renvoi

14.8 Having characterised the problem the Scots courts may, following Scots choice of law rules, decide that a foreign law applies. Suppose that that law, under its own—different—choice of law rules, does not consider its own internal rules applicable but transmits the question to a third legal system or remits it back to Scots law. For instance, Scots law holds that the law of the deceased's domicile applies, but *that* law refers the question to the law of his nationality. That is the problem of *renvoi*.[19]

Several solutions are possible. The simplest is for the Scots courts

[12] 1969 S.L.T. 325.
[13] (1804) 4 Pat. 581.
[14] Corbett, pp. 617–620; Morris, p. 413.
[15] Anton, pp. 455–458 and 507–508.
[16] Anton, pp. 536–537; Morris, p. 402; *Westerman's Exr.* v. *Schwab* (1905) 8 F. 132.
[17] Corbett, pp. 618–620; *Pitluk* v. *Gavendo*, 1955 (2) S.A. 573 (T).
[18] [1945] Ch. 5.
[19] Anton, pp. 55–67; and see cases in Currie, pp. 267–268.

to apply only the *internal* law of the foreign legal system: thus ignoring its choice of law rules and preventing *renvoi*. This is the purpose of the provision in section 1 of the Wills Act 1963 that a will is treated as properly executed if its execution conformed to the internal law in force in, *inter alia*, the territory where it was executed.

Alternatively the courts may accept the foreign choice of law and its *renvoi* back to Scots law. Or they may apply the whole foreign law including its internal rules. There is no uniform doctrine.[20]

4. Incidental questions

14.9 Once the courts have decided to apply a foreign law in a question of succession, a subsidiary issue may then emerge concerning some other area of law: for instance, a beneficiary's legitimacy. What legal system governs that? Logically the foreign *or* the Scots choice of law rules could decide, but again there is no universal principle.

In deciding legitimacy the Scots courts usually apply the parents' domiciliary law as at the date of the child's birth, except for succession to heritage where legitimacy under the *lex situs* is also required.[21]

INTESTATE SUCCESSION

1. General

14.10 The general rule is that intestate succession to moveables is governed by the *lex situs*, to immoveables by the law of the deceased's last domicile.[22] Characterisation as moveable or immoveable is made by the *lex situs*.[23]

The Succession (Scotland) Act 1964 largely abolished the distinction between heritable and moveable property in succession: henceforth heritage devolves in the same way as moveables. The old distinction is preserved for purposes of legal rights and private international law.[24] Immoveables therefore do not become moveables for these purposes; they merely devolve as if moveable in ordinary domestic Scots questions. In particular, immoveables still devolve by the *lex situs*, not the *lex ultimi domicilii*.

---

[20] *Re Annesley* [1926] Ch. 692; *Re Ross* [1930] 1 Ch. 377.
[21] *Fenton* v. *Livingstone* (1859) 3 Macq. 497; Anton pp. 67–72, and pp. 347–351.
[22] Anton, pp. 512–515.
[23] *Macdonald* v. *Macdonald*, 1932 S.C. (H.L.) 79.
[24] Succession (Scotland) Act 1964, ss. 1 and 37(2).

2. Legal rights

14.11 Scots law treats legal rights as rights of succession; they are indefeasible except by *inter vivos* disposition and so arise on both testacy and intestacy.

The existence, nature and extent of legal rights[25] over moveables is governed by the *lex domicilii*. So *ius relictae, ius relicti* and legitim may be claimed out of the deceased's moveable property, wherever situated, if he died domiciled in Scotland. Conversely moveables in Scotland belonging to a domiciled foreigner are subject to any appropriate foreign legal rights.

Rights over immoveables are governed by the *lex situs*; since such rights were abolished in Scots law in 1964 the point will only arise in connection with analogous rights recognised by foreign legal systems over immoveables situated outwith Scotland.

Note that English law recognises no such legal rights. Payments may be made out of the deceased's estate under the Inheritance (Provision for Family and Dependants) Act 1975 to dependants of the deceased for whom he has not made reasonable provision: but the deceased must have been domiciled in England (so immoveables in England belonging to a domiciled Scot are not affected); and payments are at the discretion of the High Court (so the Scots courts apparently could not make payments out of the moveables in Scotland of a domiciled Englishman).

3. Prior rights

14.12 Again the *lex domicilii* and *lex situs* apply in respect of moveables and immoveables respectively. The existence of three types of prior rights makes for complexity:[26]

(1) In respect of the deceased spouse's interest in a dwelling-house: this (being immoveable) applies to dwelling-houses situated in Scotland but not abroad, whatever the deceased's domicile. Where a cash sum is given in lieu, this is a surrogate for the house and so probably to be treated as immoveable likewise.

(2) In respect of furniture and plenishings: though these are moveable, the right *may* only apply if they are in a Scottish house. The answer is unclear and depends on how one interprets section 8 of the 1964 Act.

(3) Cash sum: this is borne by and paid out of heritage and moveables in proportion to their relative values. In the case of a domiciled Scot, his heritage in Scotland and his moveables every-

---

[25] Anton, pp. 505–511.
[26] Meston, pp. 92–94; Leslie, 1988 S.L.T. (News) 105.

where are affected. If the deceased was domiciled elsewhere, only his heritage in Scotland is affected: only that is subject to Scots law, so it bears the whole cash sum however large the rest of his estate may be; immoveables outwith Scotland and moveables everywhere are disregarded.

4. Law reform

14.13 The current rules have been widely criticised. Their *raison d'être*—the need for each state to control ownership of its land lest its dignity and independence be threatened—is suspect; their principles outdated, since in many legal systems the *lex domicilii* governs both moveables and immoveables; and their effects arbitrary, since relatives' succession rights differ greatly depending on the chance of where property is located. Consequently the Scottish Law Commission advocates[27] that both moveables and immoveables devolve according to the law of the deceased's last domicile, in line with its proposed abolition of the heritable-moveable distinction in domestic Scots law.

TESTATE SUCCESSION[28]

1. Capacity

14.14 Capacity to make a will may depend on age, understanding, or status (such as marriage or legitimacy). Capacity to make a will of moveables is governed by the domiciliary law at the time the will is made; of immoveables, by the *lex situs*. The Scottish Law Commission thinks[29] that section 28 of the Succession (Scotland) Act 1964, by which minors have "the like capacity to test" on heritage as moveables, might suggest that minors' capacity is always judged by their domiciliary law; it is hard to see how this stands with the express preservation (by section 37(2)) of existing choice of law rules.

The moveable-immoveable distinction has been widely questioned, and again the Commission advocates that the *lex domicilii* govern wills of both types of property.[30]

14.15 Capacity of a legatee to take under a will is judged by his, rather than the testator's, domiciliary law: presumably at the date of the testator's death.[31]

[27] Memorandum No. 71, paras. 6.2–6.7.
[28] See generally Anton, pp. 519–540.
[29] Memorandum No. 71, para. 6.14.
[30] Memorandum No. 71, para. 6.14.
[31] Anton, pp. 502–503; Corbett, pp. 640–641.

2. Formal validity

(a) The common law

14.16 In *Purvis's Trustees* v. *Purvis's Executors*[32] it was held that a will of moveables was valid if executed according to the law of the place of execution or that of the testator's domicile. This might be the domicile at the date of execution, validity being unaffected by a later change of domicile, or—as was confirmed in *Chisholm* v. *Chisholm*[33]—at date of death. English law accepted only the last. The Wills Act 1861, of importance in England, was little used in Scotland because of the breadth of the Scots rules. Similar rules governed wills of heritage—not permitted at common law—after the Titles to Land Consolidation (Scotland) Act 1868 allowed their execution in the same way as wills of moveables.

(b) The Wills Act 1963

14.17 The Wills Act 1963 implemented the 1961 Hague Convention on Conflicts of Laws relating to the form of testamentary dispositions and other calls for reform. By its main provisions:

(1) A will is treated as properly executed if (section 1) its execution conformed to the internal law of either (a) the territory where it was executed, (b) the territory of the testator's domicile or habitual residence at the time of its execution or his death, or (c) a state of which he was a national at either time; *or* (section 2(1)(*b*)) in the case of wills of immoveables only, the territory where the property was situated.

(2) A will executed on board a vessel or aircraft is treated as properly executed if its execution conformed to the internal law of the territory with which, having regard to registration and other relevant circumstances, the vessel or aircraft was most closely connected (section 2(1)(*a*)).

(3) A will exercising a power of appointment is properly executed if its execution conforms to the law governing the essential validity of the power: despite its failure to comply with formal requirements specified in the instrument creating the power (sections 2(1)(*d*) and (2)).

(4) Conformity to a law is judged by its requirements at the time of execution, but account is taken of subsequent changes if they enable the will to be treated as properly executed (section 6(2)).

(5) If a state or territory has more than one legal system—as does

---

[32] (1861) 23 D. 812.
[33] 1949 S.C. 434.

the UK—the system applicable is that indicated by the state's rules or, failing that, with which the testator was most closely connected at the time in question (section 6(3)).

(c) The Administration of Justice Act 1982

14.18 The Act gives effect *inter alia* to the 1973 Convention providing a Uniform Law on the Form of an International Will. Schedule 2 to the Act, which sets out the Annex to the Convention, establishes a new form of "international will." Such a will, apart from being valid for purposes of internal Scots law alongside existing methods of execution, will be recognised in any state which has signed and ratified the Convention, and may be recognised in other countries whose choice of law rules so permit. The place of execution is irrelevant. The will need not be "international" in, say, the sense of involving a foreign testator or foreign property.

Schedule 2 stipulates the formalities to be followed by such a will. Invalidity as an international will does not affect validity as a will of another kind, *e.g.* under domestic Scots law.

3. Essential validity

14.19 Rules of essential validity must be distinguished from those of formal validity. The Wills Act 1963 will, of course, only apply to the latter. *Irving* v. *Snow*[34] illustrates the contrast. A will was notarially executed in Carlisle by a solicitor on behalf of a domiciled Scot; under the will the solicitor was entitled as executor to charge for his services. Such execution would have been formally invalid had it happened in Scotland, but was valid by English law which Scots law accepted as the *lex loci actus*. Quite separate was the question whether Scots law would give effect to a bequest in a will: the solicitor's charges might still be struck down under the principle that a notary must not take an interest under a will he executes.

The essential validity of a will of immoveables is governed by the *lex situs*; of a will of moveables, by the law of the testator's last domicile. Again the Scottish Law Commission proposes that the domiciliary law should apply to both.[35] In some cases the validity of a legacy is instead judged by the law of the place where it is to take effect.[36]

The law of the testator's last domicile will govern whether a legatee is required to elect between a legacy and other benefits such as legal

---

[34] 1956 S.C. 257.
[35] Memorandum No. 71, para. 6.15.
[36] Anton, pp. 527–528.

rights. This is the rule even if those benefits concern immoveables situated abroad. See, for instance, *Brown's Trustees* v. *Gregson*:[37] a will purported to create a trust over Argentine land; under Argentine law the trust was invalid and the beneficiaries took the land as outright owners; as the legacy was null by the *lex situs* Scots law did not require election.

4. Construction

14.20 As a general principle a will must be construed according to the intention of the testator.[38] The courts must ascertain by which legal system he intended its provisions to be construed. The tendency is to presume that a will of moveables is to be construed by the testator's domiciliary law. This is determined as at the date of the will, not of the testator's death; under section 4 of the Wills Act 1963 the construction of a will is not altered by reason of any subsequent change of domicile. The presumption may be rebutted by circumstances pointing to a different intention, such as the location of the property and the technical legal terms used in the deed.

Where the will is of immoveables, the Scots courts tend to construe according to the *lex situs*. Thus in *Mitchell and Baxter* v. *Davies*,[39] where a domiciled Englishwoman disposed of heritage in Scotland by a deed which used Scots legal terms, these factors displaced the usual presumption of construction by the domiciliary law. Again the rule is not conclusive: use of English legal forms may—even in respect of Scottish heritage—lead to construction by English law.[40]

Where foreign property is owned jointly by the testator and others, the title may be construed according to the foreign law. Thus shares in an English company will be joint property, with the deceased's portion passing to the survivor, whereas under Scots rules of construction it would pass as common property to the deceased's estate: *Connell's Trustees* v. *Connell's Trustees*.[41] The Scottish Law Commission point out[42] that this will scarcely square with the deceased's intention, which would be given better effect by application of Scots law as the domiciliary law.

5. Revocation

14.21 There is little Scottish authority on questions whether a will

---

[37] 1920 S.C. (H.L.) 87.
[38] *S.N.O. Society Ltd.* v. *Thomson's Exr.*, 1969 S.L.T. 325.
[39] (1875) 3 R. 208.
[40] *Studd* v. *Cook* (1883) 10 R. (H.L.) 53.
[41] (1886) 13 R. 1175.
[42] Memorandum No. 71, paras. 6.17–6.22.

has been validly revoked. The position may vary according to the method used.[43]

(1) Revocation by later will or codicil: the usual tests will decide the validity of the second deed. In addition, under section 2(1)(c) of the Wills Act 1963, a will (so far as it revokes a will or provision in a will) is also treated as properly executed if its execution conforms to any law by reference to which the revoked will or provision is so treated. Note too that where revocation is by implication, insofar as inconsistent with the earlier will, the extent of revocation must be determined by construing according to the *lex domicilii* at date of execution.

(2) Revocation by destruction or deletion: probably the *lex domicilii* at date of revocation applies, but there is no UK authority. It would be odd if a later change of domicile revived the will. The issue arises because some legal systems prescribe formalities for destruction, such as the testator being present.

(3) Revocation by operation of law: this may be by marriage (as in English law) or by the birth of a child (Scots law). Probably the rule in (2) applies. The only Scots authority, *Westerman's Executor* v. *Schwab*,[44] concerned the effect on an English spinster's will of her later marriage to a domiciled Scotsman: taking the spouses' (and therefore at that time the husband's) domicile at date of marriage to be the criterion, the court held that the will was not revoked. In fact that is probably a question, not of succession, but matrimonial property (and English law so regards it); if so the *lex domicilii* applies to wills of any property, both moveables and immoveables.

6. Administration of estates[45]

(a) Appointment of executor

14.22 (1) *Right to appointment.* In Scotland a deceased's estate is administered by an executor, whose title to ingather and deal with the property derives from a grant of confirmation by the sheriff court. While the English system of a grant of probate or letters of administration is similar, many foreign legal systems are radically different. The estate may pass directly to heirs, or through the medium of a public administrator; where there is an ofice of executor his role may be merely to advise the heirs.

The Scots courts can grant confirmation only if the deceased left property located in Scotland. His domicile determines which sheriff court makes the grant.[46]

---

[43] See Morris, pp. 400–402.
[44] (1905) 8 F. 132.
[45] See generally Anton, pp. 485–503.
[46] See para. 13.3.

By contrast, the law of the deceased's last domicile determines who has the right to be confirmed executor.[47] It will be necessary to aver the foreign law, prove his entitlement, and also the validity of any will from which it derives.[48] It is unnecessary to have previously obtained a grant of administration in the country of domicile. Nor need the executor reside in Scotland: he may grant someone resident here a power of attorney to seek confirmation in his name and administer the estate on his behalf.

The exception is an executor-creditor. He is regarded as doing diligence in order to realise the estate for the benefit of the deceased's creditors. Consequently Scots law determines who is entitled to be appointed.

14.23 (2) *Recognition of foreign appointments.* It is obviously convenient for the person entitled to administration under the domiciliary law to deal with the whole estate wherever situated. But in principle confirmation gives no title to administer property outwith Scotland, and a separate grant of confirmation must be sought afresh within each jurisdiction where property is located.

The major exception concerns England and Wales and Northern Ireland.[49] Under the Administration of Estates Act 1971 a grant of confirmation in Scotland, stating the deceased's Scottish domicile, is automatically treated in England and Wales and Northern Ireland as a grant of representation; and an English or Northern Irish grant of representation has the same effect in Scotland as a grant of confirmation.

The 1971 Act only applies if the deceased was domiciled (if outside Scotland) in England, Wales or Northern Ireland. Otherwise a grant of representation in respect of property there will not dispense with the need to obtain separate confirmation in Scotland. The Act does not extend to the Channel Islands or the Isle of Man. Resealing is possible of grants of representation made in Commonwealth countries.[50]

(b) Administration

14.24 Questions of executry administration (as opposed to rights of inheritance) are governed by the law of the country where the administration takes place; the deceased's domicile is irrelevant. Thus Scots law will govern the rights and duties of executors in a Scottish executry, such as their duty to find caution. It also dictates the order of priority in which they pay the deceased's debts.

---

[47] *Marchioness of Hastings* v. *Marquess of Hastings' Exrs.* (1852) 14 D. 489.
[48] Currie, pp. 266–273.
[49] Currie, pp. 238–247, and 258–266.
[50] Colonial Probates Act 1892. See Currie, pp. 258–266.

These points were illustrated in the complex case of *Scottish National Orchestra Society Ltd.* v. *Thomson's Executor.*[51] The testatrix, born in Scotland, made a will in Sweden while separated from her Canadian husband. Though she was thus then domiciled in Canada, all the circumstances pointed to it being her intention that Scots law should govern the construction of the will (and in particular a legacy "free of Government duties"). She died domiciled in Sweden leaving property in Sweden and Scotland, to which separate executors or administrators were appointed. Swedish law decided who the beneficiaries were. Scots law decided whether the Scottish executor could remit Swedish inheritance tax to the Swedish administrator: under normal rules he could not (foreign taxes are unenforceable in Scotland), but this case was an exception, since until he did so he could not fulfil his duty to pay the legatees.

Further reading

A. E. Anton, "The Formal Validity of Wills," 1958 S.L.T. (News) 217.
"The Wills Act 1963," 1963 S.L.T. (News) 161 and (1964) 9 J.L.S. 75.
M. Brandon, "U.K. Accession to the Wills Conventions" (1983) 32 I.C.L.Q. 742.
R. D. Leslie, "Prior Rights in Succession: the International Dimension," 1988 S.L.T. (News) 105.
M. C. Meston, "Prior Rights in Scottish Heritage" (1967) 12 J.L.S. 401.
J. H. C. Morris, "Intestate Succession to Land in the Conflict of Laws" (1969) 85 L.Q.R. 339.

---

[51] 1969 S.L.T. 325.

CHAPTER 15

LAW REFORM

INTRODUCTION

The Scottish Law Commission issued its *Report on Succession* (Scot. Law Com. No. 124) in January 1990, with a draft Bill annexed. This chapter sets out its main proposals. Given that this is by way of an appendix, I have tried to deal with the various topics in the same order as in the body of this book, rather than that in the report itself. Consequently, to assist cross-reference, paragraph numbers follow those in the main text. References marked [ ] are to the clauses in the draft Bill.

DEATH AND SURVIVORSHIP

1.10 To be able to inherit property from the deceased, a beneficiary must survive him for at least five days from the beginning of the day on which the deceased died. This applies to testate and intestate succession, legal shares, special destinations, *mortis causa* donations, and nominations. Otherwise he is deemed to have predeceased the deceased, as regards any third person's right to inherit that property. However, a testator is permitted to stipulate a longer or shorter period of survivance. (The latter is best avoided: the effect may be that the beneficiary, while surviving for the purpose of inheriting under the testator's will, "predeceases" him for purposes of legal shares.) [Clause 28.]

A presumption of survivorship will rarely now be needed; the above rule will cover the typical "common calamity". But it will not deal with every case; so there is a new, simplified, presumption. Where two or more persons die in such circumstances that it cannot be established whether either survived the other for five days (or any other period required under a will), each person's estate is disposed of as if the other(s) predeceased [clause 28(4)].

The five-day rule is concerned with the order in which A (a beneficiary) and B (someone from whom he inherits) die. By contrast, property may pass directly to either A or B from a third person, C, depending on who lives longer. This may occur (say) under a will (by a destination-over) or under life assurance. In this case the five-day rule will not apply. If A and B die simultaneously, or the order is uncertain, the property is divided equally between the estates of A and B [clause 28(5)].

Clause 28(4) and (5) both apply *unless* the will (or other document regulating the transfer) makes some other provision for the event.

The new rules will apply to all deaths occurring after the proposed Act comes into force. If it is uncertain whether someone died before or after that date, he will be deemed to have died afterwards [clause 34 (1), (2)].

ENTITLEMENT TO INHERIT

1. Forfeiture

2.9 The Parricide Act 1594 will be repealed. A new forfeiture rule will apply when someone has been convicted of murder or culpable homicide in the United Kingdom, Channel Islands or Isle of Man (or of an analogous crime elsewhere) and the conviction is no longer open to appeal. In that case the killer:

(a) automatically forfeits any rights to inherit from his victim, *or* to property which was previously held in trust and which would have gone to him on the victim's death, *or* to property which he received from the victim by a *mortis causa* donation;

(b) is deemed for this purpose not to have survived the victim.

So the killer's issue, or alternative beneficiaries under the victim's will, can inherit in his place. For other purposes—such as the disposal of his own estate—the killer is of course still alive [clause 19, Schedule 2].

The common law rules of public policy are not repealed, and will govern cases where the killer has not been convicted under the above criteria.

The civil courts may grant relief from statutory or common law forfeiture. The time limit will be six months after the conviction ceases to be appealable; where there is no conviction there is no time limit. Relief may now be complete or partial [clause 20].

2.11 Judicial separation of spouses will no longer affect their right to inherit from each other. Section 6 of the Conjugal Rights (Scotland) Amendment Act 1861 will be repealed, but existing decrees of separation will remain effective [Schedule 2].

2. Adoption

2.12 Sections 23 and 24 of the 1964 Act, together with section 5 of the Law Reform (Miscellaneous Provisions) (Scotland) Act 1966, will be re-enacted as section 39A of the Adoption (Scotland) Act 1978. Two minor amendments are to be made. To answer previous doubts about the scope of section 23A, it will now clearly cover references in deeds to "issue". Section 24(1A), which dealt with the relative seniority of adopted children, is to be repealed.

PAYMENT OF DEBTS

3.5 The draft Bill abolishes the right of the deceased's family to claim an allowance for mourning expenses. Similarly the right to aliment from his estate disappears [clauses 25–27].

3.15 Anyone succeeding to property under a special destination will be personally liable for the previous owner's debts, up to the value of the property when the owner died. Thus his own assets may be subject to diligence by the previous owner's creditors. This reverses the effect of *Barclay's Bank* v. *McGreish*.[1] He can avoid liability by disclaiming his right to the property [clause 29(6)].

INTESTATE SUCCESSION

4.1 There are substantial changes. To summarise: prior rights in their current form disappear; the surviving spouse gets more extensive rights in the intestate estate; the rules for dividing the "free estate" remain largely unchanged. Legal rights of spouse and issue are renamed and re-shaped as a "legal share"; they become primarily a means to protect against disinheritance by a testator, and cease to provide (as at present) a means for dividing up the intestate estate after prior rights and before the free estate.

1. The intestate estate

The relevant estate is the "net intestate estate": this is any "net estate" which is not disposed of by will or special destination. Legal shares are not deducted first. The "net estate" is the deceased's estate *less* his debts (other than IHT) and funeral expenses [clause 36(1)].

IHT and expenses of administration will thus be deducted from the estate *after* ascertaining its value and division for purposes of intestacy and legal share. As regards IHT, the Inheritance Tax Act 1984 will, as before, govern its incidence on the assets of the estate. Expenses of administration will fall on the assets in the intestate

[1] 1983 S.L.T. 344.

estate and residue, implicitly *pro rata* in accordance with their values; then on the legal shares and general legacies *pro rata*; lastly on special legacies [clauses 10, 36(5)].

The estate is valued at the date of death; but where estate is realised in ordinary course and without due delay after the death, the realised value is used, except insofar as the estate could be accurately valued as at the date of death. This simply aims to make the existing common law explicit [clause 24].

2. Rights of spouse and issue

Where the deceased is survived by a spouse and no issue (or vice versa), the spouse or issue (respectively) inherit the whole intestate estate. If both spouse and issue survive, the spouse takes the first £100,000 and—if applicable—half the excess estate over that figure; the issue take the other half of the excess. The Secretary of State will have power to raise or lower the figure by statutory instrument [clauses 1(2), (3)].

Thus prior rights are replaced by a blanket cash sum. But the surviving spouse has a new right, reminiscent of the old prior right under section 8 of the 1964 Act, but wider. Suppose she is entitled to a share of intestate estate—*or* to residue under the deceased's will—which includes his interest in the matrimonial home and furnishings. In that event she will have the option to acquire that interest in satisfaction (in whole or in part) of her entitlement; she can do so even if the interest exceeds her entitlement, provided she pays the estate the difference between the two figures. "Matrimonial home" is wider than the section 8 "dwelling-house" test: it clearly includes caravans and other structures (there was doubt under section 8), and the home may have been a family residence even if the surviving spouse was not ordinarily resident in it at the date when the deceased died.[2] The exclusion from section 8 of certain tenancies, property used for trade, and (as regards contents) business assets and heirlooms is broadly reproduced [clause 23].

The right to the matrimonial home is not automatic. The surviving spouse has six months after the executors' confirmation to intimate to them her intention to claim. She cannot claim if, in the meantime, the executors have disposed of the property. As under section 8, there is provision for valuing the claim, by arbitration if need be.

If the spouse is herself the sole executor, she intimates to any children who have claimed legal shares and to all beneficiaries whom she can trace by reasonable inquiry. Her transaction with the estate

---

[2] Matrimonial Homes (Family Protection) (Scotland) Act 1981, s. 22.

will not be voidable on the grounds (applicable at common law) that she is *auctor in rem suam* and has a conflict of interest as beneficiary and executor.

3. General rules

The order of succession to the intestate estate otherwise remains much the same [clauses 1, 2, 4]. The rules of *per stirpes* division are now spelled out clearly in plain English [clause 3]. Collaterals of the full blood will no longer have preference over those of the half blood; all will have equal rights [clause 1(4)].

WILL SUBSTITUTES

1. Special destinations

5.2 The proposed Act will restrict the scope of special destinations in two complementary ways [clause 29]:

(a) Simple survivorship destinations will remain valid. But where a document of title to property—moveable or heritable—contains a destination in favour of some person other than the original grantee or (if there was more than one grantee) the survivor, the destination is invalid in respect of that person. The grantee or the survivor, as appropriate, has an outright title which simply passes as part of his estate by the ordinary rules of succession. This rule does not apply to destinations to "X in liferent and Y in fee", nor to "X as trustee [*or* as an officeholder] and his successors in office".

(b) Destinations-over in wills may instruct conditional institution or substitution. The first remains valid. The second will be ineffective in respect of the substitute beneficiary; the original institute will, by analogy with (a), take an outright right.

The Act will govern title deeds and wills (respectively) executed after its commencement, with one exception: deeds after the Act which implement a provision contained in a pre-Act will [clause 34 (4)].

In all cases where a post-Act title deed contains a destination, the owner may validly evacuate it either by will or during his lifetime. If the destination is contractual, that would not prevent evacuation: it would merely leave the owner liable for damages for breach of contract [clause 29(3)].

Special rules will cover destinations in leases. More generally, special destinations will include "class" destinations [clause 36(1)].[3]

---

[3] Reversing the effect of *Cormack* v. *McIldowie's Exrs.*, 1975 S.C. 161.

Property subject to a destination will be excluded from the deceased's estate for the purpose of administration under the 1964 Act—unless a transfer by the executor is necessary—only if, in the circumstances, the destination actually takes effect [Schedule 1, paras. 12 and 14].[4]

The Bill provides that the construction of title deeds to moveable property will—unless the document says otherwise—be determined in accordance with the law of the deceased's last domicile. This aims to reverse the rule in *Connell's Trustees* v. *Connell's Trustees*[5] that English law applied to shares held by a Scotsman in English companies, so that where shares were held in joint names there was an implied survivorship destination.

2. Donations *mortis causa*

5.13 These will not be deemed to be part of the donor's estate for the purpose of legal shares, so will not be forfeited if the recipient claims on the estate. They will be returnable if the recipient forfeits his rights by killing the donor, or fails to survive him for five days [clauses 19(1), 28(8), 36(1)].

WILLS: FORMAL VALIDITY

6.27 The Court of Session and the sheriff court will have power to declare formally valid a writing which purports to be a will, an alteration to one, or a revocation of one, notwithstanding failure to comply with the normal requirements for formal validity. The court must be satisfied that the testator intended it to take effect as his will (or alteration or revocation); extrinsic evidence will be permitted for this purpose. In validating the will, the court may also declare when (or within what period) and where the will was made [clause 12].

The validating power would apply so long as the testator dies after the Act comes into force, whatever the date of the will.

REVOCATION OF WILLS

7.16 Marriage will not revoke a previous will. But divorce or annulment of marriage is to have the effect of revoking provisions made by one spouse in the other's favour—*e.g.* legacies, nominations and special destinations, and appointment as trustee, executor, tutor or curator, or donee of a power of appointment—unless the

---

[4] Amending Succession (Scotland) Act 1964, ss. 18(2), 36(2).
[5] (1886) 13 R. 1175.

document indicates that provision is to take effect nevertheless. The benefiting ex-spouse will be deemed not to have survived [clause 14].

However, suppose someone, unaware of the new rule, sells property which she believes she has inherited from her ex-spouse under a destination. The destination does not reveal the true position. The buyer, if he bought in good faith, has a protected title [clause 14(4), (5)]. The seller must pay over the proceeds of her ex-spouse's share (if she still has them) to his estate.

The *conditio si testator sine liberis decesserit* will be abolished [clause 15].

If a will is revoked in whole or in part, the will (or part) is not revived *unless* (a) it is subsequently re-executed, or (b) another document which expressly revives it is executed or is validated by a court order [clause 16].

WILLS: ESSENTIAL VALIDITY

8.6 Neither the courts nor curators bonis are to be given power to make a will on behalf of someone who lacks testamentary capacity.

8.18 The Court of Session and sheriff court will have a limited power to order a will to be rectified so as to give effect to a testator's instructions, if satisfied that it fails to do so. The will must have been prepared by someone other than the testator. An application for rectification must be brought within six months after the executor is confirmed, unless the court on cause shown allows one later. A trustee or executor shall not be personally liable for having distributed, in good faith, estate which vested in him under the unrectified will [clause 13].

TESTAMENTARY FREEDOM

1. Legal shares

9.1 "Legal rights" are replaced by "legal shares" in favour of the surviving spouse and issue. As before, these will be fixed proportions of the estate, rather than discretionary awards made by the courts on the English model. They will be exigible from both heritage and moveables.

The surviving spouse's legal share will in all cases be 30 per cent of the first £200,000 of the net estate, and 10 per cent of any excess estate over that figure.[6] The issue take a similar share if there is no surviving

---

[6] The Secretary of State can amend the figure by statutory instrument.

spouse. If there is, then (a) their share is halved; (b) they cannot claim out of the first £100,000 of any net estate of which the spouse inherits the fee (as opposed to a liferent) under the deceased's will or intestacy. The purpose of (b) is to avoid the position in *Kerr, Petitioner*[7] where the spouse inherited the whole estate under a will, but was worse off than under intestacy (because she had no prior rights with which to defeat the legal rights of issue): (b) gives the spouse the *same* protected right as she would take under intestacy [clauses 5, 7].

Legal shares will not vest automatically by mere survivance of the deceased. They must be claimed within two years after the death by the spouse or child, or (if legally incapacitated for some reason) by someone entitled to act on his behalf in the management of his affairs: *e.g.* a parent or a curator bonis. If the spouse or child dies before claiming, his own executor may claim within the two years or within six months after his death, whichever ends later. Where the court grants a decree under the Presumption of Death (Scotland) Act 1977, it may extend the period for up to six months after the decree [clause 6].

Legal shares may be renounced before or after the deceased died, by or on behalf of the spouse or issue. If a share is renounced or merely not claimed, it does not pass to any other potential claimant. Nor does that constitute a transfer of value under the Inheritance Tax Act 1984 [clauses 5(5), 7(5); Schedule 1, para. 24].

Anyone claiming a legal share forfeits all rights under the deceased's will (unless the will provides otherwise) *and* under intestacy. The claimant is treated as failing to survive, but only so as to debar his own rights: they do not pass to his issue (under intestacy or the *conditio si institutus*) or to a conditional institute (under a destination-over), as they would have done had he really not survived. But a claimant may withdraw his claim before payment and keep his rights [clause 8].

The net estate is calculated before the legal share is divided. The different parts of the estate bear the share in the following order, unless the deceased's will stipulates a different order: (a) intestate estate; (b) residue; (c) general legacies; (d) special legacies, and property passing by nomination or special destination. Assets within each class bear the share *pro rata* according to value. Conversely, the spouse's "protected £100,000"—free from the issue's legal share—is attributed to the estate in the reverse order; the effect is to minimise the conflict between legal share and protected sum. Finally, the legal share will now bear expenses of administration (throughout the executry) *pro rata* along with general legacies [clauses 5(4), 9, 10].

---

[7] 1968 S.L.T. (Sh. Ct.) 61.

Legal rights will be abolished and, along with them, collation *inter liberos* [clause 5(6)].

Where legal shares are payable out of agricultural property, it will be possible to pay by 10 equal annual instalments starting from the date of death. Each instalment bears interest at 7 per cent from its due date, or such other rate as the Secretary of State may prescribe [clause 11].

2. Forfeiture and equitable compensation

9.8 If property is left in liferent and fee, and the liferent for any reason lapses before the liferenter's death, the Bill allows accelerated vesting in the fiar. Unless the document creating the liferent expressly provides otherwise, the fee vests on the date when it would have done if the liferenter had in fact died at the date of lapse (which may of course not be at once: other conditions may have to be fulfilled) [clause 18]. In that situation there will presumably be no opportunity for equitable compensation to occur.

INTERPRETATION OF WILLS

10.21 The *conditio si institutus sine liberis decesserit* survives in an altered form.[8] It will apply only to direct descendants, and then only unless "the will clearly intends otherwise". A survivorship clause or destination-over will be taken to show clear intention, thus defeating the *conditio*. The beneficiary's issue will take the share he would have taken had he survived, including accresced shares. Finally, the rules for *per capita* and *per stirpes* division among a predeceased beneficiary's issue are set out in clear English [clause 17].

EXECUTRY ADMINISTRATION

13.8 The Bill updates the rules which state who is entitled to be appointed executor-dative. Entitlement as "next-of-kin", derived from pre-1964 succession law, is abolished. Instead, anyone entitled to inherit by the rules of intestacy can apply; or, if the sheriff is satisfied that no such person is going to do so, any blood relation of the deceased. (The relation will, as now, be best to get a written declinature from the entitled beneficiary.) If more than one relation applies, the sheriff shall—unless there is good reason not to do so—

---

[8] The change applies only to wills executed after the new Act becomes law [clause 34(3)].

appoint one or more of those most closely related to the deceased [Schedule 1, para. 2].[9]

13.14 Caution will be required for the whole estate administered by the executor-dative: not just that confirmed to by him [Schedule 1, para. 1].

13.17 It will be competent for an executor to be confirmed to the estate of someone who died domiciled in Scotland, even if none of that estate was in Scotland [clause 21].[10]

13.43 It will remain competent for an executor or trustee to use the deceased's will as a link through which to deduce title in a conveyance to a third party or to complete title in his own name by notice of title [Schedule 1, para. 4]. That option will now be open to legatees and general disponees under the will—thus avoiding the need to seek confirmation if no other property has to be transferred. But, as before, only a purchaser acquiring in good faith from a confirmed executor will get a protected title under section 17 of the 1964 Act, so the new option may be little practical use if the heritage is to be sold.

13.44 Replacing the rules which apply in the case of illegitimate beneficiaries, there is a new general protection for a trustee or executor distributing the estate. He is not personally liable for any error in distribution based on ignorance of the (non-) existence of persons, or their (lack of) relationship to any other person; *provided* he acted in good faith and made such inquiries as a reasonable and prudent trustee or executor would make in such circumstances [Schedule 1, para. 7].[11]

13.45 Section 17 of the 1964 Act, which protects the title of those who acquire heritage from a confirmed executor, is to be extended to moveables. It will also be made clear that it is not confined to purchase; it will, say, apply where someone acquires assets in lieu of an alternative claim on the estate, *e.g.* a house or moveables instead of a legal share or intestacy [Schedule 1, para. 11].

13.46. New rules govern the transfer of a lease by an executor, and (reversing the effect of *Inglis* v. *Inglis*)[12] permit him to acquire it for himself without the transaction being challengeable as being in breach of the common law *auctor in rem suam* rule [clause 22].[13]

---

[9] Inserting new Confirmation of Executors (Scotland) Act 1858, s. 2.
[10] Inserting new Succession (Scotland) Act 1964, s. 14A.
[11] Inserting new Trusts (Scotland) Act 1921, s. 29A.
[12] 1983 S.L.T. 437.
[13] Amending Succession (Scotland) Act 1964, s. 16.

INDEX